Black Designers in American Fashion

Black Designers in American Fashion

Edited by
Elizabeth Way

BLOOMSBURY VISUAL ARTS
LONDON • NEW YORK • OXFORD • NEW DELHI • SYDNEY

BLOOMSBURY VISUAL ARTS
Bloomsbury Publishing Plc
50 Bedford Square, London, WC1B 3DP, UK
1385 Broadway, New York, NY 10018, USA
29 Earlsfort Terrace, Dublin 2, Ireland

BLOOMSBURY, BLOOMSBURY VISUAL ARTS and the Diana logo
are trademarks of Bloomsbury Publishing Plc

First published in Great Britain 2021

Cover design: Adriana Brioso
Cover image: Model Beverly Johnson wearing an outfit by Scott Barrie, with a hat by Don Marshall,
and an envelope bag by I. Miller. (© Francesco Scavullo/Condé Nast/Getty Images)

A catalogue record for this book is available from the British Library.

Library of Congress Cataloging-in-Publication Data
Names: Way, Elizabeth (Writer on fashion), editor.
Title: Black designers in American fashion / edited by Elizabeth Way.
Description: London ; New York : Bloomsbury Visual Arts, 2021. |
Includes bibliographical references and index.
Identifiers: LCCN 2020051658 (print) | LCCN 2020051659 (ebook) |
ISBN 9781350138476 (paperback) | ISBN 9781350138469 (hardback) |
ISBN 9781350138483 (pdf) | ISBN 9781350138490 (epub)
Subjects: LCSH: Fashion–United States–History. |
African American fashion designers–History.
Classification: LCC TT504.4 .B59 2021 (print) | LCC TT504.4 (ebook) |
DDC 746.9/2–dc23
LC record available at https://lccn.loc.gov/2020051658
LC ebook record available at https://lccn.loc.gov/2020051659

ISBN: HB: 978-1-3501-3846-9
         PB: 978-1-3501-3847-6
         ePDF: 978-1-3501-3848-3
         eBook: 978-1-3501-3849-0

Typeset by Integra Software Services Pvt. Ltd.
Printed and bound in India

To find out more about our authors and books visit www.bloomsbury.com
and sign up for our newsletters.

Contents

Illustrations

Notes on Contributors

Elizabeth Way (MA, New York University; BS, BA, University of Delaware) is Assistant Curator of Costume at The Museum at the Fashion Institute of Technology, USA. Her co-curated and curated exhibitions include *Global Fashion Capitals* (2015), *Black Fashion Designers* (2016), and *Fabric In Fashion* (2018). Her personal research focuses on the intersection of Black culture and fashion, and published works include, "Strands of the Diaspora: Black Hair in the Americas 1800–1920" in *A Cultural History of Hair in the Age of Empire* (2018) and "Elizabeth Keckly and Ann Lowe: Recovering an African American Fashion Legacy That Clothed the American Elite" (2015).

Contributors

Joy Davis is an independent scholar of fashion history and the director of Waller Gallery in Baltimore, Maryland, USA. She created Waller Gallery in 2018. She also co-hosts and produces for *Unravel Podcast*, a fashion history and culture podcast. Her scholarly projects include subject matter that is underdeveloped in academia and transcends many fields of study: fashion, history, art, media, and performance among people of color throughout history. She holds two BA degrees, one in history and one in media studies from the University of Maryland, and her MA in Fashion and Museum Studies is from the Fashion Institute of Technology in New York.

Nancy Deihl is Director of the Costume Studies graduate program at New York University, USA. Her research interests focus on twentieth-century fashion, in particular on the American fashion industry. She lectures and publishes on fashion history topics and is the editor of *The Hidden History of American Fashion: Rediscovering 20th-Century Women Designers* (2018) and co-author of *The History of Modern Fashion* (2015).

Ariele Elia (MSL, Fordham University School of Law; MA, Fashion Institute of Technology; BA, Saint Mary's College, California, USA) is Assistant Director of the Fashion Law Institute at Fordham Law, USA. She previously served for seven years as the Assistant Curator of Costume and Textiles at The Museum at Fashion Institute of Technology, where she curated, *Faking It: Originals,*

Copies, and Counterfeits (2014) and co-curated *Black Fashion Designers*. She has lectured at the United Nations, Oxford University, and Columbia Law School, and developed the course *Cultural Awareness, Design Responsibility, and the Law*. Recent publications include, "Fashion's Destruction of Unsold Goods: Responsible Solutions for an Environmentally Conscious Future."

Katie Knowles is Curator of the Avenir Museum of Design and Merchandising and an assistant professor in the Department of Design and Merchandising at Colorado State University, USA. She holds a PhD in history from Rice University, Houston, Texas, USA, and is currently completing a book manuscript from her dissertation on enslaved people's clothing in the antebellum US South. Knowles has worked in museums for more than a decade, including at the Avenir Museum, the Smithsonian National Museum of African American History and Culture, Winterthur Museum, Garden & Library, and the Bayou Bend Collection and Gardens of the Museum of Fine Arts, Houston.

Darnell-Jamal Lisby is a fashion historian and curator. His projects include curatorial contribution to the *Willi Smith: Street Couture* exhibition at Cooper Hewitt, Smithsonian Design Museum, USA (2020). His research delves into contextualizing the impact of Blackness within the history of fashion during the twentieth and twenty-first centuries. In addition to contributing curatorial efforts at The Museum at FIT and Metropolitan Museum of Art, he has published works related to his research on various platforms, including *The Fashion and Race Database*, *Teen Vogue*, and for the Smithsonian Institution.

Kristen J. Owens is an arts administrator, curator, and researcher with interests in visual culture, fashion, and African American studies. She has co-created exhibitions, including *Performing Fashion: New York City* at New York University's 80WSE Gallery (2017) and *Dressed* at Rutgers University-Newark's Paul Robeson Galleries (2018). Owens holds an MA in Visual Culture: Costume Studies and an MS in Library and Information Science from New York University's dual degree program with Long Island University Palmer, USA. She holds a BA in fashion studies from Montclair State University, USA.

Eric Darnell Pritchard is the endowed Brown Chair in English Literacy and Associate Professor of English at the University of Arkansas, USA. Pritchard is the author of *Fashioning Lives: Black Queers and the Politics of Literacy* (2016), which received three book awards, and editor of "Sartorial Politics, Intersectionality, and Queer Worldmaking," a special issue of *QED: A Journal in GLBTQ*

Worldmaking (2017). Currently, he is completing the book, *Abundant Black Joy: The Life and Work of Patrick Kelly*, a biography of the 1980s international fashion design superstar.

Jonathan Michael Square teaches in the Committee on Degrees in History and Literature at Harvard University, USA, and has taught at University of Pennsylvania, Fashion Institute of Technology, and Parsons School of Design. He has a PhD in history from New York University, MA from the University of Texas at Austin, and BA from Cornell University. His teaching and book projects focus on the fashion and visual culture of the African Diaspora. A proponent of the power of social media as a platform for radical pedagogy, he founded and runs the digital humanities project *Fashioning the Self in Slavery and Freedom*.

Kristen E. Stewart is the Nathalie L. Klaus Curator of Costume and Textiles at the Valentine, the museum of the history of Richmond, Virginia, USA. Her research interests focus on the intersection of established gender identity norms within dress and the fashion industry. She has explored these themes in recent exhibitions at the Valentine, including *The Virginia Man: Respect, Responsibility, Rebellion* (2016–2017) and *Pretty Powerful: Fashion and Virginia Women* (2018–2019).

Tanya Danielle Wilson Myers is the Cultural Arts Portfolio Manager for the Washington, DC Department of Parks and Recreation, USA. She holds a BS in Retail Management and Marketing from Syracuse University and a MA in Visual Communication: Costume Studies from New York University, USA. Her academic research focuses on the power of artifacts and the way in which citizens of the world connect art and culture as it relates to socio-cultural aspects of dress. Her most recent publication is *Imprint (NYC): The Evolution of Motifs in Fashion* (2012) in which she contributed a chapter on Animal Print.

Acknowledgments

This book represents a wealth of original scholarship on a subject that is unfortunately rare in fashion studies. As editor, I am extremely proud, grateful, and humbled by the dedication and determination of the authors in this book. They are professionals, curators, independent scholars, professors, partners, and parents, and yet they devoted countless hours to help fill in a vital space on the fashion history bookshelf. Thank you. A special thanks to Nancy Deihl who encouraged me to propose this volume.

On behalf of all the authors, thank you to the institutions and individuals that opened their archives, shared their memories, and permitted their images to be used in this book. A special thank you to Robbie and Stephen Marks and to Valerie Steele and The Museum at FIT.

Thank you to Yvonne Thouroude, and the entire team at Bloomsbury, especially Frances Arnold and Rebecca Hamilton.

Every effort has been made to locate copyright holders and acquire permissions to reproduce copyrighted material. The publisher apologizes for any omissions or errors and would appreciate notification of any amendments that should be incorporated into any subsequent reprints or editions.

Introduction

Elizabeth Way

When Lois K. Alexander was interviewed by model-turned-journalist Norma Jean Darden in 1979 on the opening of the Black Fashion Museum, Alexander explained that the impetus for her project was to reveal the forgotten histories of Black fashion makers. She pointed out a disconnect in the perception of contemporary Black designers by both the mainstream fashion industry and the designers themselves: "We always begin with the current generation without knowing the investment of past generations." Darden, herself a pioneering Black model, praised Alexander for her determination to "shatter the myth that Blacks are newfound talent in the fashion world."[1] Funded by the National Endowment for the Arts, Alexander traveled the United States collecting clothing objects and the stories of those who had taught and nurtured the Black designers of the 1970s, stating, "it is their grandmothers who worked long, hard and anonymously, that I am looking for."[2] The Black Fashion Museum not only preserved and traced a rich and relevant history for the public, it also served as inspiration and motivation for the students at the neighboring Harlem Institute of Fashion, founded by Alexander in 1966.[3] This book picks up Alexander's mantle. Fashion history was still developing as an academic discipline when she published *Blacks in the History of Fashion* in 1982. Since then countless scholars and curators have exponentially expanded the canon of fashion scholarship. More recently, insightful academics from various fields, including history, anthropology, and literature, as well as fashion scholars and curators, have examined the role of fashion and style in Black communities and in the visual culture that Black individuals create.

Fashion, clothing, and style have undoubtedly served as transformative tools for African Americans. In her seminal work, *Slaves to Fashion: Black Dandyism and the Styling of Black Diasporic Identity*, Monica L. Miller details the deep and syncretic understanding of clothing that West African people exercised

Figure 0.1 Lois K. Alexander's Black Fashion Museum preserved the work of often unknown fashion makers including this ornate coat (1870–1900) from the collection of Lucy Louvenia Cordice of Boston. Collection of the Smithsonian National Museum of African American History and Culture. Gift of the Black Fashion Museum founded by Lois K. Alexander-Lane.

in their self-expression, and how those knowledges followed them across the Atlantic. Miller, as well as Graham White and Shane White in their book, *Stylin' African American Expressive Culture from Its Beginnings to the Zoot Suit*, note the influence of West African aesthetic practices on African American style, the "embrace of the new and unusual … [the] ability to inventively manipulate or blend the traditional and the novel."[4] They and other scholars have demonstrated that Black people have exercised agency in styling their bodies since they arrived on American shores, doing their best to combat oppression and violence, both physical and psychological, by taking control of their appearance, expressing their creativity, and shaping their identities through fashion. These efforts were not always seen or understood by mainstream America and were in no way monolithic. Black Americans have created unique cultures across the country, differentiated by enslavement or freedom, as well as geography and class. These differences were manifested in active discourses within the larger African American population about how Black people should dress and how their fashion choices affected their treatment by mainstream society. Ideas about respectability politics in fashion are debated into the twenty-first century.

Within this wider history of Black style, designers and makers are only one part, but they are an important one. Black makers have been crucial in dressing Black Americans, but they have also significantly contributed to mainstream American fashion culture. Yet few scholarly works have focused specifically on Black fashion makers. Throughout this book, a group of scholars have dug deep into the history of makers—people who have turned inanimate material into forms that have adorned the bodies and shaped the identities of a wide variety of people, from enslaved laborers to First Ladies to hip hop stars. These makers, called seamstresses, mantuamakers, modistes, dressmakers, and designers, have used their skills, not only to create beautiful, interesting, and provocative clothing, but also to buy their freedom, obtain property, fund migrations, and head companies. Producing fashionable clothing could be a lucrative form of empowerment for Black people, but just as importantly, it was and is an outlet to assert their humanity, express artistic impulses, and to achieve visibility, even fame, in a society that has sought to render them invisible.

Black Designers in American Fashion is divided into four sections. The first, "Anonymous Histories," focuses on eighteenth-, nineteenth-, and early twentieth-century Black fashion makers, people—mostly women—who were largely uncredited or lost to history. Yet, evidence of their work exists. Katie Knowles and Jonathan Michael Square draw from rare extant garments, slave narratives, historic newspapers—especially runaway slave ads—and a host of non-fashion scholarship to piece together the histories of individual enslaved fashion makers and those one or two generations removed from slavery, telling stories of agency and empowerment through clothing. The third chapter uses advertisements placed by New York City dressmakers during the nineteenth and early twentieth centuries, as well as census data, to trace their businesses in America's burgeoning fashion capital. This section amplifies what is discernable throughout the book, that the history of Black fashion is the history of the United States, and that the material culture made by Black people, whether extant or not, is vital in confronting and understanding American society.

The designers featured in the second section, "In the Atelier: Modistes and Independent Designers," operated in autonomous shops during the early to mid-twentieth century, much like nineteenth-century artisanal makers. Unlike production processes that were employed in the industrialized fashion system, they performed most of the labor themselves or with a small staff, from the design concept to the final execution. However, these designers were increasingly modern in their approaches, whether in the labeling of their clothing with their own names, or their melding of fashion with art and image-making. Kristen E. Stewart uses an archive of Fannie Criss's material culture, in conjunction with textual documents and records, to investigate a highly successful dressmaker who thrived in the Jim Crow South. Joy Davis and Kristen J. Owens look at Ruby Bailey and Art Smith, respectively, as artists who worked in the vernacular of fashion. Bailey transitioned from a traditional designer to a sculptor, recreating fashion dolls as innovative art pieces that she called cotton sculptures or "manikins." Smith, a well-respected mid-century jeweler, created biomorphic, surrealist jewelry that incorporated the body as part of the sculpture. His bold, organic designs spoke to the burgeoning cultural shifts that would transform America between the post-World War Two era and the radical 1960s.

The third section of the book, "Into the Mainstream: Seventh Avenue and Beyond" focuses on designers working within, adjacent to, or in conversation with the mainstream fashion industry during the second half of the twentieth century. Nancy Deihl explores the career of Wesley Tann, an early Black designer working in New York during the 1950s and 1960s when the "fashion industry," with all the glamorous connotations of the fashion designer, was emerging from the garment trade. He not only carved out a space for himself through versatility and hard work, but also organized and mentored other designers and fashion students. Darnell-Jamal Lisby's study of Jay Jaxon follows the designer from the New York industry to Paris, where he rose to the very top. Jaxon took over the

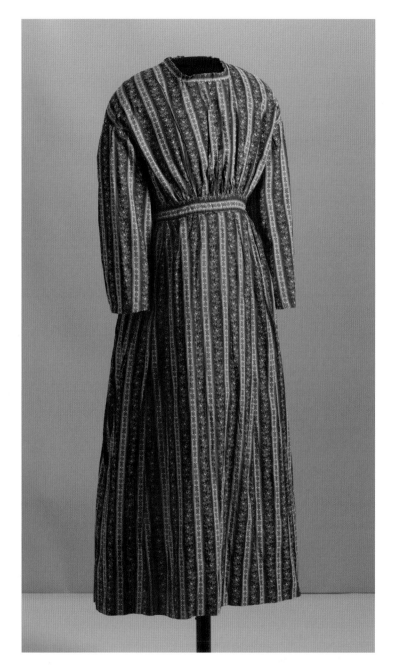

Figure 0.2 Although rare, clothing objects made by enslaved makers exist in archives and help to reveal anonymous fashion histories. Cotton dress made by an unidentified enslaved woman or women, 1845–1865. Collection of the Smithsonian National Museum of African American History and Culture. Gift of the Black Fashion Museum founded by Lois K. Alexander-Lane.

design leadership of the haute couture house Jean-Louis Scherrer in 1970 when the titular designer stepped away to confront legal issues. In leading an haute couture house, Jaxon took on a highly visible role as a Black American within fashion's most elite circle. Ariele Elia contextualizes Dapper Dan, a Harlem hip hop institution, within the wider fashion culture, examining his self-taught skills and innovations, as well as the dialog he created between American hip hop fashion and European luxury fashion brands. Dapper Dan originated influential trends in fashion culture that went unacknowledged for decades.

The final section, "The Star Designer: National and International Impact," looks at the most well-known of the designers researched for this book. By the 1970s Black designers were having an undeniable moment in American fashion. Tanya Danielle Wilson Myers follows this period in Stephen Burrows's career, defining the characteristics of his style, weaving it into a diasporic history, and identifying his impact on later designers. The chapter on Scott Barrie traces the rise of a celebrated designer, relying on interviews with Barrie's business partners who reveal the New York fashion industry during the late 1960s and 1970s as a smaller, more intimate world than its twenty-first-century iteration. They shed light on the hard-won status of Barrie's company as a mainstay on Seventh Avenue. Eric Darnell Pritchard compares and contrasts Willi Smith and Patrick Kelly, two wildly successful Black designers whose premature deaths disrupted the even greater success they were on track to achieve. Both designers embraced Black culture and humor in their designs, making these concepts accessible to mainstream audiences. While Smith created an all-American sportswear brand, Kelly took his distinctly Southern American perspective to Paris.

The majority of the makers covered in this volume have not previously received scholarly attention, and the details of their work and their contributions to fashion culture are now academically considered for the first time. Other designers featured in this book are evaluated in new ways and contextualized into broader narratives. Each chapter can stand alone as an important piece of scholarship, yet taken together, themes arise that help illuminate, not only the history of Black American fashion makers, but also the American fashion system and African American history. For example, the importance of skills taught and passed down through families recurs in many narratives. Elizabeth Keckly took the sewing skills her enslaved mother taught her and transformed this knowledge into free labor in the same way that Ann Lowe's grandmother and mother passed their skills through the family from the antebellum period, through emancipation, and into the Jim Crow era. It is hard to overemphasize the significance of this practice. Designers working during the mid to late twentieth century, including Wesley Tann, Scott Barrie, and Stephen Burrows, had their first sewing lessons from mothers and grandmothers, all highly skilled, professional dressmakers. The book is organized in an approximately chronological order, and there is a clear divide between the predominance of female fashion makers and male designers that occurs during the mid-twentieth century. The mainstream fashion industry overwhelmingly favored male designers for womenswear, and the Black designers who found mainstream success were subject to this bias.

It is not surprising that the cultural movements that shaped the lives of African Americans, from the Great Migration to the Harlem Renaissance to the Civil Rights era also shaped the careers of Black designers. These movements helped bring the majority of the twentieth-century designers covered in this book to New York City, a creative hub that served as an essential site for American fashion makers. Harlem drew Fannie Criss from Richmond, Virginia; her townhouse, located near Madam C. J. Walker's, was a symbol of her success as a Black American. Harlem was also a crucial environment that nurtured the careers of both Ruby Bailey and Dapper Dan, yet they drew different inspirations from the neighborhood during their respective eras. Harlem was recognized as a mecca of Black culture from the 1920s, yet it formed as an enclave over the nineteenth century because Black New Yorkers were pushed out of other areas of Manhattan. The neighborhood housed all classes of Black Americans, creating a dynamic cultural mix that readily expressed itself in highly visible fashion and style, but Black Harlemites were also subject to higher rents and lower standards of living compared to many other parts of the city. Both Bailey and Dapper Dan channel and capture the intense creativity of Harlem's fashionable expression in their work, while bypassing traditional networks within the established Seventh Avenue fashion industry. Other parts of New York nurtured Black designers into the twentieth century. Art Smith's jewelry design thrived in the cultural stimulation and liberal attitudes of mid-century Greenwich Village where Black creativity, expressed through literature, jazz music, and modern dance, as well as in fashion and art, mingled with Beat and countercultural ideas. The boutique culture of the late 1960s changed fashion retailing in the city and was vital to the early careers of Stephen Burrows and Scott Barrie—both broke into the industry by selling early designs to boutiques, such as Allen & Cole on Manhattan's east side. Willi Smith, a streetwear pioneer, tied up a century of New York's style

ELIZABETH KECKLEY.

Figure 0.3 Elizabeth Keckly transformed the skills she received from her enslaved mother—dressmaking as well as literacy—into free labor. The frontispiece of her 1868 book, *Behind the Scenes, or, Thirty Years a Slave, and Four Years in the White House*, shows her portrait. National Portrait Gallery, Smithsonian Institution.

development, taking a myriad of influences from around the city and distilling them into a modern and distinctly American way of dressing.

While Barrie, Burrows, and Smith went on to achieve fame and win industry accolades as the face of their brands, it is as important to recognize the careers of designers who worked across the industry for several companies or outside the orbit of Seventh Avenue. Wesley Tann and Jay Jaxon both helmed their own companies and worked for others. Tann made a name for himself working slightly outside the hub of the Garment District and designed fashion goods ranging from lingerie to sportswear before establishing a company under his own name. Jaxon worked for European couturiers and New York manufacturers, such as Yves Saint Laurent and Pierre Cardin's New York license, in addition to Jean-Louis Scherrer. Fashion history privileges the narrative of the star designer, who might apprentice under others at first, but eventually creates his or her own brand and sustains it throughout a career. Yet many more designers, especially in the twentieth-century New York industry, had successful and influential careers working at multiple manufacturers and firms under others' names. These stories are vital for understanding the historical impact of Black designers on American fashion.

The authors of this volume utilized untapped resources, from theoretical discourses outside of fashion studies, to new oral histories that were documented for the first time for this work. They brought out hidden treasures from archives, including those of the Historic New Orleans Collection, the Valentine museum, the North Carolina Museum of History, the New York Public Library, The Museum at the Fashion Institute of Technology, the Museum of the City of New York, the Brooklyn Museum, and the Smithsonian National Museum of African American History and Culture, which now holds Lois Alexander's Black Fashion Museum collection. This research was done with the hope that *Black Designers In American Fashion* will serve as one of many more scholarly works that documents and rediscovers the work of not just Black, but of other marginalized designers in American fashion, and throughout the world.

Notes

1 Norma Jean Darden, "Harlem's Fashion Museum: Lois Alexander Traces Our Fashion Roots," *Essence,* November 1979, 82.

2 Ibid.

3 Ibid., 152.

4   Monica L. Miller, *Slaves to Fashion: Black Dandyism and the Styling of Black Diasporic Identity* (Durham: Duke University Press, 2009), 90; Shane White and Graham White, *Stylin' African American Expressive Culture from Its Beginnings to the Zoot Suit* (Ithaca: Cornell University Press, 1998), 23–4.

Bibliography

Darden, Norma Jean. "Harlem's Fashion Museum: Lois Alexander Traces Our Fashion Roots." *Essence*, November 1979, 82–3, 152.

Miller, Monica L. *Slaves to Fashion: Black Dandyism and the Styling of Black Diasporic Identity*. Durham: Duke University Press, 2009.

White, Shane and Graham White. *Stylin' African American Expressive Culture from Its Beginnings to the Zoot Suit*. Ithaca: Cornell University Press, 1998.

Section 1

Anonymous Histories

1

The Fabric of Fast Fashion: Enslaved Wearers and Makers as Designers in the American Fashion System

Katie Knowles

On June 1, 1830, Lucy Ann Brown was taken to the Baltimore jail as a runaway. She was wearing "a green bonnet, a common cotton shawl, a red plaid frock, a blue and yellow plaid apron" but "no shoes or stockings."[1] Sources such as this runaway slave advertisement, taken out by enslavers to help track down and reclaim enslaved people who escaped their bondage, reveal a visualization of slavery, demonstrating that the everyday wear of enslaved Southerners in the antebellum period was highly individualized and comprised a multitude of fabrics, colors, and styles. By providing low quality and limited wardrobes to enslaved people, enslavers created a code of dress that was meant to mark enslaved people as outsiders. Although many runaway advertisements list quite a quantity and variety of clothing worn by enslaved people, such as the description of Brown's apparel, other advertisements speak of desperate conditions. One advertisement, which gave no name for the thirty-year-old man who freed himself in Virginia in the late spring of 1852, noted that "his clothes were so filthy and tattered that their color cannot be known."[2] The jailor who incarcerated Jacob as a runaway did not even attempt to explain Jacob's apparel, stating simply that his "clothing [was] so much worn out that a description cannot be given."[3] Yet, enslaved people manipulated and supplemented the clothing allowance provided to them. During the antebellum period, enslaved people designed alternative dress codes that were usually misunderstood, unacknowledged, or appropriated by the dominant American fashion system. Necessity created by limited access to quality apparel inspired enslaved people to design new methods of expressing fashionability. Enslaved fashion creators seized opportunities to assert their personal identities and tastes.

When Lucy Ann Brown was jailed in Baltimore, she wore a riot of colors and patterns in her clothing. The blue and yellow plaid apron she wore over her red plaid frock presented a clashing palette of brightness. She covered her head with a green bonnet, but her feet had nothing to protect them. Her ensemble is both typical of the everyday clothing worn by enslaved people, and uniquely styled to her own personality. Brown's limited access to apparel marked her as an outsider in mainstream American fashion culture. Her lack of footwear speaks to the conditions of enslavement that reflect the domination and suffering of enslaved people's lived experiences, but her color combination choices demonstrate the pleasure she took for herself in styling her appearance.[4]

Designers and the Fashion System

The goals of enslavers in using clothing to dominate and cause suffering to enslaved people created tension with the ways enslaved people found pleasure within their everyday dress practices. This fraught relationship provides a complex understanding of how enslaved people affected the early American fashion system. To fully appreciate their contributions requires a reframing of terminology. In the past decade, fashion studies has shifted as a field toward a more inclusive and more accurate consideration of fashion as "changing styles of dress accepted by a group of people, at a specific time, and in a specific place."[5] This definition, developed by Linda Welters and Abby Lillethun, does not limit the phenomenon of fashion to Western Europe and North America, nor to only capitalistic societies. They further define the social phenomenon of a fashion system as "a process of innovation in dress and appearance practices, and diffusion to others."[6] Multiple fashion systems exist in a single place and time, dependent on the relational identities of individuals within a social power system. In the antebellum United States, fashion systems operated simultaneously at global, national, regional, and local levels. In each of these settings, the social identities of people were both defined by others and self-determined through fashion.

Enslaved Americans affected changes in fashion from the micro level of a single rural plantation to the macro level of global industrialization. Recognition of their contributions requires a reframing and redefinition of the term and role of the designer. Traditionally, the term designer is used in reference to the creative maker of innovative apparel that is then adopted by society to become the next fashionable garment, style, or silhouette. But this limited concept of apparel designers as the only innovators does not align with expanding definitions of fashion and how it changes. This chapter argues that designers are indeed the innovators that drive changes in fashion systems. However, the people who develop products used to make apparel, and who use textiles and clothing to stylize existing apparel in inventive ways, should also be considered as designers. Rivana Boynton's recollection of the methods enslaved women used to achieve the mainstream fashionable silhouette of the 1850s cage crinoline is one example of fashion design through resourcefulness and improvisation: "My missus, she made me a pair of hoops, or I guess she bought it, but some of the slaves took thin limbs from trees and made their hoops. Others made them out of stiff paper and others would starch their skirts stiff with rice starch to make their skirts stand way out."[7]

As wearers and makers, enslaved people were at the forefront of the nascent modern American fashion system that began to develop during the late eighteenth century and was solidifying its position by the mid-1800s. The patterns of consumption and approaches to wearing textiles and clothing that ultimately became what is today called fast fashion were first experienced by enslaved people. By expanding the history of the rise of fast fashion much further back than the standard narrative of its birth during the 1960s, it is evident that enslaved people were also implementing the tools of resistance that are resurfacing in the early twenty-first century to combat a fashion system driven by poor quality, ill-fitting, impersonal products.[8] When Sylvia Cannon was not provided with warm undergarments for the winter, she made a "petticoat out of old dress an patch en patch till couldn' tell which place weave."[9] Her description of a repurposed dress so heavily patched that the original parts could not be distinguished from the added scraps is an example of visible mending. In her case, the need for winter clothing resulted in a moment for self-expression and individualization.

Industrialization aided enslavers and others invested in a racially exclusionary American fashion system by promoting the mass production of fabrics and ready-made clothing. Enslaved people were at the center of the shift from older, slower methods of textile-making and use that prioritized long-lasting fabrics and made-to-measure fit, to the current system that encourages producing fabrics that do not last (thus driving the need for an ever-increasing purchasing cycle) and clothing constructed according to ranges of size rather than individual bodies.

Enslaved people negotiated a space within these shifting fashion systems, forging new ways of self-expression while experiencing the gradual loss of direct knowledge of making textiles and clothing. By recognizing the experiences of enslaved makers and wearers, this chapter reveals the importance of Black style and culture to the current fashion industry. Enslaved Southerners in the antebellum United States were among the first people to experience the wearing of standard-sized clothing and disposable fabrics. This chapter presents extant objects and supporting archival evidence centered on the use of ready-to-wear tailored menswear and homemaking practices, including the making of cloth and dyestuffs. Understanding how enslaved people designed space for their bodies through clothing centers them in this historical moment and within the longer history of the modern American fashion system.

The Roots of Ready-to-Wear

Willis Woodsen, describing his job as a carriage footman, remembered that his enslaver "got me a uniform, most like a soldier's uniform, ceptin mine was red, wid black stripes down de sides ... I wore my red suit when I went to church wid de white folks, and held de horses, while dey listened to do sermon."[10] Woodsen's comparison of his livery to a military uniform speaks to his sense of importance when dressed in the garb of a footman. Livery, worn by servants both free and enslaved throughout the United States during the nineteenth century, did indeed harken back to military uniforms because both relied upon styles that were popular during the late eighteenth century but had long since gone out of fashion.

Woodsen's livery coat was probably similar to one that was used by a man enslaved by Dr. William Newton Mercer in Louisiana, and that is now part of the Historic New Orleans Collection.[11] The livery coat is one of two Brooks Brothers coats purchased by Mercer for men he enslaved. The dark tan fulled wool coats were likely purchased by Mercer in 1858 during one of his many trips to New York City, where he bought plantation tools and bulk purchases of cloth and "negro shoes" each year in addition to expensive wines and luxury goods for his own use.[12]

Only one of the coats, a frock coat, has a Brooks Brothers brand label in it, but both were made with similar lining materials and construction methods, though the frock coat is of a slightly higher quality wool than the livery coat. The label for Brooks Brothers of New York, a firm that was known for its men's tailored clothing, in the interior collar of the frock coat is an early example of the branded labeling of ready-made clothing. The firm began selling ready-made suits in 1849 and changed the name to Brooks Brothers in 1850.[13] The buttons on the coats are decorated with a raised design of a bird, said to be

Figure 1.1 Brooks Brothers. Livery coat, circa 1860. Wool, linen, cotton, and metal. The Historic New Orleans Collection, 2013.0115.1.

the Mercer family crest.[14] The enslaved men who wore these coats clearly did important work for Mercer, and their bodies were marked as belonging to the Mercer family through the wearing of similar looking apparel embellished with the same buttons.

These coats represent a newer way of purchasing fitted, tailored clothing that was used by lower and working-class people in addition to enslavers. In buying them, Mercer was exercising his ability to consume goods sourced in a far-off metropolitan city in the North. He also used the coats to identify the bodies of the enslaved men who wore them as belonging to him—a uniform that signified to others that he had the monetary capital to own people and to clothe them well—thus increasing his cultural capital as a man of wealth and prestige. The value of well-clothed enslaved bodies served to indicate to other enslavers that certain enslaved bodies belonged to particular persons of importance within the social world of the ruling class.[15]

These coats were noted within the historical record and preserved into the twenty-first century because of their purchaser and the social standing of Mercer and his relatives before and after the Civil War. The actual wearers of the coats are lost within the story, reflecting the social function that the coats provided Mercer: a space to display his wealth upon the bodies of enslaved men. These men experienced the movement of their bodies dressed in ready-made tailored menswear, a relatively new category of clothing that had been a growing market from the second quarter of the 1800s.[16] The standardization of sizing using clothing patterns to create men's suit components such as jackets, vests, and trousers led to poorer fitting garments that were constructed using methods designed to maximize output rather than strength, durability, and fit. This poor fit due to the lack of custom measurements also led to the wearers being identified as lower class in public spaces. The mismatched seam lines and sloppy finishings on both Brooks Brothers coats were noticeable details that indicated that the men who wore them were not of a high social status. In response to limited access to clothing, enslaved people wore combinations of apparel that were considered to clash in terms of the fabric patterns or colors, or were too small or large for their frames according to mainstream fashion standards. These ways of combining cut and style contributed to the creation of an alternative dress code practiced by enslaved people.

In the regional fashion system of the antebellum South, enslaved people who dressed in livery uniforms were recognized as being of a higher stature than other enslaved people. Willis Woodsen's understanding of his social status

Figure 1.2 Brooks Brothers. Frock coat, circa 1860. Wool, linen, cotton, and metal. The Historic New Orleans Collection, 2013.0138.

and his sense of self-worth, derived from his access to a livery uniform, is an expression of fashionability. Enslaved people like Woodsen and the men who wore these Brooks Brothers coats had increased power in relation to other enslaved people. They usually had access to a greater variety and a higher quality of apparel, and their livery allowed them to inhabit places off-limit to most Black Southerners. Woodsen's pride in his appearance is an instance of a dominated person within a power system understanding his position as above that of other oppressed people through his access to clothing. The role of his body as a site of display for his enslaver's wealth not only solidified the power of the enslaver, but also awarded Woodsen greater power within and beyond the enslaved community.

Homemaking and Resistance

Ready-to-wear clothing was the result of the rise of industrial textile manufacturing, which prioritized output and continuous consumption over long-lasting products. Enslaved people and their clothing played a fundamental role in changing the textile industry, in particular through their use of a product called negro cloth. Negro cloth was cheap and rough. Unlike other fabrics of the period that were still being designed to last, sometimes for several years with proper care, negro cloth was made to be used up, worn through, and thrown out. Both textile factory owners and enslavers embarked on a project to create fabrics that would last exactly until the next period when enslaved people were to receive new clothing but would cost the factory owner minimal money to make and the enslaver minimal money to purchase. This is a very basic reduction of a complicated global supply system built on a capitalist economy.[17] At the heart of it were enslaved people in the US South who both provided the labor to supply factories with cheap raw cotton and were the ultimate end-users of the finished cheap goods.

Negro cloth was a consumer good designed specifically for the race-based slave system that developed in the Americas. The term itself helped contribute to efforts by the ruling powers to define enslaved people as raced and to define all people of African descent as slaves. To fully understand the product negro cloth, it must be understood as a raced product–one that could only exist in a racist capitalist economy.[18] The word negro in the name of the fabric further solidifies its position as a product designed to reinforce race-based slavery by equating the textile with Black skin. Jacob Blunt was incarcerated in Richmond as a runaway wearing "common negro clothing, and very ragged and dirty," despite his claim to be a free person of color and his even having free papers with him.[19] Enslaved people were well aware of efforts to define and restrict their bodies through visual displays.

Negro cloth was usually bought in bulk, resulting in the distribution of the same fabric across the entire population on a single plantation. The attempts by enslaved people to individualize their clothing or to obtain higher quality goods were more than vanity; these were people resisting a product meant to mark them as enslaved laborers, indistinguishable from one body to the next. Because most enslaved people in the antebellum South lived on large, rural plantations, understanding the relationship between local, regional, and global fashion systems is a key component of this story. While there were likely specific styles or tastes evident to those on a single plantation or within small regions of neighboring rural plantations, there were shared patterns of behavior in the responses of enslaved people in very different areas who described similar methods of resistance through their fashion choices.

While industrially produced negro cloth was increasing as the nineteenth century progressed, the work of textile production done by enslaved people remained a crucial part of the Southern economy. Three vibrantly colored fabric samples in the collection of the American Civil War Museum provide a window into the continued textile-making practices of enslaved people throughout the antebellum period. According to museum records, the blue, yellow, and red wool fabrics were made in 1863 by an unidentified enslaved woman on the Woodruff, South Carolina plantation belonging to Mary Pilgram. The catalog record for the blue and white checked fabric notes, "The indigo used to dye the cloth was raised on the homeplace as well."[20] This brief notation indicates that cultivating indigo and processing it into a dyestuff was a knowledge and skillset developed and maintained on this South Carolina plantation by at least one enslaved woman up until the legal ending of slavery in the United States in 1865. People on this plantation also knew how to harvest, clean, spin, and weave the wool thread used to make these woven samples, and in a manner that required setting up a loom to create checked patterns. These and other fabric samples in the American Civil War Museum's collection suggest that home production of cloth on plantations in the South existed simultaneously with the increasing industrialization of the textile industry and emerging global supply chains. The knowledge some enslaved people maintained about processing, constructing, and caring for fabric and clothing allowed them to individualize their appearances in ways not available to all.

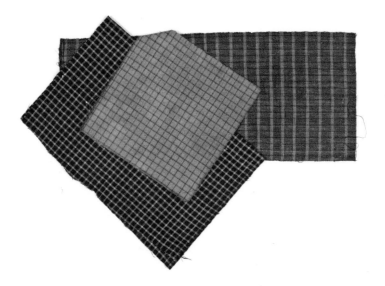

Figure 1.3 Unidentified enslaved woman. Fabric samples, 1863. Wool. American Civil War Museum, 985.10.247, 248a, 248b.

Enslaved women in particular were closely involved with the production of their apparel. On some plantations, this meant growing cotton and linen and raising sheep for wool and cows for leather. On some cotton plantations, a portion of the cash crop was set aside for home use rather than shipped to market. Rose Williams gave an abbreviated summary of the months of work that went into transforming cotton from boll to fabric. Her recollections demonstrate the close relationship enslaved people had to their clothing through this process. Williams stated, "clothes dat we wore was made right dar what we lives, first we picks de cotton in baskets, den feeds it ter a little ole gin … Den it was carded, spinned, and den weaved and made into our clothes."[21] Breaking down the many steps listed by Williams shows that nearly every day of enslaved people's lives involved textile production of some kind, whether it was plowing land that would eventually grow cotton to be manufactured in England or hand sewing the sleeves of a jacket.

Enslaved people often took great time and energy to color the thread, yarn, and cloth that they produced. Dyeing was done either before the thread or yarn was woven, in order to create colored designs such as stripes and checks, or it was done after weaving to achieve a solid colored fabric. Dyestuffs could be procured from locally available natural items, or they could be purchased.

Enslavers and enslaved people procured a variety of coloring agents. Indigo, the dyestuff mentioned in the catalog record for the blue and white wool check in the American Civil War Museum's collection, was a popular crop grown in some parts of the South into the antebellum period and used locally to dye textiles.[22] Emma Tidwell gave a detailed description of how she cultivated, harvested, and prepared indigo for use as dye:

> We planted indigo an hit growed jes like wheat. When hit got ripe we gathered hit an we would put hit in a barrel an let hit soak bout er week den we would take de indigo stems out an squeeze all de juice outn dem, put de juice back in de barrel an let hit stay dere bout nother week, den we jes stirred an stirred one whole day. We let hit set three or four days den drained de water offn hit an dat left de settlings an de settlings wuz blueing jes like us have dese days. We cut our in little blocks. Den we dyed clothes wid hit. We had purty blue cloth. De way we set de color we put alum in hit. Dat make de color stay right dere.[23]

A wide array of other dyestuffs was available either cultivated or wild, including sumac, walnut hulls, red clay, and poke berries.[24] All of these dyes, particularly those available in the wild or through local cultivation, provided opportunities for enslaved people to personalize their clothing without incurring expenses.

Knowledge about dyeing and dyestuffs came from many sources. Some of it was passed down through the generations from African ancestors.[25] Dyeing, weaving, and spinning also had long histories in Western Europe, where many women knew how to spin, and increasingly also how to weave and dye as the network of the guild system was broken down over the eighteenth century.[26] Weaving and spinning were likely skills taught by women of both races to each other, though by the antebellum period these tasks were seen as below the station of elite white women.[27] In the North American colonies, both Europeans and Africans encountered new plants that contained multiple possibilities as dyestuffs. The natural dyes used in the antebellum South were likely a combination of several world cultures adapting previous knowledge; this was a shared knowledge of skills that created a uniquely American dye culture.

Once dyed, thread could be woven into stripes, checks, and—if someone skilled enough in weaving was available—multicolored plaids. Cloth dyed in the piece or finished garments that were dyed could set a person apart from the crowd. In places where dozens of people were given the same textile supplies or clothing allotments, such differences in appearance could have a big impact. These efforts to create individualized fabrics and garments, despite the heavy use they would see as work clothing, demonstrate the value many enslaved people placed on looking unique. Over the antebellum period an increasing number of enslavers, especially in the Old Southwest where short-staple cotton production was concentrated, relied on industrial negro cloth and ready-to-wear apparel to supply clothing for enslaved people. Opportunities for enslaved people to make their own fabric or apparel, or to customize it, decreased due to a lack of time and lost knowledge of these making skills.

Conclusion

Black style and the alternative dress codes created by both free and enslaved Black people within rural and urban local fashion systems were dismissed and ridiculed through the process of nationalistic culture-making undertaken by white people in the antebellum United States. Despite these efforts of dismissal or erasure, African Americans designed space for themselves by fashioning alternative dress codes that allowed them to extend their self-evaluation and that of their communities into subcultures that sometimes affected the dominant ways of dressing and styles in mainstream American fashion. The observations of formerly enslaved woman Laura Moore that "De white folks would say, 'I wishes I could wear hances [handkerchiefs] on my head 'cause they looks so pretty,'" reveals the importance enslaved women attached to their head coverings as beautifying and stylish objects, and their recognition that white women sometimes envied their style choices.[28] Moore's statement also indicates the pride in Black style that enslaved people expressed. Their valuation of themselves as fashionable was not strictly tied to the acceptance of their choices by white people or mainstream fashion culture.

Enslavers expressed their desire for a monochromatic workforce by purchasing ready-made livery uniforms for enslaved personal servants, by distributing the same shoes and clothing to all of the people they enslaved, and by limiting the amount of apparel to the bare minimum. But it seems that by the antebellum period enslavers had given up trying to actually enforce uniformity within the appearance of the enslaved population. Through centuries of collective resistance, enslaved people had gained the upper hand in terms of personalizing their clothing and appearance. Lucy Ann Brown fashioned a distinctively colorful, patterned ensemble for herself. Willis Woodsen flipped the notion that livery was undesirable attire, instead expressing power in this fashion. Emma Tidwell labored over the arduous process of indigo dyeing to brighten the fashions of the people in her community. By the early nineteenth century, this insistence on fashionability was a continuation of an established pattern of everyday resistance.

Enslaved people were at the center of the transition in apparel and textile supply and fashion that occurred over the long nineteenth century, a transition that created the modern American fashion system. They used home production to defy the uniformity of the industrializing and monotonizing negro cloth industry, they improvised ways of expressing fashionability while making do with inadequate supplies of fabric and apparel, and they experienced their bodies wearing mass-produced ready-made tailored clothing by adapting what a fashionable fit to the uniformed body meant.

Ultimately, knowing more about the clothing of enslaved people in the antebellum South demonstrates how deeply entrenched race and racism were in the United States by the antebellum period. Fashion, and by extension the fashion system, is often trivialized. Yet, it was deliberately used by white people in their attempts to exclude African Americans from participating in American culture, from expressing themselves individually and collectively, and from being recognized as contributors to fashionable society. But enslaved Southerners designed behaviors of consumption and uses of mass-produced fabrics and apparel that continue into the twenty-first century. Current methods of resistance against fast fashion such as slow-making, customizing, and repurposing clothing can be traced back to enslaved people seeking to sustain their very souls.

Notes

1   "Advertisement," *Baltimore Gazette and Daily Advertiser*, June 1, 1830, 3.
2   "Advertisement," *Richmond Enquirer*, May 11, 1852, 3.
3   "Advertisement," *Richmond Enquirer*, October 25, 1836, 1.
4   The concept that enslaved people lived within three bodies—the body of domination, the body of suffering, and the body of pleasure—is a method of analysis drawn from the work of Stephanie M. H. Camp. All three of the bodies that Camp identifies existed within the one physical body of every enslaved individual at the same time. One did not exist without the other, and the conditions of enslavement caused the existence of all three. The dominated, suffering, and pleasurable bodies Camp defines represent the experience of a single person who lived in all of those bodies simultaneously. See Camp, *Closer to Freedom: Enslaved Women and Everyday Resistance in the Plantation South* (Chapel Hill: University of North Carolina Press, 2004).
5   Linda Welters and Abby Lillethun, *Fashion History: A Global View* (London: Bloomsbury, 2018), 13.
6   Ibid., 5–6.

7   George P. Rawick, ed., *The American Slave: A Composite Autobiography* (1941, Westport: Greenwood Publishing Company, reprint ed., 1972), 17.1: 44.

8   Stephanie O. Crofton and Luis G. Dopico, "Zara-Inditex and the Growth of Fast Fashion," *Essays in Economic and Business History* 25, no. 1 (2007): 41–53.

9   Rawick, *American Slave*, 2.1: 189.

10 Ibid., S2-10.9: 4279.

11 Object file, 2013.0115.1, Historic New Orleans Collection, New Orleans, Louisiana.

12 William Newton Mercer papers, Manuscripts Collection 64, Louisiana Research Collection, Howard-Tilton Memorial Library, Tulane University, New Orleans, Louisiana; William Newton Mercer papers, Mss. 292, 1051, 1233, Louisiana and Lower Mississippi Valley Collections, Louisiana State University Libraries, Baton Rouge, Louisiana. The Mercer papers were accessed in the microfilm collection, "Records of Ante-bellum Southern Plantations from the Revolution through the Civil War."

13 Kate Betts, ed., *Brooks Brothers: 200 Years of American Style* (New York: Rizzoli, 2017), 14. For more on the company's ties to slavery see Jonathan Michael Square, "A Stain on an All-American Brand: How Brooks Brothers Once Clothed Slaves," Vestoj, accessed August 5, 2020, http://vestoj.com/how-brooks-brothers-once-clothed-slaves/

14 Object file, 2013.0138, Historic New Orleans Collection, New Orleans, Louisiana.

15 The valuation of an enslaved person's clothed body by the enslaver of that person and the enslavers' peers speaks to Daina Ramey Berry's theory of the multiple values of enslaved bodies. The external values used by enslavers that Berry discusses are based upon monetary values, but there was also a value of cultural capital that enslavers practiced upon enslaved bodies. Daina Ramey Berry, *The Price for Their Pound of Flesh: The Value of the Enslaved, from Womb to Grave, in the Building of a Nation* (Boston: Beacon Press, 2017), 6–7.

16 Michael Zakim, *Ready-Made Democracy: A History of Men's Dress in the American Republic, 1760–1860* (Chicago: University of Chicago Press, 2003). See especially chapters 2 and 3.

17 Sven Beckert, *Empire of Cotton: A Global History* (New York: Alfred A. Knopf, 2015).

18 Seth Rockman, "Negro Cloth: Mastering the Market for Slave Clothing in Antebellum America," in *American Capitalism: New Histories*, ed. by Sven Beckert and Christine Desan (New York: Columbia University Press, 2018), 170–89.

19 Advertisement, *Richmond Enquirer*, May 11, 1838, 1.

20 Online collections catalog record for unidentified enslaved woman, 985.10.247, American Civil War Museum, accessed September 18, 2019, https://moconfederacy.pastperfectonline.com/webobject/11606447-7AFD-4EF5-B833-358282270476.

21 Rawick, *American Slave*, S2-10.9: 4125.

22 Jenny Balfour-Paul, *Indigo: From Mummies to Blue Jeans* (London: British Museum Press, 2011).

23 Ibid., 10.5: 331. For information on indigo cultivation in South Carolina specifically, see Andrea Feeser, *Red, White, and Black Make Blue: Indigo in the Fabric of Colonial South Carolina Life* (Athens: University of Georgia Press, 2013).

24 For a useful table of the dyestuffs and mordants mentioned in the Works Progress Administration interviews, see "Appendix III" in Helen Bradley Foster, "*New Raiments of Self*": *African American Clothing in the Antebellum South* (Oxford: Berg, 1997).

25 Colleen E. Kriger, *Cloth in West African History* (Lanham: AltaMira Press, 2006); Judith Perani and Norma Hackelman Wolff, *Cloth, Dress, and Art Patronage in West Africa* (Oxford and New York: Berg, 1999), 120.

26 Adrienne D. Hood, *The Weaver's Craft: Cloth, Commerce, and Industry in Early Pennsylvania* (Philadelphia: University of Pennsylvania Press, 2003); Marla R. Miller, *The Needle's Eye: Women and Work in the Age of Revolution* (Amherst: University of Massachusetts Press, 2006); Zara Anishanslin, "Industry, Idleness, and Protest: The Spitalfields Weaver as Guild Member and Cultural Symbol," in *Portrait of a Woman in Silk: Hidden Histories of the British Atlantic World* (New Haven: Yale University Press, 2016), 124–39.

27 Drew Gilpin Faust, "Chapter Ten: If I Were Once Released: The Garb of Gender," in *Mothers of Invention: Women of the Slaveholding South in the American Civil War* (Chapel Hill: University of North Carolina Press, 1996), 220–33; Elizabeth Fox-Genovese, *Within the Plantation Household: Black and White Women of the Old South* (Chapel Hill: University of North Carolina Press, 1988).

28 Rawick, *American Slave*, S2-7: 2744–5.

Bibliography

"Advertisement," *Baltimore Gazette and Daily Advertiser*, June 1, 1830, 3.

"Advertisement," *Richmond Enquirer*, October 25, 1836, 1.

Advertisement, *Richmond Enquirer*, May 11, 1838, 1.

"Advertisement," *Richmond Enquirer*, May 11, 1852, 3.

Anishanslin, Zara. "Industry, Idleness, and Protest: The Spitalfields Weaver as Guild Member and Cultural Symbol," in *Portrait of a Woman in Silk: Hidden Histories of the British Atlantic World*, 124–39, New Haven: Yale University Press, 2016.

Balfour-Paul, Jenny. *Indigo: From Mummies to Blue Jeans*. London: British Museum Press, 2011.

Beckert, Sven. *Empire of Cotton: A Global History*. New York: Alfred A. Knopf, 2015.

Berry, Daina Ramey. *The Price for Their Pound of Flesh: The Value of the Enslaved, from Womb to Grave, in the Building of a Nation*. Boston: Beacon Press, 2017.

Betts, Kate. ed., *Brooks Brothers: 200 Years of American Style*. New York: Rizzoli, 2017.

Camp, Stephanie M. H. *Closer to Freedom: Enslaved Women and Everyday Resistance in the Plantation South*. Chapel Hill: University of North Carolina Press, 2004.

Crofton, Stephanie O. and Luis G. Dopico. "Zara-Inditex and the Growth of Fast Fashion." *Essays in Economic and Business History* 25, no. 1 (2007): 41–53.

Faust, Drew Gilpin. "Chapter Ten: If I Were Once Released: The Garb of Gender," in *Mothers of Invention: Women of the Slaveholding South in the American Civil War,* 220–33, Chapel Hill: University of North Carolina Press, 1996.

Feeser, Andrea. *Red, White, and Black Make Blue: Indigo in the Fabric of Colonial South Carolina Life.* Athens: University of Georgia Press, 2013.

Foster, Helen Bradley. *"New Raiments of Self": African American Clothing in the Antebellum South.* Oxford: Berg, 1997.

Fox-Genovese, Elizabeth. *Within the Plantation Household: Black and White Women of the Old South.* Chapel Hill: University of North Carolina Press, 1988.

Hood, Adrienne D. *The Weaver's Craft: Cloth, Commerce, and Industry in Early Pennsylvania.* Philadelphia: University of Pennsylvania Press, 2003.

Hunt, Patricia K. "'Round Homespun Coat & Pantaloons of the Same': Slave Clothing as Reflected in Fugitive Slave Advertisements in Antebellum Georgia." *Georgia Historical Quarterly* 83, no. 4 (Winter 1999): 727–40.

Hunt, Patricia K. "The Struggle to Achieve Individual Expression through Clothing and Adornment: African American Women Under and After Slavery," in *Discovering the Women in Slavery,* ed. Patricia Morton, 227–40. Athens: University of Georgia Press, 1996.

Kriger, Colleen E. *Cloth in West African History.* Lanham: AltaMira Press, 2006.

Miller, Marla R. *The Needle's Eye: Women and Work in the Age of Revolution.* Amherst: University of Massachusetts Press, 2006.

Miller, Monica L. *Slaves to Fashion: Black Dandyism and the Styling of Black Diasporic Identity.* Durham: Duke University Press, 2009.

Perani, Judith, and Norma Hackelman Wolff. *Cloth, Dress, and Art Patronage in West Africa.* Oxford and New York: Berg, 1999.

Putman, Tyler Rudd. "The Slop Shop and the Almshouse: Ready-made Menswear in Philadelphia, 1790–1820." Master's thesis, University of Delaware, 2011.

Rawick, George P., ed. *The American Slave: A Composite Autobiography,* 1941. Westport: Greenwood Publishing Company, reprint ed., 1972.

Rockman, Seth. "Negro Cloth: Mastering the Market for Slave Clothing in Antebellum America," in *American Capitalism: New Histories,* ed. Sven Beckert and Christine Desan, 170–189. New York: Columbia University Press, 2018.

Tucker, Barbara M. *Industrializing Antebellum America: The Rise of Manufacturing Entrepreneurs in the Early Republic.* New York: Palgrave Macmillan, 2008.

Welters, Linda, and Abby Lillethun. *Fashion History: A Global View.* London: Bloomsbury Academic, 2018.

White, Shane, and Graham White. *Stylin': African American Expressive Culture from Its Beginnings to the Zoot Suit.* Ithaca: Cornell University Press, 1998.

Zakim, Michael. *Ready-Made Democracy: A History of Men's Dress in the American Republic, 1760–1860.* Chicago: University of Chicago Press, 2003.

2

Slavery's Warp, Liberty's Weft: A Look at the Work of Eighteenth- and Nineteenth-Century Enslaved Fashion Makers and Their Legacies

Jonathan Michael Square

Rosa Parks received her first sewing lessons from her mother and maternal grandmother, both of whom made quilts. Parks was enrolled at the Montgomery Industrial School for Girls in 1924, at first with her mother Leona paying her tuition, and later as a work-study pupil who cleaned classrooms at the end of every day in exchange for free tuition. In 1954, she was employed as a tailor's assistant and seamstress at the Montgomery Fair Department Store in downtown Montgomery, Alabama.[1] She also sewed at home for private clients, family members, and herself. On December 1, 1955, after a full day of work, Parks left the store and boarded a bus home at around six o'clock. Onboard, she refused to give up her seat to a white passenger. This act of civil disobedience launched the Montgomery Bus Boycott, a seminal event in the American Civil Rights Movement. Just two generations out of slavery, Parks is but one example of the many African American fashion makers whose sewing acumen dovetailed with their work as activists.

Very little scholarly attention has been devoted to Black fashion in the late twentieth and twenty-first centuries. There is even less scholarship on Black fashion that reaches further back into the era of slavery (and even into precolonial Africa). Nevertheless, it is not hard to find examples of early Black fashion makers who used their sewing and dressmaking skills as a means of gaining more autonomy within a system of chattel slavery predicated on subservience. From Grace Wisher, an African American indentured servant who is believed to have helped in the creation of the Star-Spangled Banner,[2] to Nancy Prince, the free African American woman who documented her travels in one of the first travel narratives penned by a Black woman and who later worked as a

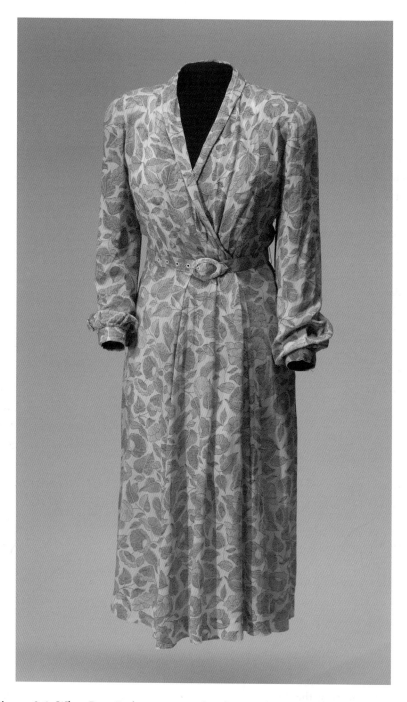

Figure 2.1 When Rosa Parks was arrested on her way home from Montgomery Fair where she worked as a seamstress, she was working on this wrap-style dress. Collection of the Smithsonian National Museum of African American History and Culture, Gift of the Black Fashion Museum founded by Lois K. Alexander-Lane.

seamstress.[3] Examples of early Black fashion makers abound. Moreover, their skills as seamstresses cannot be divorced from their efforts to end slavery and the discrimination against themselves and other African Americans.

Critical inquiries into fashion history are often viewed as separate from the study of African American freedom struggles, but a number of scholars have shown that these two seemingly disparate areas of study are intimately linked. For example, Tanisha C. Ford explores the Civil Rights Movement, Black Power, and the anti-apartheid eras through the lens of Black fashion, hair, and beauty.[4] In a similar way, Monica Miller examines how dandyism in Black diasporic communities was not just a fashion statement, but also an act of resistance.[5] In her tentatively titled book, *Intentional Tourists: International Leisure Travel and the Making of Black Global Citizens*, Tiffany Gill argues that African American fashion designer Freddye Henderson was responsible for promoting Ghana as a site of pan-Africanist roots tourism after its independence from Great Britain in 1957.[6]

Taking inspiration from the work of these scholars, this chapter focuses on free and enslaved makers' contributions to the development of the American fashion system and nascent African American freedom struggles during the eighteenth and nineteenth centuries. It will thus contribute to the burgeoning literature on the integral role that free and enslaved people played in the birth of the fashion system during the eighteenth and nineteenth centuries. Although they made their livings as dressmakers and seamstresses, many of these women are better known as abolitionists and early Civil Rights activists. What is essential to understand is that their labor as makers and caretakers of clothing cannot be divorced from their efforts to gain greater self-determination for themselves and other African Americans. By failing to consider fashion as a tool strategically wielded by enslaved seamstresses and their descendants, historical research and fashion scholarship miss a key dimension through which African Americans understood themselves and with which they fought for their place in American society. This chapter uses slave narratives, runaway slave ads, published journalistic accounts, and artistic and photographic evidence alongside analyses of extant garments to trace the histories of free and enslaved women of African descent who were on the vanguard of the United States-based fashion system. This chapter argues that, with their technical skills and creative ingenuity, these early Black designers laid the groundwork for the genesis of the American fashion industry. Black female designers not only sewed and mended simple articles of clothing; they designed original garments, and sometimes, as small business owners, even established ateliers and hired seamstresses. Through their fashion labor, enslaved seamstresses and their descendants promoted self-reliance, cultural pride, and resistance against racial oppression. Although their garments are understudied (and, in most cases, have not survived), their work was foundational to later generations of Black designers who benefited from the ground they broke.

Unsewn Histories

Enslaved people were treated as units of labor, and they were identified—and valued—by their marketable skills. In runaway slave ads, particular attention was given to the enslaved person's sewing skills. In one ad, Kate is described as a mulatto capable of "work[ing] well with a needle." Kate had lived in the same household since she was an infant, but she ran away from her enslaver on July 21, 1777. This was not the first time she had tried to escape. Earlier, she had attempted to pass as a free woman and headed toward the Caribbean. Her enslaver suggested that she again might be "lurking about some of the shores, in order to get off." Runaway slave ads are important resources for historians interested in self-fashioning among formerly enslaved people. Her enslaver's runaway slave ad further mentions that Kate took "a great number of very good clothes" with her. These pieces of clothing would have allowed her to pass as a free woman, make multiple outfit changes, and elude capture. Thus, Kate's sewing skills, in conjunction with her knowledge of the power of fashion, equipped her with the tools to escape the brutality of slavery.[7]

Charlotte was a seamstress for Martha Washington at Mount Vernon, where her primary responsibility was making and maintaining Martha's wardrobe. As an enslaved domestic, Charlotte would have been provided with clothing finer than the more utilitarian workaday garments allocated to the enslaved people engaged in agricultural work and other menial tasks. Moreover, as Martha's seamstress, she may have developed a taste for elite fashion and acquired her own fashionable attire through second-hand clothing markets.[8] On one of her Sundays off, Charlotte traveled to nearby Alexandria, Virginia, where she crossed paths with a Mrs. Charles MacIver. Mrs. MacIver believed Charlotte was wearing a dress that she had once owned. During the late eighteenth century, all clothing was custom made, so it is plausible that Mrs. MacIver could have positively identified a previously owned garment. According to Mrs. MacIver's husband the dress was "altered for the worse, particularly in the Flouncing which went all round the Tail. The Lining originally overshot the Chintz at the Sleeves, which used to be concealed by Cuffs, as they were very short. I understand the Boarder is turned upside down."[9] Charlotte's alterations of these dress embellishments contested the authority of the master class and the institutional structures that maintained slavery, as she had used "the language of clothing to assault the hierarchies of race."[10] This run-in with Mrs. MacIver reveals that Charlotte understood the power of fashion and wielded it as a means of greater self-determination.[11]

In another notable case, Cumber constructed a cotton dress for her mistress Janie Wright Robeson MacKethan in 1864, during the height of the Civil War. A brief biography of Cumber (or Combo, as she is referred to) was written inside the hem of the dress. Cumber worked on the Robeson Plantation near Tar Heel, North Carolina, and was married to Jim Dry, the plantation's carriage driver, with whom she had seven children. Because the import of cloth and clothing decreased radically during the Civil War, with textile production earmarked for the armies, the calico from which Cumber constructed the dress for Robeson MacKethan was imported by a blockade runner and cost eight dollars per yard,

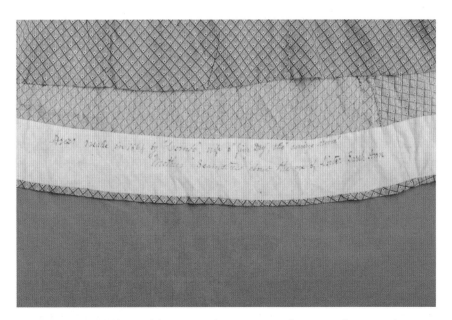

Figure 2.2 On the hem of this cotton dress is written, "Dress made in 1864 by 'Combo' wife of 'Jim Dry,' the 'carriage driver'/mothers 'seamstress' about the age of sister Sarah Ann." Photo by the North Carolina Museum of History.

a highly inflated sum. Nonetheless, Robeson MacKethan insisted on maintaining an up-to-date wardrobe during the war, requiring great efforts by Cumber. Yet, it was this sewing work that also allowed her to eke out a living for herself and endure the remaining days of slavery in the United States.[12]

These are just three examples of enslaved fashion makers whose collective lives traversed eighteenth- and nineteenth-century United States, as the country shifted from the auspices of British colonization to its existence as an independent nation divided by sectarian strife. This chapter seeks to draw a connection between enslaved seamstresses and dressmakers and the later generations of African American designers who began making clothing during the nineteenth century, some working well into the twentieth century.[13] Many of these women, such as Harriet Jacobs and Margaret Mahammitt Hagan, are not known primarily as dressmakers, instead being recognized as abolitionists and early Civil Rights leaders. However, these women supported themselves (and sometimes their families and even their enslavers) with their fashion labor.

Harriet Jacobs

The life of Harriet Jacobs illustrates the degree to which needlework was embedded in freedom struggles for African American seamstresses. Jacobs, best known for her book, *Incidents in the Life of a Slave Girl*, published in 1861, was born into slavery in Edenton, North Carolina, in 1813. Jacobs sewed her way through slavery, her flight from bondage, and her struggle as an abolitionist. Orphaned at the age of six, she was taught to read and sew by her enslaver Margaret Horniblow.[14] When Horniblow died, Jacobs was willed to her three-year-old niece, whose father, Dr. James Norcom, became her de facto enslaver. Her time in the Norcom household was marked by neglect and abuse, and the Norcoms did not provide adequate food and clothing for their enslaved bondsmen. Jacobs famously described her dress during this period as such: "I have a vivid recollection of the linsey-woolsey dress given me every winter by Mrs. Flint [a pseudonym for Norcom's wife Matilda Horniblow Norcom]. How I hated it! It was one of the badges of slavery."[15] As the passage here elucidates, Jacobs, from a young age, understood the use of clothing to mark her identity as an enslaved person. After years of repeated emotional and physical abuse at the hands of Norcom, James gave her an ultimatum between remaining with him and her own children on his plantation or working on his son's plantation six miles away. She chose to free herself of his abuse and work for his son. Clothing other slaves was one of her many tasks as the de facto superintendent of this other plantation.[16]

At age twenty-two, Jacobs escaped from slavery, prompted by the continued predations of James Norcom, which never ceased despite her move to another plantation. Her runaway slave ad read: "Being a good seamstress, she has been accustomed to dress well, has a variety of very fine clothes, made in the prevailing fashion, and will probably appear, if abroad, tricked out in gay and fashionable finery."[17] Evidenced again is that Jacobs is not only a gifted needle worker, but also a fashionable dresser. For the next seven years, she lived as a fugitive slave in her grandmother's attic, during which time she sewed and read the Bible. "My eyes had become accustomed to the dim light, and by holding my book or work in a certain position near the aperture I contrived to read and sew," she wrote.[18] She continued living as a fugitive slave between Massachusetts and New York while supporting her children with her work as a seamstress. For the remainder of her life, she worked as an abolitionist and reformer with her siblings and children. Although she is known for her abolitionist activism, her life was supported and punctuated by her ability to sew. Although there are no known surviving pieces that she constructed, her legacy as a fashion creator lives on through her writing and the abolitionist efforts that her sewing enabled.

Elizabeth Keckly

Fortunately, there are some surviving pieces made by Elizabeth Keckly.[19] Keckly and Jacobs had a lot in common, beginning with the fact that both were born to elite enslavers. Both were also enslaved domestics who were survivors of sexual harassment or assault, and both had fair complexions and were identified as "mulattos." Further, both used money from their sewing to support themselves and their loved ones (and, in the case of Keckly, her enslavers). One important difference is that Keckly is known primarily as a dressmaker, while Jacobs is more often remembered as an abolitionist and author. Keckly was born just five years after Jacobs in 1818, and unlike Jacobs, who escaped from slavery, Keckly bought her freedom and that of her son primarily through her own hard work, but also with money borrowed from her white dressmaking clientele in St. Louis, Missouri.[20]

As a child, Keckly learned to read and sew from her mother, who made clothing for her enslaver's family and his slaves. Sewing was a skill that Keckly continued to hone within the various households in which she was enslaved.

At one point during the late 1840s or early 1850s, she was supporting the entire seventeen-person household of Anne Burwell Garland and her husband Hugh A. Garland in St. Louis with money that she made from dressmaking. Keckly developed such a loyal clientele that these elite St. Louis women willingly lent her $1,200 to buy her and her son's freedom in 1855. Newly freed, Keckly moved to Washington, DC and quickly became the dressmaker of choice for the Washingtonian elite, working first with Varina Howell, wife of Jefferson Davis. Keckly, however, is best known for serving as Mary Todd Lincoln's dressmaker during her time as First Lady and directly afterward. Keckly penned *Behind the Scenes, or, Thirty Years a Slave, and Four Years in the White House*, in 1868, a memoir of her years in the White House, in which she reveals intimate details about the Lincoln household during the Civil War.[21] Beyond her experience

Figure 2.3 Elizabeth Keckly designed this purple silk velvet and satin dress for Mary Todd Lincoln who wore it during the 1861–1862 winter social season. Division of Political and Military History, National Museum of American History, Smithsonian Institution.

as a dressmaker for the crème de la crème of Washington's elite, and alongside her involvement in the inner circles of the White House, Keckly was an activist who fought fiercely for the end of slavery. Although she maintained a cordial relationship with her former enslavers, Keckly was a staunch abolitionist. She founded the Contraband Relief Association in August 1862, receiving donations from both President and Mrs. Lincoln, as well as other white patrons and well-to-do free Black people in Washington, DC. The organization provided food, shelter, clothing, and emotional support to recently freed slaves and sick and wounded soldiers.[22]

Thankfully, later generations of scholars and others have been able to learn of both Jacobs's and Keckly's sewing skills and activist work because both were literate and had the power to tell their own stories through their published memoirs. Although Keckly is remembered as an expert "mantua-maker," while Jacobs is better known as an abolitionist, both women simultaneously utilized their needlework and advocacy skills throughout their lives.

Laying the Groundwork: Ann Lowe

The task of studying other early Black fashion designers' histories and material culture is often difficult because during the eighteenth and nineteenth centuries, most enslaved and even free seamstresses of color worked in relative obscurity for little or no pay. This is despite the fact that prior to the mechanization of the fashion system, with the widespread use of sewing machines and industrial systems emerging by the end of the nineteenth century, all clothing was made by hand, and the constructing of garments required skill and precision. These early dressmakers' work informed the careers of more widely recognized twentieth-century designers, such as Ann Lowe. Unfortunately, only a small number of handmade garments positively identified as having been made by a free or enslaved maker of color survive in museums and cultural institutions. There are three reasons why it is still difficult—two centuries later—to match surviving garments to the craftsmanship of enslaved people. First, most of these women were not credited for their work at the time. Second, records describing enslaved peoples and their occupations are not a reliable guide in differentiating those who worked as dressmakers and seamstresses—designing, sewing, and mending clothes—from those who performed other household duties, such as cooking or childcare. In other words, most women who worked as seamstresses would have also performed these other domestic duties. Third, the garments themselves are often "silent" as to their origin, as the enslaved seamstresses had to ply their craft under duress within slave societies. For these reasons, many African American dressmakers have been under-acknowledged in studies of Black fashion history.

Although the majority of women in eighteenth- and nineteenth-century America possessed basic sewing abilities, dressmaking, especially on a professional level, was a specialized skill. Women such as Margaret Mahammitt Hagan and Eliza Ann Gardner possessed such skills and could rely on them to support themselves and their families. They were also able to engage in other professional pursuits and activist work at different points in their lives. Hagan worked as an entrepreneur and dressmaker throughout her life, but she is most remembered as a reformer and groundbreaking business owner. Born in 1826, she lived in Maryland during the mid-1800s. In 1861, she moved to Philadelphia, where she owned a laundry. By the late 1800s, Hagan had moved to Washington, DC and had established a dressmaking business at 1109 F Street North West. While in Washington, DC, she also studied medical electricity—what is today more often called electrotherapy—and became a certified practitioner. After obtaining her certification, Hagan set up business in Williamsport, Pennsylvania. By the age of eighty, Hagan had owned and operated three medical electricity businesses, including two in Pennsylvania and one in New Jersey.[23] Although she does not appear to have been directly involved in abolitionist efforts, Hagan, as a wealthy Black female landowner and entrepreneur during slavery, disrupted white male supremacy and served as a living example of the potential of enterprising African Americans. Her progeny would go on to become prominent African American educators, athletes, religious leaders, and even an astronaut.[24]

Eliza Ann Gardner also worked as an entrepreneur and dressmaker throughout her life, but this work is eclipsed by her abolitionist efforts and her position in Boston's elite African American artisanal class. She also used her home as a stop on the Underground Railroad. Gardner was born in 1831 in New York City to free parents who made a living making sails for ocean vessels. The family moved to Boston in 1854, where they opened a sailmaking business on Grove Street in the West End. Gardner became active in her church and in the anti-slavery movement while making her living as a dressmaker, and was later employed as a keeper of a boarding house. She founded the missionary society of the African Methodist Episcopal Zion Church and was a strong advocate for women's equality within the church. As an activist, she knew and worked with many abolitionist leaders including Frederick Douglass, William Lloyd Garrison, and Wendell Phillips. She was also a cousin of W. E. B. Du Bois.[25]

The early Black fashion designers described above laid the groundwork upon which a later generation of Black designers made their names. For example, designer Ann Lowe's maternal grandmother was an enslaved seamstress named Georgia, whose freedom was bought by her grandfather "General" Cole, a free Black carpenter. The two married soon thereafter. Their daughter Janey followed the métier of her mother, and later gave birth to her own daughter, Ann.[26] Lowe was thus a third-generation clothier. Trailblazing fashion makers, such as Lowe's mother and grandmother, can be understood as the literal and metaphorical forebears to early twentieth-century Black designers. The talents of these enslaved seamstresses were not directly molded by the formal fashion apprenticeship system that was active in the great metropolises of the time. During the eighteenth and nineteenth centuries, it was rare for free and enslaved seamstresses to be formally trained in fashion design; the same was true for the generation just out of slavery. They learned in the home, as many people have historically learned to create and care for clothing. However, Georgia Cole possessed professional-level skills that stood out among those of the typical home-sewers, and she passed these, along with a successful dressmaking business, down to her family; her granddaughter thus emerged as an African American designer who learned how to sew at home, but who would also go on to train at a design school.

Lowe was born in Alabama, where she worked for her family's business in Montgomery. In 1916, at the approximate age of eighteen, she moved to Tampa, Florida, where she opened a successful dress shop.[27] She then participated in the Great Migration of African Americans from the South to major metropolises in the North in pursuit of greater employment opportunities and less racial discrimination. In an *Ebony* profile, Lowe described her early years in New York City as lonely and difficult. She was the only Black student at a design school in the city and was segregated from the other students in a separate classroom.[28] Although she spent most of her life living in Harlem like other early Black New York-based designers Ruby Bailey (see Chapter 5 by Joy Davis) and Zelda Wynn Valdes, Lowe designed for New Yorkers who lived in a different part of the city—the old-moneyed Upper East Side, where her studios were also located. Lowe is documented as saying that she only designed for elite families, such as the Du Ponts, Roosevelts, Astors, and Auchinclosses. "I love my clothes and I'm particular about who wears them. I'm not interested in sewing for café society or social climbers. I do not cater to Mary and Sue. I sew for the families of the Social Register," she told *Ebony* in her 1966 feature.[29] Although Lowe decided to work primarily with New York's upper crust, her very presence in these elite circles was an intervention into what was still a bastion of whiteness. She opened two shops of her own on the Upper East Side and even had a short-lived made-to-order salon in a Saks Fifth Avenue department store.

Figure 2.4 This ivory dress decorated with handmade roses is representative of Ann Lowe's precision and attention to detail. Silk dress, 1966–1967. Collection of the Smithsonian National Museum of African American History and Culture. Gift of the Black Fashion Museum founded by Lois K. Alexander-Lane.

Figure 2.5 Ann Lowe was known for her careful embroidery and handmade details. Silk dress, back detail, 1966–1967. Collection of the Smithsonian National Museum of African American History and Culture. Gift of the Black Fashion Museum founded by Lois K. Alexander-Lane.

Lowe's biggest claim to fame was designing Jacqueline Kennedy's wedding dress, which was worn at her 1953 wedding to future president, John Kennedy. Inauspiciously, a few weeks before the wedding, a flood in Lowe's New York studio destroyed the wedding dress and the gowns of most of the wedding party. Lowe had just two weeks to remake all the dresses and ended up losing money on the order. Regardless of her hard work and the loss of any potential profit, Lowe was not widely or publicly credited for designing the extensively photographed Kennedy wedding dress.[30] Despite the lack of acknowledgment of her work, it is through Lowe—who died in 1981—that scholars can draw a direct through line from enslaved fashion makers to the current generation of Black fashion designers.

Conclusion

Ann Lowe is one of the last Black American designers whose design acumen can be directly and positively traced back to the era of slavery. However, the legacy of enslaved seamstresses lived and lives on in the subsequent generations of Black seamstresses and designers. Many of these designers have drawn inspiration from their progenitors. Today, Black designers are less obligated to juggle fashion design with greater freedom struggles, though a number of twentieth- and twenty-first century designers have drawn inspiration from Black history and have made commitments to address social justice in their work. Patrick Kelly, for example, was born and raised in Vicksburg, Mississippi, but made his name as the creative director of his eponymous Parisian label (as Eric Darnell Pritchard discusses in Chapter 12). In 1988, Kelly became both the first American and the first person of color to be admitted as a member of the *Chambre syndicale du prêt-à-porter des couturiers et des créateurs de mode,* the organizing body of Parisian ready-to-wear designers. Rather than eschewing his Southern roots, Kelly liberally drew inspiration from African American culture; he appropriated and reframed the racist imagery popularized in American popular culture after slavery, such as the golliwog, which he prominently featured on his shopping bags. Ever the provocateur, Kelly reclaimed a controversial symbol of racism and transformed it into the logo for his chic Parisian design house.[31]

Likewise, Kerby Jean-Raymond, the creative director of Pyer Moss, designed "American, Also," a three-part series of fashion collections beginning in the fall of 2018 to address the erasure of African American narratives in United States history. With each successive collection, Jean-Raymond has pushed forward the concept of the brand's ethos of broadening the definition of Blackness. His immersive shows are staged at important places for American Africans, such as the Weeksville Heritage Center, the site of a community founded by free African Americans in the early nineteenth century. Jean-Raymond's work is grounded in the reality of Black genius rising out of a collective history of enslavement. Twentieth- and twenty-first century African American designers such as Jean-Raymond have taken inspiration from the United States' legacy of slavery and, in the process, have helped change the meaning of African American and American identity.[32]

Rosa Parks's work as a seamstress provided her with the livelihood with which she could launch a seminal moment in the Civil Rights Movement. The same is true for Harriet Jacobs, Elizabeth Keckly, Margaret Mahammitt Hagan, Eliza Ann Gardner, Ann Lowe, and numerous other less prominent early Black fashion designers and their progeny. Sewing was part of the broader social activism in which these designers were engaged. They mobilized needlework in the fight for the enfranchisement and elevation of African Americans, weaving slavery's warp into liberty's weft.

Notes

1 Joyce A. Hanson, *Rosa Parks: A Biography* (Santa Barbara, California: Greenwood, 2011), 17.

2 Seth Rockman, *Scraping By: Wage Labor, Slavery, and Survival in Early Baltimore* (Baltimore: Johns Hopkins University Press, 2009), 260–1.

3 Nancy Prince, *A Narrative of the Life and Travels of Mrs. Nancy Prince* (Boston: Self-Published, 1853).

4 Tanisha C. Ford, *Liberated Threads: Black Women, Style, and the Global Politics of Soul* (Chapel Hill: University of North Carolina Press, 2015).

5 Monica Miller, *Slaves to Fashion: Black Dandyism and the Styling of Black Diasporic Identity* (Durham: Duke University Press, 2009).

6 Tiffany M. Gill, "How a Black Female Fashion Designer Laid the Groundwork for Ghana's 'Year of Return,'" *The Washington Post*, January 10, 2020, accessed April 13, 2020, https://www.washingtonpost.com/outlook/2020/01/10/how-black-woman-fashion-designer-laid-groundwork-ghanas-year-return/.

7 "Virginia Gazette (Purdie), Williamsburg, August 8, 1777," *The Geography of Slavery: Virginia Runaways*, accessed April 8, 2020, http://www2.vcdh.virginia.edu/gos/search/relatedAd.php?adFile=vg1777.xml&adId=v1777082448.

8   In 1799, it is assumed that George Washington prepared an eight-page document that was found to have accompanied his will, which lists 317 enslaved peoples at Mount Vernon. Charlotte is identified as a seamstress on this list. To view the entire list, see "List of Slaves at Mount Vernon," Mount Vernon Collection, accessed April 8, 2020, https://www.mountvernon.org/preservation/collections-holdings/browse-the-museum-collections/object/il.2016.019.015/#-. For more information on Charlotte, see Mary V. Thompson, "Charlotte," George Washington's Mount Vernon, Mount Vernon Collection, accessed April 8, 2020, https://www.mountvernon.org/library/digitalhistory/digital-encyclopedia/article/charlotte/.

9   "MacIver to Washington, June 17, 1786," *The Papers of George Washington Digital Edition*, accessed April 8, 2020, https://rotunda.upress.virginia.edu/founders/GEWN-04-04-02-0113.

10 Drew Gilpin Faust, *Mothers of Invention: Women of the Slaveholding South in the American Civil War* (Chapel Hill: University of North Carolina Press, 1996), 223.

11 For more information on this episode, see Sara Georgin, "An Indian Chintz Gown: Slavery and Fashion," *The Junto*, accessed April 8, 2020, https://earlyamericanists.com/2018/09/12/an-indian-chintz-gown-slavery-and-fashion/.

12 "Cotton Dress," H.1993.535.1, Combo, North Carolina Museum of History, accessed March 16, 2019, http://collections.ncdcr.gov/RediscoveryProficioPublicSearch/ShowItem.aspx?70491+

13 Although the use of the word "designer" in this chapter may seem anachronistic in describing nineteenth-century fashion makers, it is an intervention that places their dressmaking skills on equal footing with the work of white couturiers who often could only sketch or conceptualize garments. For this reason, "seamstress" and "dressmaker" are used interchangeably with "designer."

14 Jean Fagan Yellin, *Harriet Jacobs: A Life* (New York: Civitas Books, 2004), 43.

15 Harriet Jacobs, *Incidents in the Life of a Slave Girl: Written by Herself* (New York: Barnes and Noble Books, 2005), 17.

16 Ibid., 100.

17 Ibid., 229–30.

18 Ibid., 129.

19 Though Keckly is often spelled "Keckley," Jennifer Fleischner has shown that Keckly spelled her name without the second "e." See Jennifer Fleischner, *Mrs. Lincoln and Mrs. Keckly* (New York: Broadway Books, 2003), 7.

20 Elizabeth Keckley, *Behind the Scenes, or, Thirty years a Slave, and Four Years in the White House* (New York: G. W. Carleton & Co., Publishers, 1868). Online edition is available, produced by Documenting the American South, 1999, 54–60, accessed March 16, 2019, https://docsouth.unc.edu/neh/keckley/keckley.html.

21 Ibid., online edition, 21, 45, 55–6, 65–6.

22 Ibid., 113–16.

23 Rosemary E. Reed Miller, *Threads of Time, The Fabric of History: Profiles of African American Dressmakers and Designers, 1850 to the Present* (Washington, DC: Toast

and Strawberries Press, 2002), 26–31. Much of what we know about Hagan can be credited to the genealogical work of her great-granddaughter Sheila Gregory Thomas. See Sheila Gregory Thomas, "Margaret Mahammmitt of Maryland," Lycoming College Archives, accessed March 16, 2019, http://digitalcollections. powerlibrary.org/cdm/ref/collection/alycc-wmhis/id/15914.

24 Her great-great-grandson is astronaut Frederick Drew Gregory, the first African American to pilot an American spacecraft.

25 Miller, *Threads of Time*, 14–26. For more information on the connection to Du Bois, see David Levering Lewis, *W. E. B. Du Bois: Biography of a Race* (New York: Henry Holt and Company, Inc., 1993), 106–7.

26 Ann Smith, "Ann Lowe: Couturier to the Rich and Famous," *Alabama Heritage* 53 (Summer 1999): 8.

27 Elizabeth Way, "Elizabeth Keckly and Ann Lowe: Recovering an African American Fashion Legacy That Clothed the American Elite," *Fashion Theory: The Journal of Dress, Body & Culture* 19, no. 1 (February 2015): 118.

28 Gerri Major, "Dean of American Designers," *Ebony*, December 1966, 135.

29 Ibid.

30 Christopher Andersen, *Jack and Jackie: Portrait of an American Marriage* (New York: Avon Books, 1997), 11.

31 "Mississippi in Paris," Philadelphia Museum of Art, accessed April 14, 2020, https://www.philamuseum.org/exhibitions/799.html?page=2.

32 M. H. Miller, "The Designer Changing How We Think About Fashion and Race in America," *The New York Times*, March 5, 2020, accessed April 14, 2020, https://www.nytimes.com/2020/03/05/t-magazine/pyer-moss-kerby-jean-raymond.html.

Bibliography

Collections
The Geography of Slavery: Virginia Runaways
Library of Congress
Lycoming College Archives
Mount Vernon Collection
National Museum of African American History and Culture
North Carolina Museum of History
Philadelphia Museum of Art

Andersen, Christopher. *Jack and Jackie: Portrait of an American Marriage.* New York: Avon Books, 1997.
Faust, Drew Gilpin. *Mothers of Invention: Women of the Slaveholding South in the American Civil War.* Chapel Hill: University of North Carolina Press, 1996.
Fleischner, Jennifer. *Mrs. Lincoln and Mrs. Keckly.* New York: Broadway Books, 2003.

Ford, Tanisha C. *Liberated Threads: Black Women, Style, and the Global Politics of Soul.* Chapel Hill: University of North Carolina Press, 2015.

Georgin, Sara. "An Indian Chintz Gown: Slavery and Fashion." *The Junto*, September 12, 2018, accessed April 8, 2020, https://earlyamericanists.com/2018/09/12/an-indian-chintz-gown-slavery-and-fashion/.

Gill, Tiffany M. "How a Black Female Fashion Designer Laid the Groundwork for Ghana's 'Year of Return.'" *The Washington Post*, January 10, 2020, accessed April 13, 2020, https://www.washingtonpost.com/outlook/2020/01/10/how-black-woman-fashion-designer-laid-groundwork-ghanas-year-return/.

Hanson, Joyce A. *Rosa Parks: A Biography.* Santa Barbara, California: Greenwood, 2011.

Jacobs, Harriet. *Incidents in the Life of a Slave Girl: Written by Herself.* New York: Barnes and Noble Books, 2005.

Keckley, Elizabeth. *Behind the Scenes, or, Thirty years a Slave, and Four Years in the White House.* New York: G. W. Carleton & Co., Publishers, 1868. Online edition by Documenting the American South, 1999, accessed March 16, 2019. https://docsouth.unc.edu/neh/keckley/keckley.html

Lewis, David Levering. *W. E. B. Du Bois: Biography of a Race.* New York: Henry Holt and Company, Inc., 1993.

Major, Gerri. "Dean of American Designers." *Ebony*, December 1966, 136–42.

Miller, M. H. "The Designer Changing How We Think About Fashion and Race in America." *The New York Times*, March 5, 2020, accessed April 14, 2020, https://www.nytimes.com/2020/03/05/t-magazine/pyer-moss-kerby-jean-raymond.html.

Miller, Monica. *Slaves to Fashion: Black Dandyism and the Styling of Black Diasporic Identity.* Durham: Duke University Press, 2009.

Miller, Rosemary E. Reed. *Threads of Time, The Fabric of History: Profiles of African American Dressmakers and Designers, 1850 to the Present.* Washington, DC: Toast and Strawberries Press, 2002.

Prince, Nancy. *A Narrative of the Life and Travels of Mrs. Nancy Prince.* Boston: Self-Published, 1853.

Rockman, Seth. *Scraping By: Wage Labor, Slavery, and Survival in Early Baltimore.* Baltimore: Johns Hopkins University Press, 2009.

Smith, Ann. "Ann Lowe: Couturier to the Rich and Famous." *Alabama Heritage* 53 (Summer 1999): 6–15.

Thomas, Sheila Gregory. "Margaret Mahammmitt of Maryland," Lycoming College Archives, accessed March 16, 2019. http://digitalcollections.powerlibrary.org/cdm/ref/collection/alycc-wmhis/id/15914.

"Virginia Gazette (Purdie), Williamsburg, August 8, 1777," *The Geography of Slavery: Virginia Runaways*, accessed April 8, 2020, http://www2.vcdh.virginia.edu/gos/search/relatedAd.php?adFile=vg1777.xml&adId=v1777082448.

Way, Elizabeth. "Elizabeth Keckly and Ann Lowe: Recovering an African American Fashion Legacy That Clothed the American Elite." *Fashion Theory: The Journal of Dress, Body & Culture* 19, no. 1 (February 2015): 115–42.

Yellin, Jean Fagan. *Harriet Jacobs: A Life.* New York: Civitas Books, 2004.

3

A Matrilineal Thread: Nineteenth- and Early Twentieth-Century Black New York Dressmakers

Elizabeth Way

Many of the Black fashion designers that emerged into visibility in the New York fashion industry during the later twentieth century cite older relatives, usually female, as the source of their construction skills and interest in clothing design. These grandmothers, mothers, aunts, and family friends were the first nurturers of their talent. However, these women who influenced later designers through familial contact or simply through visibility are largely invisible in both fashion culture and African American history. With the exception of precious few instances in which nineteenth-century dressmakers such as Elizabeth Keckly left documentation describing their personal and professional lives, these women seem to be anonymous contributors to a legacy of Black fashion design. Yet dressmaking was a lucrative skill and business that needed networks to thrive. Not only did dressmakers advertise their services, leaving crucial information about their working lives, dressmaking also enabled Black women to own businesses and property and employ others, rendering them visible in the historical record. Dressmaking was also highly respectable work for Black women and could elevate them to financial security and into the Black elite. As early as 1860, for example, the New York City census listed the three most financially successful Black women as dressmakers and seamstresses. One, Sarah Susset, owned twenty thousand dollars in money and property.[1]

The previous two chapters have elucidated the vast amount of knowledge that enslaved fashion makers brought into the post-bellum period, as well as the vital importance of Black fashionable expression. This legacy of knowledge and skill was also present in free Black communities in the North and South. This chapter will focus on New York City during the nineteenth and early twentieth centuries, examining Black female dressmakers and the urban environment in which they lived during a period that established New York as the American fashion capital and also saw a dramatic increase in the city's Black residents (from approximately 14,000 in 1830 to nearly 60,000 in 1910).[2] Although Black women worked in far greater numbers than white women, Black dressmakers were a minority in the trade. However, those who established dressmaking businesses within the harsh and increasingly racist urban environment laid a foundation of Black design in New York that quietly continued into the late twentieth century. During the late 1960s and 1970s, Black designers such as Scott Barrie, Stephen Burrows, Jon Haggins, and Willi Smith attained visibility and success in the mainstream fashion industry. From the perspective of the fashion press, they seemed to burst onto the New York fashion scene fully formed as a young, yet sophisticated group of fashion designers. However, the creative skills of Black dressmakers had continually existed even as ready-to-wear clothing became dominant. The designers of the 1960s and 1970s can trace their professional presence back through a community of Black dressmakers that worked in the city decades earlier. This chapter aims to document nineteenth- and early twentieth-century Black dressmakers in an effort to tease out the circumstances of their work, place them in the context of New York City's Black community and fashion industry, and provide a missing link to later generations of designers.

As historian Wendy Gamber notes, dressmakers were artisans who interacted with their clients on a regular and ongoing basis during the nineteenth century. Far from a sporadic indulgence for special occasions or the preserve of the very wealthy, women on all economic levels sought the services of custom fashion makers. For example, "as early as the 1840s, New York City had a group of dressmakers who catered to domestic servants ... By 1900, 'fashion,' though in varying quantities and qualities, was within the reach of all but the most destitute."[3] Gamber also emphasizes that dressmakers and milliners, together with their customers, formed a female economy that existed "apart from—but in integral relation to—the larger commercial and industrial economies of nineteenth- and early twentieth-century America."[4] Due to the intimate nature of dressmaking, these economic relationships often crossed class boundaries and necessitated "emotional labor" on the part of the dressmaker.[5] For Black dressmakers in New York City, all of these components would have been magnified. Black society was far less socially stratified—all but the wealthiest Black New Yorkers would have lived in Black neighborhoods housing both working and professional classes—and work such as dressmaking did not bar Black women from the social elite. The economic and emotional connections of the female economy would have also existed in a concentrated microcosm. Discrimination from white dressmakers and later from retailers, as well as conscious efforts to support Black businesses, would have led Black women to patronize Black dressmakers. Additionally, following fashion and looking respectable was a major concern within Black communities, making dressmakers integral members of Black New York's struggle for safety, equality, visibility, and economic stability.

Until the second half of the nineteenth century, the majority of clothing was made to fit individuals by professional dressmakers and tailors and by home production. Those who could not afford custom-made clothing typically acquired garments second-hand. During the late nineteenth century, the American fashion industry was evolving. It increasingly incorporated ready-to-wear clothing manufacture, a process that began decades earlier (as Katie Knowles described in Chapter 1). This industrial fashion system cropped up in different urban areas throughout the country but was largest in New York City. Ready-to-wear manufacture altered the fashion system, decreasing reliance on highly skilled cutters, fitters, and drapers who performed multiple tasks, and increasing reliance on lesser-skilled sewers and factory workers who performed a single function. However, the transition to ready-to-wear clothing was not abrupt or complete, especially for women's wear. Loose and simple garments, such as cloaks, wrappers, petticoats, and chemises, could be industrially produced from the 1860s, and the shirtwaist or blouse was the first popularly mass-produced women's garment; however, these items represented a small part of the female wardrobe, which was dominated by a corseted silhouette and elaborate detailing during the nineteenth century. (Figures 3.1 and 3.2 illustrate how styles changed over the mid to late nineteenth century, but maintained, and even increased, a reliance on tightly fitting bodices.) The quality and fashionability of these garments relied on a close, custom fit, and they were less adaptable to industrial production than men's suiting. Into the turn of the twentieth century, dressmakers, working at varying price points, were still highly relevant to women's fashion.[6] Yet, as the nineteenth century progressed, New York ready-to-wear manufacturers grew exponentially, demanding more, mostly female, labor. Due to the intensification of racial discrimination during this period, Black women were generally shut out of factory work, as well as home- or out-sewing for clothing manufacturers.[7] This discrimination from the mainstream fashion industry would keep the number of Black garment workers, especially skilled technicians and creative makers, low into the late twentieth century, and this discrepancy is still felt in the New York fashion industry into the twenty-first century.

Figure 3.1 Abraham Bogardus, "Portrait of woman seated next to tasseled curtain," New York City, circa 1860. Schomburg Center for Research in Black Culture, Photographs and Prints Division, The New York Public Library.

Figure 3.2 "Studio portrait of woman wearing hat and gloves and dress with bustle," circa 1875. Schomburg Center for Research in Black Culture, Photographs and Prints Division, The New York Public Library.

Sarah Johnson: The Role of Black Dressmakers during New York's Emancipation

On May 2, 1828, an advertisement purchased by Sarah Johnson appeared in *Freedom's Journal*. The ad read, "Mrs. Sarah Johnson. No. 551 Pearl Street, respectfully informs her Friends and the Public, that she has commenced Bleaching, Pressing, and Refitting Leghorn and Straw Hats, in the best manner. Ladies dresses made, and Plain Sewing done on the most reasonable terms."[8] Johnson announced the formation of her millinery and dressmaking business, possibly run out of her home, to her potential clientele. It was located on one of the most historic streets in lower Manhattan, not far from the busy South Street seaport. She took out this advertisement specifically to reach the Black community in the first Black-owned and Black-operated newspaper in the country. It cost her seventy-five cents. Johnson invested another fifteen dollars and eighteen cents in advertising with *Freedom's Journal* over the next eleven months, repeating her ad in every issue at a rate of thirty-three cents, until the newspaper's last issue on March 28, 1829.[9]

Johnson began her business at a dynamic time for Black New Yorkers. In 1790 enslaved African Americans outnumbered free Black people approximately two to one in New York City (2,369 enslaved people compared to 1,101 free people), and enslaved Black people made up just over 77 percent of the 10,727 Black people living in the area around the metropolis.[10] In 1799 the state government made tentative movements toward emancipation. By 1820 enslaved people made up approximately 5 percent of the 10,886 Black people living in New York City and 14.7 percent of the 18,307 Black people in the Greater New York City area as recorded by the census that year. On July 4, 1827 a law that had been passed ten years before by the governor and state legislature went into effect, freeing the majority of New York's enslaved population. New York City, however, continued to play a dominant role in financing American slavery and slavery-dependent businesses into the Civil War.[11]

With the abolishment of slavery in New York came new opportunities and Sarah Johnson took advantage of them. She advertised in *Freedom's Journal* among a population of Black business owners offering a variety of goods and services, from boarding houses to tobacco shops and catering to New York's growing Black population. Johnson specialized in fashionable dress; she led her advertisement with "LEGHORN BONNETS," in bold capital letters, offering Black women care and refurbishment of their stylish hats made from fine,

Figure 3.3 Edward Williams Clay, *Life in Philadelphia*. "What you tink of my new poke bonnet …?" Etching, Philadelphia: Published by S. Hart, 65 So. 3d. St, circa 1830. Library Company of Philadelphia.

Leghorn straw, a variety imported from Italy. That Black women used fashion in their fight for respect and humane treatment, as well as an outlet for their individuality and creativity, has been well established.[12] The popular straw hat, shaped into the poke style with a deep brim extending over and surrounding the face, was an accessory that marked Black women as fashionable, but also played a subversive role by hiding their faces. When venturing into public, poke bonnets worn with fashionable dresses, shawls, and gloves, could afford Black women a modicum of privacy. Illustrator E. W. Clay expressed the discomfort that white urban populations felt about these styles. His cartoons of Black urbanites in late 1820s Philadelphia used racist tropes to undermine and harass the Black middle class, typically ridiculing their engagement with fashion. In *Life in Philadelphia, No. 14* (1828), Clay uses base racial slurs and a distortion of vernacular English to specifically criticize the anonymity that poke bonnets provided Black women.

Sarah Johnson's advertisement continued, "Mrs. J begs leave to assure her friends and the public that those who patronize her may depend upon having their Work done faithfully, and with punctuality and dispatch."[13] Yet, she provided so much more to Black women who needed fashionable, respectable clothing and accessories to proclaim their dignity and survive in New York. Considering the attitudes reflected in Clay's work, Sarah Johnson's dressmaking and millinery shop not only illustrates the entrepreneurial initiatives undertaken by Black women during this period and the growing economic opportunities possible under freedom in New York City, but also the significant role that dressmakers and fashion played in helping Black communities, and Black women in particular, assert their humanity and control their visibility in the urban landscape.

Late Nineteenth-Century Black Dressmakers in a Changing City

The Black population of the city increased after emancipation to reach 16,358 in 1840, accounting for about 19 percent of the city's total population. However, as European immigration increased, economic opportunities decreased, and political policies chipped away at Black rights, African Americans left the city. After the violent Draft Riot in 1863, the city's Black population fell to under 10,000, when the overall city population was growing toward 900,000. The city's Black population steadily rebounded during the next decades to reach 19,509 by 1880, fed by Black immigration from the nearby northeastern area, as well as regions south.[14] Black New Yorkers lived all over the city throughout the nineteenth century, although increasing housing discrimination would work to concentrate Black populations in enclaves.[15] Historian Marcy Sacks notes that before the Civil War most Black people in New York lived in Five Points at the lower tip of Manhattan—one of the poorest and most dangerous places in the city. From there, Black populations moved to Greenwich Village until the influx of Italian immigrants pushed the Black population up to the Tenderloin District, between 24th and 42nd Streets. After the Draft Riot, racist terrorism forced many Black residents farther northward in Manhattan.[16]

Johnson's business had been located downtown during the late 1820s, and Black dressmakers continued to work in the area into the late nineteenth century. In *A Respectable Woman* historian Jane Dabel notes that Harriet Harding not only operated, but also owned, a dressmaking shop located on the lower west side of Manhattan during the 1860s.[17] An 1884 announcement in *The New York Freeman* (later *The New York Age*) proclaimed, "Miss Mary Mason, the artistic dressmaker" would "be pleased to see her patrons at 61 Broadway, for a short season only."[18] Mason's shop was slightly south and east of where Johnson's shop had been located half a century earlier. Yet, advertisements from the end of the century show a northward drift of dressmakers following the movements of the Black population. An 1886 "help wanted" ad in *The New York Freeman* asked applicants to inquire with the dressmaker at 50 East 8th Street, and dressmaker Miss Adella R. Richardson operated her shop at 106 MacDougal Street in Greenwich Village.[19] Moving northward, additional dressmakers' advertisements from the late nineteenth century show that their shops were located between 17th and 47th Streets and between Sixth and Eighth Avenues. This movement reinforces the idea that Black patrons made up the majority of Black dressmakers' clientele, and that the businesses, which were often located within domestic residences, followed the population.

Dressmaking could be lucrative work, though its profitability depended not only on a dressmaker's skills, experience, and reputation, but also on the dressmaker's network and the money she could invest in equipment, assistants, renting or buying a shop, and advertising through local newspapers. There was a wide divide between dressmakers who owned their own businesses and the burgeoning apprentices they might train. Gamber cites data on white dressmakers from 1859, which she notes could be based on "observations that often were hasty or impressionistic," but nonetheless give some idea of the hierarchies within dressmaking in New York City. At that time, weekly wages for fitters and forewomen in shops ranged from four to seven dollars, while dressmakers who worked out by the day could make between three-and-a-half to seven-and-a-half dollars a week, plus meals. Apprentices and finishers made between one-and-a-half and four-and-a-half dollars a week.[20] Almost three decades later, Gertrude Mossell wrote for the "Our Women's Department" column in *The New York Freedman* that Black women in 1886 could earn fifteen or twenty dollars a week as a dressmaker or teacher, compared to three dollars a week as a servant.[21]

Miss Adella R. Richardson of MacDougal Street advertised herself as a "fashionable dressmaker" several times in the *The New York Age* in 1891,[22] but her appearance in the paper's society pages marked her as a member of the city's Black elite and implied her success as a dressmaker. In February 1891 Richardson's presence at the annual reception of the Edmonia Social Club at Tammany Hall was reported, along with her gown of "electric blue silk."[23] In November 1891, a description of her dress—"white surah, black ostrich feathers, V back and front"—was listed second in an article that described the gowns of twenty-four women at the forty-second annual Terry Lodge Reception.[24] For Thanksgiving of that year, Richardson and a Mrs. L. B. Mann threw a reception for their friends at their home at 322 West 37th Street.[25] Richardson was clearly a fashion leader, both as a dressmaker and a socialite. Her visibility in *The New York Age* also confirms that she did not run her dressmaking business out of her home and could afford to rent or own the property on MacDougal Street. Given her social connections, Richardson's shop likely produced a number of the gowns described in the newspaper alongside her own at the events of the Black elite.

Other dressmakers did not operate out of their own shops. Julia Hunt, for example, advertised in October of 1888, "A good dressmaker wants work with a first-class dressmaker, by the day or week."[26] Hiring herself out, Hunt most likely did not have the space to run a small business out of her lodgings, but she could have also preferred an opportunity to tap into an established dressmaker's network of clients instead of building up her own clientele from scratch. Conversely, Victoria Peterson advertised herself in November 1891 as a dressmaker who "Will receive work at home or Sew at residences by the day or week."[27] This type of short-term employment and commission-based work offered flexible opportunities to dressmakers who might need to supplement other income. Fashion was also notoriously seasonal—when new styles were reported from Europe during the spring and fall, dressmakers would have plenty of work, however, orders could be slow during other times of year. Miss Mary Mason, who announced in December 1884 that she would take clients for a short season, may have been taking advantage of the demand for holiday gowns, and may not have found dressmaking worth her while at other times of the year.[28]

Most dressmakers at this time were women; however, men also made women's wear. As reported in the "New York News" section of the *Age* in 1890, "Anthony F. White, ladies' tailor and dressmaker" was located at "235 West 47th street, three doors from Broadway." White was setting up his own shop and told his future patrons, "Having spent five years with J. Krakawer, ladies' tailor of Fifth Avenue, I am prepared to execute all orders at the above address … Anthony F. White, cutter and fitter."[29] While Charles Frederick Worth, the first couturier in Paris, had faced ridicule as a male dressmaker when he established his atelier during the 1850s, the fashionable "tailor-made" styles for women, based on masculine wool tailoring techniques, helped make male ladies' tailors more common. White was sure to note for propriety's sake, however, that he had "Ladies in attendance."[30]

Dressmakers among Working Black Women at the Turn of the Century

The varying working situations of dressmakers illustrate the ways in which Black women leveraged their skills to gain employment opportunities. At this time most Black women in New York City worked. In 1911 Mary White Ovington, a white journalist and co-founder of the National Association for the Advancement of Colored People, wrote, *Half a Man: The Status of the Negro in New York*, examining the lives of Black New Yorkers using census and other statistical data from the first decade of the twentieth century. Ovington states that of Black women between the ages of sixteen and twenty (she presumed these women were mostly unmarried), 66 percent were gainfully employed, compared to 59 percent of white women. However, 53 percent of Black women over the age of forty-five (presumably mostly married) worked compared to 13.5 percent of white women of the same age.[31] Ninety percent of working Black women were employed in the domestic service trade. While the variety of employment for women was limited compared to Black men, the high demand for domestic service actually created more opportunities for Black women to immigrate to New York City from the South, as well as the Caribbean, during the late nineteenth and early twentieth centuries. Although discrimination, racial tensions, and violence increased from both European immigrants and white New Yorkers who competed with the Black population for jobs, Black women could move to New York and be almost guaranteed a position in domestic service at double the salary earned in smaller towns.[32] Ovington notes that while theaters and trains employed maids, "the bulk of the girls are servants in boarding-houses, or are with private families as nurses, waitresses, cooks, laundresses, maids-of-all-work, earning from sixteen and eighteen to twenty-five and even thirty dollars a month. Occasionally a very skillful cook can command as high a monthly wage as fifty dollars."[33] Yet domestic work, among many other drawbacks, including long hours and backbreaking work, often required Black women to live in the homes of their employers. This situation inevitably lengthened their working days, restricted their movements during their off-work hours, and subjected them to the constant scrutiny of those who employed them.[34] Black women were eager to use the skills they possessed to carve out better employment opportunities for themselves. As previously noted, dressmaking provided flexibility and higher wages, as well as opportunities for independence and property ownership.

Black people represented 1.9 percent of the population of Manhattan and the Bronx in 1900, and 1.8 percent of the population the Greater New York area.[35] Black women made up approximately four percent of city's female workforce at this time. Among this number, 813 were listed in the census that year as dressmakers, out of a total of 37,514 New York City dressmakers or about 2 percent. Black seamstresses were recorded at 249 out of a total of 18,108, or about 1 percent (although women who regularly repaired or even made clothing might consider homemaking, domestic service, or laundry work as their main occupation). Black male tailors were much less prevalent, listed as 69 out of a total of 56,094 working in the city, or about 0.1 percent.[36] Although white New Yorkers patronized Black dressmakers—Ovington's dressmaker, for instance, was a Black Caribbean woman—most Black dressmakers served the Black community, which accounted for their low overall numbers, and their increase in step with the growing Black population.[37] Ovington writes that the number of Black dressmakers in the entire country quadrupled between 1890 and 1900, and that comparable increases occurred in New York City, but because they could not find employment in white shops, "numbers of these dressmakers and milliners earn a livelihood, though often a scanty one, from the patronage of the people of their own race."[38] For historical comparison, Dabel counted only four milliners and five "tailoresses" in New York in 1860. Those numbers dropped to one and three respectively a decade later, and although the number of milliners rebounded to four again in 1880, the number of tailoresses dropped to two. The number of recorded seamstresses dropped from 240 in 1860 to 170 in 1870, and 124 in 1880.[39] It is important to note that these numbers only account for the dressmakers, seamstresses, and milliners who were visible in the public record. Yet Dabel also points to the increasingly discriminatory social environment of the city in the later nineteenth century that pushed Black people out of skilled trades.[40]

The Dressmaking Trade

Dressmaking was indeed skilled work. The fashionable women's silhouettes relied on tight-fitting bodices and elaborately draped skirts during the 1880s and 1890s, best achieved by an experienced dressmaker working with an individual's measurements. Gamber describes dressmaking as "mental as well as manual labor," noting that creativity and a sense of style was required as well as advanced technical skill. Seamstresses worked a needle and thread to sew pieces of cut fabric together, a process that required nuanced knowledge and skill and could not be entirely replaced by turn-of-the-century sewing machines. However, the dressmaker was responsible for the far more difficult task of cutting out the fabric in the specific shapes needed to form the dress. She also fitted the garment to the customer's body at various points in the production process.[41] Costume historian Claudia Kidwell describes the draping technique used to create women's bodices, used as early as the eighteenth century, as the "pin-to-form" method. This technique required a skilled practitioner to lay inexpensive fabric or paper pieces onto a customer's corseted body and pin it in place to create the pattern pieces used to cut the expensive fashion fabric. The method was slow, but accurate, and created garments that molded to the wearer's body.[42] Miss M. A. Felton of "No. 12 Ormond Place, Brooklyn" made sure to inform potential clients that she was well versed in the skills needed to create stylish, well-fit clothes. She advertised herself as a "Fashionable Dressmaker, cutter fitter, and draper" in *The New York Age* during the fall of 1891.[43]

Professional dressmakers typically learned their trade through apprenticeship, though the formal workshop system may have been more fluid in Black communities.[44] Gamber notes, for example, that white dressmakers who had worked long enough to own their shops were typically unmarried, however it was not uncommon, as statistics showed, for Black married women to continue to work.[45] Filling multiple personal and professional roles, Black women may have learned advanced dressmaking skills within their families, or they even taught themselves to make clothing. A well-established way to learn was to take apart and copy existing garments.[46] Professional training schools also taught Black women sewing and dressmaking during the early twentieth century as Ovington writes,

From 1904 to 1910, the Manhattan Trade School graduated thirty-four colored girls in dressmaking, hand sewing, and novelty making. The public night school on West Forty-sixth Street, under its able colored principal, Dr. W. L. Bulkley, since 1907, has educated hundreds of women in sewing, dressmaking, millinery, and artificial flower-making. While the majority of the pupils have taken the courses for their private use, a large minority are entering the business world.[47]

She also, however, notes that racist attitudes made it hard for Black women to find work placements after graduating.[48]

Innovations in dressmaking techniques both opened the trade up to more practitioners and threatened existing dressmakers' businesses. Pattern drafting systems became popular during the late nineteenth century.[49] These drafting systems were "characterized by odd assortments of 'tools,' 'charts,' 'scales,' and 'machines'" and "were designed with the difficult task of cutting bodices in mind."[50] They were based on systems and patterns that male tailors had used from the early nineteenth century and "differed from the pin-to-form technique in a crucial respect, for they relied, not on acquired skill and the ability to mentally envision the 'shape' of a garment, but on numeric measurements and 'scientific' theories of bodily proportions."[51] They were marketed by mainly white male inventors to both amateur and professional dressmakers, and they could be difficult to understand and did not produce as precise of a fit as the "pin-to-form" method.[52] However, they were popular and their modern and technological aspects were part of their attraction. Miss Perkins and Miss Horton of 140 West 19th Street advertised their "Fashionable dress and cloak making" business in the *The New York Age* and especially noted their use of the "Tailor-made system," inviting customers to their top floor shop to "Call and see."[53] The standardization of pattern drafting through these systems led directly to both commercially available graded (or sized) patterns, invented in 1867, and women's ready-to-wear clothing manufacture.[54] Fashionable styles began to simplify at the turn of the century, also aiding the transition to ready-to-wear (see the less fitted shirtwaist and skirt style in Figure 3.4). Kidwell states, "By 1910 every article of female clothing could be purchased ready-made. Within another few years shopping for clothing off the rack became customary for women of all incomes and classes."[55] Advertisements for women's clothing stores in Black newspapers showed that retailers sought out Black women as customers as a part of this movement. Dressmakers found a niche in this changing fashion system by making alterations to ready-to-wear clothing. However, custom dressmaking in general declined significantly.[56]

The Madison Art Studio. 249 Sixth Ave., N.Y.
BET. 15TH & 16TH STS.

Figure 3.4 "Woman in hat decorated with flowers, and striped blouse." The Madison Art Studio, 249 Sixth Ave., New York, circa 1900. Schomburg Center for Research in Black Culture, Photographs and Prints Division, The New York Public Library.

The modern American fashion industry has its roots in this late nineteenth-century rise of ready-to-wear clothing manufacturing. As new industries developed in garment production and other areas new manufacturing jobs became available for women—in 1860, 25,000 women worked for manufacturers, mostly sewing clothing.[57] The industry was centered in New York City where the number of clothing-producing businesses rose from 966 to 6,145 between 1880 and 1910. By 1895 Manhattan and Brooklyn sweatshops employed approximately 80,000 workers.[58] The majority of these factory workers, as well as the sewers producing clothing for manufacturers via homework, were female. This period in the late nineteenth century also saw a dramatic increase in the Black residents of the city—by 1880 there were nearly 20,000 Black New Yorkers and that number nearly tripled in the next thirty years. Despite the fact that Black women were much more likely to be employed than white women, Black women were generally shut out of the ready-to-wear clothing trade, due to racial discrimination.[59] This discrimination came from fellow employees as well as employers. In researching her book, Ovington spoke with some white garment workers who had no problem with Black coworkers, but converse attitudes among others prevented Black women from even taking in sewing to complete at home because "it entailed her waiting in the same sitting-room with white women."[60] Garment workers in the shirtwaist makers' union barred Black women from membership during the late nineteenth and early twentieth century. Factory work in the garment industry paid higher wages than domestic service and Black women took opportunities to earn money and possibly obtain steady employment when unions went on strike. It was only after Black women worked as strikebreakers that garment worker unions tried to recruit them. There was general distrust in the Black community of the permanence of these offers. *The New York Age*, for instance, not only published an editorial encouraging Black women to take the jobs left by union strikers, but also actively recruited workers for factories facing strikes.[61] Although unions would increasingly crack open their doors to Black workers after World War One,[62] the active discrimination of Black employees on all levels within the garment trade left a legacy that would continue to impact opportunities for Black designers into the late twentieth century.

Conclusion

A small number of Black dressmakers, along with the few Black garment workers able to break into the industry, sustained an ongoing community of Black fashion professionals in New York City. This community would grow as skilled Black professionals, and later aspiring students, moved to New York, some specifically to join the fashion industry. Over the course of the twentieth century, the creative labor of women's clothing shifted from mostly female to mostly male with the rise of the "fashion designer." By the 1970s, a new generation of Black designers commanded financial success, national publicity, and an established place in the professional fashion industry. These gains were hard won, but they also owe a debt to the Black women who sustained their fashion businesses during the nineteenth and early twentieth centuries.

Notes

1   Jane E. Dabel, *A Respectable Woman: The Public Roles of African American Women in 19th-Century New York* (New York and London: New York University Press, 2008), 74.

2   Ibid., 15; Marcy S. Sacks, *Before Harlem: The Black Experience in New York City Before World War I* (Philadelphia: The University of Pennsylvania Press, 2006), 110–13.

3   Wendy Gamber, *The Female Economy: The Millinery and Dressmaking Trades, 1860–1930* (Urbana and Chicago: University of Illinois Press, 1997), 104–5.

4   Ibid., 3.

5   Ibid., 102–3.

6   Ibid., 98, 216; Kristina H. Haugland, "Blouse," in *The Berg Companion to Fashion*, ed. by Valerie Steele (Oxford: Bloomsbury Academic, 2010), accessed February 15, 2020, http://dx.doi.org/10.5040/9781474264716.0002072.

7   Sacks, *Before Harlem,* 110–13.

8   "Advertisement," *Freedom's Journal*, May 2, 1828, accessed February 15, 2020. https://www.wisconsinhistory.org/Records/Article/CS4415.

9   Johnson may have taken advantage of a long-term advertising discount offered by the paper: 15 percent for a year's commitment, and 12 percent for six months. "Advertisement." *Freedom's Journal*, May 2, 1828; "Advertisement." *Freedom's Journal*, March 28, 1829, accessed February 15, 2020, https://www.wisconsinhistory.org/pdfs/la/FreedomsJournal/v2n52.pdf.

10 Thomas J. Davis, "Slavery," in *The Encyclopedia of New York City*, 2nd edn., ed. by Kenneth T. Jackson (New Haven and London: Yale University Press, 2010), 1191. The New York City area's free Black population in 1790, numbering 23 percent, can be compared to the number of free people of color in the country at the time, which totaled about 8 percent, Lacy Shaw, *Not A Slave!: Free People of Color in Antebellum America, 1790–1860* (New York: American Heritage Custom Publishing Group, 1995), lx.

11 Thomas J. Davis, "Slavery," 1191–2.

12 See *Stylin': African American Expressive Culture from Its Beginnings to the Zoot Suit* by Graham White and Shane White (1998) and *The Birth of Cool* by Carol Tulloch (2016), among other resources.

13 "Advertisement," *Freedom's Journal*, May 2, 1828.

14 Dabel, *A Respectable Woman*, 13–20.

15 Ibid., 17–19.

16 Ibid, 14–21; Sacks, *Before Harlem*, 5–6.

17 Dabel, *A Respectable Woman*, 39.

18 "Local Gossip." *The New York Age*, vol. 1 issue 4, December 13, 1884, 3. Nineteenth Century US Newspapers, accessed January 25, 2020, https://link.gale.com/apps/doc/GT3011046268/NCNP?u=nypl&sid=NCNP&xid=ae2ffb8f.

19 "Classified Advertisement." *The New York Freedman* 2 issue 35, July 17, 1886, 3. Nineteenth Century US Newspapers, accessed January 25, 2020, https://link.gale.com/apps/doc/GT3011537497/NCNP?u=nypl&sid=NCNP&xid=2e5a3944; "Classified Advertisement." *The New York Age*, vol. 4 issue 21, February 14, 1891, 3. Nineteenth Century US Newspapers, accessed January 25, 2020. https://link.gale.com/apps/doc/GT3011546362/NCNP?u=nypl&sid=NCNP&xid=c4882c0f.

20 Gamber, *The Female Economy*, 78.

21 N. F. Mossell and selected, "Our Woman's Department." *The New York Age*, vol. 2 issue 43, September 11, 1886, 2. Nineteenth Century US Newspapers, accessed January 25, 2020, https://link.gale.com/apps/doc/GT3011538257/NCNP?u=nypl&sid=NCNP&xid=027d2219.

22 "Classified Advertisement." *The New York Age*, vol. 4 issue 21, February 14, 1891, 3.

23 "The Edmonia Social Club," *The New York Age*, vol. 4 issue 23, February 28, 1891, 1. Nineteenth Century US Newspapers, accessed January 25, 2020, https://link.gale.com/apps/doc/GT3015898011/NCNP?u=nypl&sid=NCNP&xid=3ae9a6c9.

24 "Terry Lodge Reception," *The New York Age*, vol. 4 issue 20, February 7, 1891, 1. Nineteenth Century US Newspapers, accessed January, 2020, https://link.gale.com/apps/doc/GT3011742982/NCNP?u=nypl&sid=NCNP&xid=e5649796.

25 "New York City News." *The New York Age*, vol. 5 issue 11, December 5, 1891, 3. Nineteenth Century US Newspapers, accessed January 25, 2020, https://link.gale.com/apps/doc/GT3011052913/NCNP?u=nypl&sid=NCNP&xid=670fe2d8.

26 "Classified Advertisement," *The New York Age*, vol. 2 issue 1, October 13, 1888. Nineteenth Century US Newspapers, accessed January 25, 2020, 3. https://link.gale.com/apps/doc/GT3011543230/NCNP?u=nypl&sid=NCNP&xid=ddd4c81b.

27 "Classified Advertisement," *The New York Age*, vol. 5 issue 9, November 21, 1891, 3. Nineteenth Century US Newspapers, accessed January 25, 2020, https://link.gale.com/apps/doc/GT3011053222/NCNP?u=nypl&sid=NCNP&xid=7ab147bc.

28 "Local Gossip," 3; Gamber, *The Female Economy*, 81.

29 "New York City News," *The New York Age*, vol. 5 issue 9, November 22, 1890, 3. Nineteenth Century US Newspapers, accessed January 25, 2020, https://link.gale.com/apps/doc/GT3011052437/NCNP?u=nypl&sid=NCNP&xid=e87751ad.

30 Ibid.

31 Mary White Ovington, *Half A Man: The Status of the Negro in New York* (Norwood, Massachusetts: The Plimpton Press, 1911), 145–6, accessed February 15, 2020, http://www.gutenberg.org/files/39742/39742-h/39742-h.htm.

32 Ovington, *Half A Man*, 145–7; Sacks, *Before Harlem*, 135.

33 Ovington, *Half A Man*, 150–1

34 Sacks, *Before Harlem*, 115–17.

35 Ovington, *Half A Man*, 30.

36 Ibid., 149, 90.

37 Mary White Ovington, *The Walls Came Tumbling Down* (San Diego: Harcourt Brace, & Co., 1947), 6.

38 Ovington, *Half A Man*, 161–2.

39 Dabel, *A Respectable Woman,* 68.

40 Ibid., 66–7.

41 Wendy Gamber, "Reduced to Science: Gender, Technology, and Power in the American Dressmaking Trade, 1860–1910," *Technology and Culture*, 36, no. 3 (July 1995): 458, 462.

42 Claudia B. Kidwell, *Cutting A Fashionable Fit: Dressmakers' Systems in the United States* (Washington, DC: Smithsonian Institution Press, 1979), 13.

43 "Classified Advertisement," *The New York Age*, vol. 5 issue 5, October 23, 1891, 5. Nineteenth Century US Newspapers, accessed January 25, 2020, https://link.gale.com/apps/doc/GT3011053526/NCNP?u=nypl&sid=NCNP&xid=d02ed909.

44 Gamber, "Reduced to Science," 463

45 Ibid., 456.

46 Kidwell, *Cutting A Fashionable Fit*, 13.

47 Ovington, *Half A Man*, 161.

48 Ibid.

49 Gamber, "Reduced to Science," 466.

50 Ibid., 469.

51 Ibid., 469, 459, 472.

52 Ibid., 469, 472.

53 "Classified Advertisements," *The New York Age*, vol. 2 issue 4, November 3, 1888, 3. Nineteenth Century US Newspapers, accessed February 1, 2020, https://link.gale.com/apps/doc/GT3011542955/NCNP?u=nypl&sid=NCNP&xid=eeff9a37.

54 Gamber, "Reduced to Science," 477–8.

55 Claudia B. Kidwell and Margaret C. Christman, *Suiting Everyone: The Democratization of Clothing in America* (Washington, DC: Smithsonian Institution Press, 1974), 137.

56 Dabel, *A Respectable Woman,* 106; Gamber, *The Female Economy*, 197.

57 Dabel, *A Respectable Woman*, 67.

58 Sacks, *Before Harlem*, 111.

59 Ibid., 110–13, 120.

60 Ovington, *Half A Man*, 163.
61 Sacks, *Before Harlem,* 124, 129–30.
62 Ibid., 130.

Bibliography

"Advertisement." *Freedom's Journal* 2 no. 6 (May 2, 1828): 46, accessed February 15, 2020. https://www.wisconsinhistory.org/Records/Article/CS4415.

"Advertisement." *Freedom's Journal* 2 no. 52 (March 28, 1829): 412, accessed February 15, 2020. https://www.wisconsinhistory.org/pdfs/la/FreedomsJournal/v2n52.pdf.

"Classified Advertisement." *The New York Age*, vol. 2 issue 1, October 13, 1888, 3. Nineteenth Century US Newspapers, accessed January 25, 2020. https://link.gale.com/apps/doc/GT3011543230/NCNP?u=nypl&sid=NCNP&xid=ddd4c81b.

"Classified Advertisements." *The New York Age*, vol. 2 issue 4, November 3, 1888, 3. Nineteenth Century US Newspapers, accessed February 1, 2020. https://link.gale.com/apps/doc/GT3011542955/NCNP?u=nypl&sid=NCNP&xid=eeff9a37.

"Classified Advertisement." *The New York Age*, vol. 4 issue 21, February 14, 1891, 3. Nineteenth Century US Newspapers, accessed January 25, 2020. https://link.gale.com/apps/doc/GT3011546362/NCNP?u=nypl&sid=NCNP&xid=c4882c0f.

"Classified Advertisement." *The New York Age*, vol. 5 issue 5, October 23, 1891, 5. Nineteenth Century US Newspapers, accessed January 25, 2020. https://link.gale.com/apps/doc/GT3011053526/NCNP?u=nypl&sid=NCNP&xid=d02ed909.

"Classified Advertisement." *The New York Age*, vol. 5 issue 9, November 21, 1891, 3. Nineteenth Century US Newspapers, accessed January 25, 2020. https://link.gale.com/apps/doc/GT3011053222/NCNP?u=nypl&sid=NCNP&xid=7ab147bc.

"Classified Advertisement." *The New York Freedman*, vol. 2 issue 35, July 17, 1886, 3. Nineteenth Century US Newspapers, accessed January 25, 2020. https://link.gale.com/apps/doc/GT3011537497/NCNP?u=nypl&sid=NCNP&xid=2e5a39%2044.

Dabel, Jane E. *A Respectable Woman: The Public Roles of African American Women in 19th-Century New York*. New York and London: New York University Press, 2008.

Davis, Thomas J. "Slavery," in *The Encyclopedia of New York City*, 2nd edn., ed. Kenneth T. Jackson, 1191–2. New Haven and London: Yale University Press, 2010.

"The Edmonia Social Club." *The New York Age*, vol. 4 issue 23, February 28, 1891, 1. Nineteenth Century US Newspapers, accessed January 25, 2020, https://link.gale.com/apps/doc/GT3015898011/NCNP?u=nypl&sid=NCNP&xid=3ae9a6c9.

Gamber, Wendy. *The Female Economy: The Millinery and Dressmaking Trades, 1860–1930*. Urbana and Chicago: University of Illinois Press, 1997.

Gamber, Wendy. "Reduced to Science: Gender, Technology, and Power in the American Dressmaking Trade, 1860–1910," *Technology and Culture*, 36, no. 3 (July 1995): 455–82.

Haugland, H. Kristina. "Blouse," in *The Berg Companion to Fashion*, ed. Valerie Steele. Oxford: Bloomsbury Academic, 2010, accessed February 15, 2020, http://dx.doi.org/10.5040/9781474264716.0002072.

Kidwell, Claudia B. *Cutting A Fashionable Fit: Dressmakers' Systems in the United States*. Washington, DC: Smithsonian Institution Press, 1979.

Kidwell, Claudia B. and Margaret C. Christman. *Suiting Everyone: The Democratization of Clothing in America*. Washington, DC: Smithsonian Institution Press, 1974.

"Local Gossip." *The New York Age*, vol. 1 issue 4, December 13, 1884, 3. Nineteenth Century US Newspapers, accessed January 25, 2020. https://link.gale.com/apps/doc/GT3011046268/NCNP?u=nypl&sid=NCNP&xid=ae2ffb8f.

Mossell, N. F., and selected. "Our Woman's Department." *The New York Age*, vol. 2 issue 43, September 11, 1886, 2. Nineteenth Century US Newspapers, accessed January 25,2020, https://link.gale.com/apps/doc/GT3011538257/NCNP?u=nypl&sid=NCNP&xid=027d2219.

"New York City News." *The New York Age*, vol. 4 issue 9, November 22, 1890, 3. Nineteenth Century US Newspapers, accessed January 25, 2020. https://link.gale.com/apps/doc/GT3011052437/NCNP?u=nypl&sid=NCNP&xid=e87751ad.

"New York City News." *The New York Age*, vol. 5 issue 11, December 5, 1891, 3. Nineteenth Century US Newspapers, accessed January 25, 2020. https://link.gale.com/apps/doc/GT3011052913/NCNP?u=nypl&sid=NCNP&xid=670fe2d8.

Ovington, Mary White. *Half A Man: The Status of the Negro in New York*. Norwood, Massachusetts: The Plimpton Press, 1911, accessed February 15, 2020. http://www.gutenberg.org/files/39742/39742-h/39742-h.htm.

Ovington, Mary White. *The Walls Came Tumbling Down*. San Diego: Harcourt Brace, & Co., 1947, accessed February 15, 2020. https://link.gale.com/apps/doc/GT3011052913/NCNP?u=nypl&sid=NCNP&xid=670fe2d8.

Sacks, Marcy S. *Before Harlem: The Black Experience in New York City Before World War I*. Philadelphia: The University of Pennsylvania Press, 2006.

Shaw, Lacy. *Not A Slave!: Free People of Color in Antebellum America, 1790–1860*. New York: American Heritage Custom Publishing Group, 1995.

"Terry Lodge Reception." *The New York Age*, vol. 4 issue 20, February 7, 1891, 1. Nineteenth Century US Newspapers, accessed January, 2020. https://link.gale.com/apps/doc/GT3011742982/NCNP?u=nypl&sid=NCNP&xid=e5649796.

Tulloch, Carol. *The Birth of Cool: Style Narratives of the African Diaspora*. London: Bloomsbury, 2016.

White, Graham and Shane White. *Stylin': African American Expressive Culture from Its Beginnings to the Zoot Suit*. Ithaca: Cornell University Press, 1998.

Section 2

In the Atelier: Modistes and Independent Designers

4

Dressing Up: The Rise of Fannie Criss

Kristen E. Stewart

In 1904 *The Voice of the Negro*, "the first magazine ever edited in the South by Colored Men,"[1] published a regional profile on the "History of the Business of Colored Richmond." The story's author, William Patrick Burrell, was a prominent figure in Richmond, Virginia's Black community, serving as Grand Worthy Secretary of a fraternal benefit society that encompassed the first Black-owned, Black-operated bank chartered in America and a broad range of Black businesses.[2] In a segment highlighting Richmond's "Captains of Industry," Burrell dedicated two superlative laden paragraphs to local dressmaker, Fannie Criss Payne:

> The finest dressmaker in Richmond, regardless of color, is Mrs. Fannie Criss Payne. Her list of patrons is made up of the best white families in Richmond. So great is their confidence in her ability and taste that many leave to her the selection of their entire outfits. In the last six months she has made the trousseaus for the most popular brides.
>
> She buys her patterns from New York where she goes twice a year to make selections. She employs eight girls regularly and her business amounts to more than $8,000 a year. She has recently fitted up a new home with every home-comfort and convenience for her business at a cost of $6,000 cash. A few years ago Mrs. Payne was a day cooker, earning one fifty cents [*sic*] a day. Her dresses may now be seen at the most prominent watering places of the country and give the same satisfaction as many that are imported at a great cost.[3]

Fannie Criss Payne was one of only two women profiled in Burrell's extensive article. The other, Maggie Lena Walker (1864–1934), was the first African American woman to charter a bank and serve as its president. One year after their profiles were published, the dressmaker and the bank president became neighbors on a block known as "Quality Row" in Jackson Ward, a Richmond neighborhood remembered as the "Harlem of the South."[4] In 1917, Fannie

Criss left Jackson Ward and moved to Harlem.[5] This chapter will examine the progress of Fannie Criss, the free-born child of a formerly enslaved farmer who achieved remarkable success as the premier dressmaker in Virginia's capital city.[6]

The earliest official document to mark Fannie Criss's life may be the 1870 Federal Census of Cumberland County, Virginia, where a five-year-old "Fannie" is listed as a daughter of Samuel Christ [sic] and his wife, Adeline.[7] Ten years later, the census records Fannie's age as nineteen, moving her birth year from 1865 to 1861.[8] Fannie Criss would never be that old again in public record; her evolving birthdate may reflect a savvy instinct for image management in a professional field that valued youth. After an 1895 marriage registration records her age as twenty-five (making her birth year 1870),[9] her documented age varies from form to form until the final note, her 1942 death certificate, lists her birthdate as October 15, 1867.[10] Fannie Criss's birthdate associated her with a generation of Black Virginians who were framing their futures in the decades following the ratification of the Thirteenth Amendment, which formalized slavery's abolishment in America. At the same time, Virginia's white community was reframing the past through a "Lost Cause" lens, asserting, "the owning of the ignorant and helpless negroes by kind white masters was probably the best thing for the negroes themselves at that time" and that "slaves were happy and contented and were faithful to their owners."[11] These views reflect the devastating paternalism that informed early twentieth-century laws designed to restrict access to the rights that whites enjoyed, making progress exponentially more difficult for Richmond's Black community. Despite these challenges, Fannie Criss moved steadily forward toward professional success and self-determination.

The date that Fannie Criss first arrived in Richmond remains unknown. Her 1895 marriage to William Thornton Payne took place in Richmond and the 1900 Federal Census places her at 1012 West Leigh Street in Jackson Ward. The same census is the first to list her occupation as a dressmaker.[12] The 1910 census records the same profession and a new, significant address—106 East Leigh Street.[13] Lined by Italianate and Romanesque revival homes built at the turn of the century, the 100 block of Leigh Street was the most desirable address for the Black professional class among Richmond's segregated neighborhoods. The handsome brick structure ornamented with elaborate wrought ironwork made an ideal location for an exclusive atelier and was listed in Richmond City directories as both her home and business. Although the contents of Criss's home have not survived, Burrell's report noted that it was adorned, "with every

Figure 4.1 *100 Block E. Leigh Street*, October 1978, Edith Shelton Collection. Courtesy of the Valentine.

home-comfort and convenience for her business."[14] As a leading local fashion professional Fannie Criss would have felt that it was essential to maintain a home and atelier at the forefront of taste.

No examples of Fannie Criss's work have been identified in the Maggie Walker estate; however, Criss and Walker's social status, wealth, and proximity made it likely that they interacted both professionally and personally. Walker's views on women's advancement reflected the same enterprising spirit that led to Criss's considerable success; she called on women to "put their hands and their brains together and make work and business for themselves."[15] Walker was also an outspoken critic of Richmond's successful Black business owners who did not "help their brethren who are also in business" and may have felt an obligation to support Criss's work.[16] Indeed, Maggie Walker was likely one of only a handful of women in Richmond's Black community who could afford Fannie Criss's custom clothing.

Although no known business records survive, the Valentine museum's archives contain a list of some of Criss's clients recorded by one of her former employees, Lucy Ann Jackson Foster (1883–1961).[17] The list of fifty-four names comprises the most prominent white families in and around early twentieth-century Richmond, a mix of the descendants of Virginia's colonial and Confederate era elites and a new wave of entrepreneurial immigrants seeking opportunity in Richmond's burgeoning banking, manufacturing, and retail industries. Despite divisions perpetuated by anti-Semitic club membership laws and the subtle lines of professional segregation, Richmond's wealthy white community, and Fannie Criss's clients with rare exception, supported a Democratic party which endorsed segregation laws that disenfranchised Richmond's Black citizens.

As Dr. Blair L. M. Kelly outlines in her study of streetcar boycotts in the era of *Plessy* v. *Ferguson*, the discriminatory "Jim Crow laws" were targeted to condemn members of the Black professional class. Black citizens working in domestic service and childcare were welcome in white spaces, as they "reassured white passengers about their respective places in society," while Black first-class passengers "who were equal to white passengers in education and attainment" were refused equal access to shared public spaces.[18] In 1904, the same year that Burrell penned Fannie Criss's laudatory profile, the Virginia Passenger and Power Company announced plans to segregate Richmond's electric streetcars. This popular transportation system connected downtown Richmond with the growing sprawl of surrounding neighborhoods, including Jackson Ward where Fannie Criss lived and worked. Despite a boycott organized by Richmond's Black community leaders, the Virginia General Assembly legalized segregation in public transportation in 1906. Maggie Walker publicly condemned segregation laws as an intentional threat to Black business, placing the blame squarely on the "genteel white gentlemen" with whom she shared an elite economic status and significant social standing.[19]

It was in the context of this tension that Fannie Criss developed her business. At a moment when white patronage of Black-owned businesses was almost unheard of, Fannie Criss was regarded as "the finest dressmaker in Richmond, regardless of color." Her clients were wealthy and well traveled. They could afford to stock or supplement their wardrobes with designs from the growing number of French couturiers that were becoming household names. Those who chose to "buy local" had a long list of Black and white dressmakers from

Figure 4.2 Fannie Criss Payne designer label, circa 1907, V.87.151. Courtesy of the Valentine.

whom to choose in the Richmond City directory. Yet, as Burrell notes, Criss's clients were so confident in her "ability and taste" that many entrusted her with the "selection" or design of their entire outfits. This assertion of faith elevated Criss's professional status at a moment when the modern concept of the artist couturier was gaining momentum. Parisian couturier Charles Frederick Worth (1825–1895) is credited as the first to claim the artist's beret, "signing" his masterpieces with a label and selling a "vision" conceived without client input. Like other successful dressmakers of her era, Criss adopted Worth's "signature" strategy. Three of the four known Fannie Criss dresses in the Valentine museum's collection bear a narrow silk twill waist tape with the designer's married name, "Payne," in slanting script that emulates a signature. By embracing this symbol, the dressmaker proclaimed herself a member of the creative professional class.

With the exception of her labels, W. P. Burrell's report, and a vague mention in a 1907 souvenir publication,[20] Fannie Criss left little legacy of self-promotion, having built a sufficient client base by word of mouth. Word of mouth, unrecorded, is of little use to historians, but, happily, Fannie Criss's own work speaks volumes. The costume and textiles collection at the Valentine, the city history museum of Richmond, Virginia, contains a total of four dresses known to have been designed by Fannie Criss. Together, they create a small but consequential sample that hints at the dressmaker's range. Close examination reveals repeated patterns in style and technique that, with additional comparatives, may be called hallmarks of Fannie Criss's style. Although each dress was worn and donated by a different patron, they are all examples of early twentieth-century afternoon dress, and they are all cream or ivory. The color, time of day, and narrow period range (1904 to 1907) act as controls in this comparative analysis, helping to highlight the broad range of materials and techniques in which Criss shows prowess.

In an afternoon dress in ivory Irish and filet crochet lace with black bobbin lace and ivory taffeta trim (V.82.134a, b, circa 1907. Gift of Estate of Ida Massie Valentine), for example, invisible lace appliqué seams simultaneously shape and create an ornamental pattern on both bodice and skirt. Three-dimensional flowers, vines, and swags are organized within a mesh ground of Clones knot stitches in imitation of rococo boiserie, divided by broad vertical bands of filet lace. Fannie Criss moderated any fussiness on the bodice with a tailored effect created by the application of vertical bands of ivory taffeta trimmed with self-fabric covered buttons to the left and right of a center front band of filet lace. Triangular insets of black bobbin lace spaced around the hem create additional relief in the skirt. This dress was made for Laura Roy Ellerson Massie (1873–1957), a noted hostess and wife of Eugene C. Massie (1861–1924), who was an accomplished lawyer, chief of staff for Governor Claude A. Swanson (1906–1910), and member of the Virginia House of Delegates.[21] The skirt of this lingerie-style afternoon dress has been modified slightly since it was originally made. With its high collar, three-quarter length sleeves and the original modest train, this elegant reception gown would have been appropriate for afternoon events hosted by the wife of an esteemed political figure.

Like the reception gown above, an afternoon dress of off-white voile and bobbin lace trimmed with narrow yellow silk ribbon (V.87.151, circa 1907, Gift of Mrs. Helen Nolting Irvine Graham), has been altered from its original form. Once finished separately, the bodice hem and skirt waist have been roughly cut, sewn together along the bodice lining, and hidden under a yellow silk taffeta sash. Fortunately, most of the dress's original construction can still be

Figure 4.3 Dress worn by Laura Roy Ellerson Massie, circa 1905, V.82.134.06a, b. Courtesy of the Valentine, photo by Terry Brown.

seen. The high neck, yoke, cape-like collar, and tiered ruffle sleeves of machine-made bobbin lace form an effervescent froth above the voile bodice. Vertical pintucks define the bodice waist which is shaped along the princess line with vertical bands of inset bobbin lace and ruched yellow ribbon. Pintucks in the skirt waist release into a full, gored skirt trimmed with bands of bobbin lace and ruched yellow ribbon. One center back seam joining two bias-cut panels ensures lightness and flexibility in the full trained skirt. This one French seam, sewn along the bias, is the only seam not incorporated into an ornamental effect and provides evidence that Fannie Criss worked intentionally with the inherent qualities of material. (More than a decade later, acclaimed couturier Madeleine Vionnet would explore the full range of bias construction in her distinctly modern design methodology.) The skirt is finished with a train in gathered tiers of the same lace creating an effect that is both youthful and ethereal.

This dress was made for Roberta Nolting Irvine (1879–1973), daughter of Emil Otto Nolting, a Prussian immigrant who moved to Richmond to join a tobacco export firm and went on to serve as the president of the National Bank of Virginia, owner of Tobacco merchants E.O. Nolting & Co., President of the Tobacco Exchange and the Chamber of Commerce, and Belgian Consul for Richmond, VA (1852–1893).[22] In June 1907, Roberta Nolting married Robert Tate Irvine (1862–1929), a leading attorney and businessman in Big Stone Gap, Virginia, during a "boom" in coal and iron developments. Fannie Criss may have made this dress as a part of Mrs. Irvine's trousseau. In 2019 Kaaterskill Books auction house listed a selection of archival materials relating to the Irvines' wedding that included cards from the Richmond-born Italian Marquesa Virginia San Germano, iron and steel innovators Charles Page Perrin and R. Stuyvesant Pierrepont, as well as cables from Bremen and Paris.[23] A member of the early twentieth-century international elite, Mrs. Irvine required a trousseau that prepared her for entertaining in Virginia and around the world.

Despite the extensive damage evident in an afternoon dress of cream silk satin and pleated silk chiffon trimmed with embroidered mesh lace and metal-wrapped cord (V.68.1432a, b, circa 1905, Gift of James Taylor Crump), it can be determined that the bodice's original high lace neckline was bound by a satin band, trimmed with metal-wrapped cord and feather stitch embroidery. The neck extends from a jacket-style bodice of silk satin trimmed with metal-wrapped cord opening over a panel of vertically pleated chiffon. The satin sleeves are ornamented with scallop-edged embroidered lace insertion; the elbow-length cuffs are trimmed with self-fabric satin bands, bows, and metal-wrapped cord. An attached capelet of embroidered mesh lace falls over the front

Figure 4.4 Dress made for Roberta Nolting Irvine, circa 1907, V.87.151. Courtesy of the Valentine.

shoulders in imitation of a late eighteenth-century fichu. The skirt is constructed of gored panels; each vertical seam is embroidered over with lustrous silk floss in a repeating pattern of stars. Fannie Criss created additional fullness in the skirt with alternating ornamental gores of scallop-edged lace insertion and inverted box pleats edged with metal-wrapped cord. The embroidery on the lace panels, like the fichu, references colonial fashion history with floriate forms that resemble pineapple and pomegranate motifs popular in the late eighteenth century.

This dress was likely made for Nannie Moore Ellyson Crump (1871–1958). Crump's father James Taylor Ellyson (1847–1919) served in the Senate of Virginia (1885–1888) as mayor of Richmond (1888–1894) and as the state's lieutenant governor (1906–1918).[24] Her mother Lora Effie Hotchkiss Ellyson (1848–1935) served as vice-president of the Association for the Preservation of Virginia Antiquities (APVA) from 1896 and as president from 1911. The APVA worked to preserve Virginia's early history through the acquisition of colonial-era monuments and the installation of historic markers. Recent scholarship has also shown that, through the preservation of such sites, "Ellyson and the APVA sought to promote a version of Virginia's history that emphasized the virtues and traditions of elite white Virginians."[25] Nannie Moore Ellyson Crump was active in the preservation community with her mother and the colonial-era sartorial references in this reception gown may have been initiated at her request. The design's elegant balance of embellishment and relief, however, as well as the refined integration of construction and ornamentation, are hallmarks of the work of Fannie Criss.

The final Fannie Criss dress in the Valentine museum collection is a day dress of lightweight cream wool trimmed with topstitched pintucks and a layered passementerie of cream silk wrapped cord, cream silk taffeta appliqué, and bobbin lace (V.44.48.06a,b, circa 1905, Gift of Mrs. Gordon Wallace). The high lace collar extends from a bodice of lightweight wool trimmed with topstitched pintucks arranged in vertical and horizontal bands and crossed diagonals. A baroque bib of passementerie is inserted across the shoulder and bust over a central modesty panel of pleated chiffon. Fannie Criss constructed the cream wool skirt along a single seam at the center back waist, working additional skirt fullness into waist darts coordinated to correspond with a band of pintucks extending vertically from the waist. Below the hip, alternating bands of horizontal pintucks and crossed diagonal pintucks give a striped effect graded to echo the skirt's increasing fullness to the hem. Three passementerie medallions are appliquéd at center front and on the left and right sides of a wide central field bounded by the alternating bands of horizontal pintucks. Two gores formed

Figure 4.5 Dress probably made for Nannie Moore Ellyson Crump, circa 1905, V.68.1432a, b. Courtesy of the Valentine.

by adjacent right triangles add flaring fullness to the skirt below the hip along the inconspicuous center back seam. A wide ruffle trimmed with twenty-four groups of five vertical pintucks is eased into the skirt at the calf, adding dramatic fullness with the tucks' release and a shallow walking train to the hem.

This dress was made for Ellen Scott Clarke Wallace (1870–1956), the daughter of Maxwell T. Clarke, a "prominent businessman, confederate sailor and soldier" and "one of the leading citizens of Richmond of his day."[26] Previous scholarship has suggested that this dress was Mrs. Wallace's "second day dress," part of the trousseau made for her marriage to Gordon Wallace, proprietor of the Richmond Wholesale and Retail Grocers, R. L. Christian & Company. The style of this early twentieth-century dress, however, is inconsistent with the 1896 date of her wedding. In 1905, the Wallaces led the first wave of Richmond's urban exodus, now known as white flight, investing in an early "streetcar suburb" called Elderslie Place.[27] Mrs. Wallace may have worn this dress while hosting receptions at Elderslie Place. Taken together, these four dresses demonstrate parallels in style and technique that hint at the designer's brand. Of note in all four dresses is a precise finishing, a sophisticated opulence achieved with a balanced mix of textured and plain materials, and a consistent integration of construction and ornamentation that turns seams into style lines.

Existing scholarship on Fannie Criss is largely based on original research conducted by Etta Rebecca Williams for a 1982 profile of the designer in *The Richmond Quarterly* and expanded by Rosemary E. Reed Miller in her 2006 publication, *Threads of Time: The Fabric of History Profiles of African American Dressmakers and Designers 1850–2002*. While neither work is buttressed by rigorous citations and both perpetuate the myth of Mrs. Wallace's second day dress, they each provide snippets of a tantalizing memory of Fannie Criss's local fame. The truth of this history is borne out and confirmed by the contemporary references sprinkled through real estate reports and society columns in both Black and white newspapers in Richmond and New York. Although largely incidental to her career, these reports provide undeniable evidence of Fannie Criss's success.

In the 1900 Federal Census, Fannie Criss Payne was listed, remarkably, as the head of her 1012 Leigh Street household, with husband, William Payne and a housekeeper, Druscilla Wright.[28] Already, Criss enjoyed the luxury of domestic service afforded only by successful members of the professional classes. In 1903, *The Times-Dispatch* reported a property transfer from "Meyer Kirsh and wife to Fannie C. Payne for $3,400."[29] No address is given, but the coordinates listed point to the property at 106 East Leigh and suggest that Criss acquired this exclusive real estate without the aid of William Payne. In 1905, Fannie Criss purchased

Figure 4.6 Dress worn by Ellen Scott Clarke Wallace, circa 1905, V.44.48.06a, b. Courtesy of the Valentine, photo by Michael Simon.

219 West Leigh Street, a two-story brick dwelling one-quarter mile from her new home on Quality Row, for $2250."[30] Whether Criss rented out the entire property or reserved space for her business is unknown, but city directories indicate that the home was used in part for dressmaking. The business directory lists Criss's tenant, Celestia Clark, as a dressmaker at the West Leigh Street address in 1917, the same year that Fannie Criss left Richmond and moved to New York City.[31] The years between Criss's 1903 purchase of the 106 East Leigh Street home and her last professional listing in the 1917 Richmond City directory were a period of extraordinary success for Fannie Criss, paving the way for a move from Richmond's Quality Row to a New York townhouse one block south of Harlem's famed Striver's Row.

A telling statement in Lucy Ann Jackson Foster's notes (see above) on Fannie Criss hints at the dressmaker's eventual departure from Richmond. "Miss Fannie went to New York in the fall and spring to purchase her material for her dresses. She was very stylish."[32] Fannie Criss created custom-fit dresses using the latest patterns and most luxurious materials that she purchased during seasonal trips to America's burgeoning fashion center. Eventually both Criss's personal and professional life would lead her out of Richmond. In 1911, having divorced William Thornton Payne, Fannie Criss married William T. White, a Richmond native in the restaurant service industry whose ambitions, like those of Fannie Criss, led him to New York.[33] As Richmond's white elite (and Criss's clients) promoted legislative barriers to the burgeoning progress of the city's Black business community, Fannie Criss and her husband joined the migration of Southern Blacks to New York's Upper West Side that fostered the flowering of culture known as the Harlem Renaissance.

Reports of Fannie Criss's social accomplishments as Mrs. W. T. White published in *The St. Luke Herald*, *The New York Age*, and *The Freeman* began to rival those of her former clients in the *Richmond Times-Dispatch*. In 1913, Mr. and Mrs. W. T. White were listed "among those present at the opening of the Lybia Dining Rooms" at 115 West 131st Street.[34] In July 1914, *The St. Luke Herald* reported that "Mesdame [*sic*] Fannie C. White of E. Leigh Street, left the city (of Richmond) Monday for White Sulphur Springs," a summer vacation resort in western Virginia.[35] W. T. White's early ambitions led his work to summer resorts that attracted wealthy white and Black vacationers. Criss's social activities were reported from White Sulphur Springs, West Virginia, and St. Augustine, Florida, where White managed the large staff of a hotel dining room. In an article that celebrated White's professional leadership in St. Augustine, *The Freeman* reported with apparent tongue-in-cheek that, "your correspondent is so often told by the leading white people here that it would be well to get acquainted with the colored people here. They are very respectable and some are very wealthy. They are doing well in business and otherwise."[36] Fannie Criss White, who likely continued to practice her trade in Florida, was, no doubt, among them.

Between 1911 and 1917, Criss maintained her home and some professional connection in Richmond despite frequent trips to New York and Florida. In February 1917, W. T. White was made vice-president of a training school for waiters on Harlem's Lenox Avenue.[37] In April of that year, White purchased a majestic townhouse at 219 West 137th Street for $9,100.[38] Although her husband's name was listed in the real estate report, Fannie Criss likely contributed to the purchase with profits from her own business and real estate investments. In 1917, "Fannie C. White et vir (husband)" sold 106 East Leigh Street to prominent Black Richmond dentist, J. M. C. Ramsey.[39] In 1919, the couple sold the West Leigh Street building.[40] Before leaving Richmond, Criss sealed her reputation as a woman of means and influence in the community when her contribution to a fundraising effort by the Greater Memorial Hospital was reported alongside Maggie Walker's. Both women donated one hundred dollars to the effort.[41] After her move, Criss's visits to Richmond were reported in Richmond and New York society pages.[42]

Of all the Fannie Criss stories recounted by Etta Rebecca Williams in *The Richmond Quarterly* and Rosemary E. Reed Miller in *Threads of Time,* it is the New York narrative that most beguiles and bedevils. Both authors report the memories of an unnamed niece who, when visiting her aunt, went with Criss "to visit in the home of her nearby friend, Sarah Walker." The fabulously wealthy haircare entrepreneur and philanthropist, better known as Madam C. J. Walker (1869–1919), lived at 108–110 West 136th Street, less than two blocks from Fannie Criss's New York home. Like Criss, Madam Walker was the free-born daughter of formerly enslaved parents who succeeded in the beauty industry with tenacity and talent. Although neighbors only briefly before Madam Walker's death, they may, indeed, have been friends. Miller asserts that Fannie Criss designed for Madam C. J. Walker's daughter, A'Lelia Walker Robinson, as well as for other wealthy Black women, film and theater stars, and even Gloria Swanson. No concrete documentation has yet been found to link Criss with these women, but her history of success with word of mouth promotion has already been established. Criss did continue to include her professional status in the Federal Census of 1920 and 1930. Choosing the title, *modiste,* Criss distinguished herself as a creative professional in the language of the modern market, demonstrating the professional acuity that once made her the most sought-after dressmaker in Richmond, Virginia.

Notes

1 J. W. E. Bowen, *The Voice of the Negro*, January 1904, reprint (New York: Negro Universities Press, 1969), 1.

2 W. P. Burrell, and D. E. Johnson, *Twenty-Five Years' History of the Grand Fountain of the United Order of True Reformers, 1881–1905* (Richmond, Va: Grand Fountain, United Order of True Reformers, 1909), 498.

3 W. P. Burrell, "History of the Business of Colored Richmond," *The Voice of the Negro*, August 1904, ed. by J. W. E. Bowen, reprint (New York: Negro Universities Press, 1969), 320.

4 Julie Besonen, "Harlem of South Revived in Richmond," *The New York Times*, October 30, 2011, accessed December 20, 2019, https://archive.nytimes.com/query. nytimes.com/gst/fullpage-9F04E1D6163AF933A05753C1A9679D8B63.html

5 "Private Dwelling Sales," *The New York Times*, April 21, 1917, 18. ProQuest Historical Newspapers: The New York Times with Index.

6 Etta Rebecca Williams, "Fannie Criss: Turn of the Century Dressmaker," *Richmond Literature and History* Quarterly no. 4 (Spring 1982), 47.

7 United States Federal Census, Year: 1870, Place: Madison, Cumberland, Virginia, Roll: M593_1642, 54A, Family History Library Film: 553141, accessed January 15, 2020, https://www.ancestry.com/imageviewer/collections/7163/images/4268495_00 111?pId=37138003.

8 United States Federal Census, Year: 1880; Place: Madison, Cumberland, Virginia, Enumeration District: 077, Roll: 1362, 53A, accessed December 15, 2020, https://www.ancestry.com/imageviewer/collections/6742/images/4244582-00112?pId=18710148.

9 United States Census. Madison, Cumberland County. Virginia, digital image, Ancestry.com:1895 Index to Register of Marriages for the City of Richmond, Virginia, February 17, 1895, Virginia State Library: Vital Statistics, Marriages, City of Richmond 1878–1895, Microfilm Reel 68-9, February 17, 1895, Virginia State Library.

10 Fannie White, Certificate of Death, October 15, 1867, no. 4637, New York State Department of Health, copy in possession of author.

11 Edgar Sydenstricker and Ammen Lewis Burger, *School History of Virginia* (Lynchburg: Dulaney-Boatwright Company, 1914), 237–8.

12 United States Federal Census, Year: 1900, Place: Richmond, Jackson Ward, Richmond City, Virginia, Enumeration District: 0101, 17, FHL microfilm 1241739, accessed December 15, 2020, https://www.ancestry.com/imageviewer/collections/7602/images/4117946_00237?pId=72833266.

13 United States Federal Census, Year: 1910, Place: Richmond Monroe Ward, Richmond (Independent City), Virginia, Enumeration District: 0142, Roll:

T624_1645, 17B, FHL microfilm: 1375658, accessed January 15, 2020, https://www.ancestry.com/imageviewer/collections/7884/images/4454411_00757?pId=176217133.

14 Burrell, "History of the Business of Colored Richmond," 322.

15 Gertrude Woodruff Marlowe, *A Right Worthy Grand Mission: Maggie Lena Walker and the Quest for Black Economic Empowerment* (Washington, DC: Howard University Press, 2003), 64–5.

16 Ibid., 63.

17 Lucy Ann Jackson Foster, Notes relating to the work and clients of Fannie Criss, May 8, 1958, Valentine museum archives.

18 Blair M. Kelley, *Right to Ride: Streetcar Boycotts and African American Citizenship in the Era of Plessy* v. *Ferguson* (Chapel Hill: The University of North Carolina Press, 2010), 38.

19 Ibid., 128.

20 David A. Ferguson, *Souvenir Views: Negro Enterprises & Residences, Richmond.* (Richmond: D. A. Ferguson, 1907), pdf. accessed November 5, 2019, https://www.loc.gov/item/74182181/.

21 Albert Nelson Marquis, *Who's Who in America,1914–1915 VIII* (Chicago: A. N. Marquis & Company), 1576.

22 Philip Alexander Bruce and William Glover Stanard, *The Virginia Magazine of History and Biography*, no. 1 (January 1, 1893): 343–4.

23 "Marriage, Money, & Minutes in Richmond, Virginia Society Irvine, Roberta Nolting. Archive Concerning Richmond and Big Stone Gap Virginia Society, Early 20th century," Kaaterskill Books, accessed December 15, 2019, https://www.kaaterskillbooks.com/pages/books/43868/roberta-nolting-irvine/archive-concerning-richmond-and-big-stone-gap-virginia-society-early-20th-century.

24 Peter C. Luebke, "James Taylor Ellyson (1847–1919)," *Dictionary of Virginia Biography*, Library of Virginia (1998–), published 2015, accessed November 5, 2019, http://www.lva.virginia.gov/public/dvb/bio.asp?b=Ellyson_James_Taylor.

25 Alyssa Toby Fahringer, "Lora Effie Hotchkiss Ellyson (1848–1935)," *Dictionary of Virginia Biography*, Library of Virginia (1998–), published 2015, accessed November 8, 2019, http://www.lva.virginia.gov/public/dvb/bio.asp?b=Ellyson_Lora_Effie_Hotchkiss.

26 "Former Prominent Businessman Confederate Sailor and Soldier, Dead," *The Times-Dispatch*, December 21, 1911, 2, accessed December 1, 2019, https://virginiachronicle.com/?a=d&d=TD19111221&e=———-en-20-1-txt-txIN-%22maxwell+t.+clarke%22———-.

27 Doug Childers, "Elderslie Place," *Richmond Times-Dispatch*, August 2, 2014, accessed December 1, 2019, https://www.richmond.com/elderslie-place/article_c05d0379-cd32-5535-b8d6-432d102b8788.html.

28 United States Federal Census, Year: 1900, Place: Richmond, Jackson Ward,
    Richmond City, Virginia, Enumeration District: 0101, 17, FHL microfilm
    1241739, accessed December 15, 2020, https://www.ancestry.com/imageviewer/
    collections/7602/images/4117946_00237?pId=72833266.

29 "Property Transfers," *The Times-Dispatch*, October 2, 1903, 3, accessed November 1,
    2019, https://www.newspapers.com/image/145490141/.

30 "Personals and Briefs," *The Richmond Planet*, July 15, 1905, 1, accessed December
    15, 2019, http://www.newspapers.com/image/72193740/.

31 *Richmond, Virginia City Directory, 1917* (Richmond: n.p. 1917), 174.

32 Lucy Ann Jackson Foster, Notes relating to the work and clients of Fannie Criss,
    May 8, 1958, Valentine museum archives.

33 Fannie C. Payne, Certificate and Record of Marriage, April 22, 1911, file no. 9929,
    New York State Department of Health, copy in possession of author.

34 "A New Club and Cafe in Harlem," *The New York Age*, vol. 27 issue 7,
    November 13, 1913, 8, accessed December 12, 2019, https://www.newspapers.com/
    image/33462304/.

35 "Personals and Briefs," *The St. Luke Herald*, July 18, 1914, 4.

36 "Hotel Men In Florida Now in Their Glory," *The Freeman*, March 17, 1915, 4,
    accessed December 15, 2019, https://news.google.com/newspapers?nid=FIkAGs9z2
    eEC&dat=19150327&printsec=frontpage&hl=en.

37 *The Washington Bee*, February 10, 1917, 10.

38 "Private Dwelling Sales," *The New York Times*, April 21, 1917, 18. ProQuest
    Historical Newspapers: The New York Times with Index.

39 "Chancery Transfers," *Richmond Times-Dispatch*, October 24, 1917, 12, accessed
    December 15, 2019, http://www.newspapers.com/image/168464878/.

40 "Chancery Bargain and Sale," *Richmond Times-Dispatch*, June 11, 1919, 11, accessed
    December 15, 2019, https://www.newspapers.com/image/168582869/.

41 "Must Raise $68,346 for Hospital Today," *Richmond Times-Dispatch*, June 24, 1916,
    3, accessed December 15, 2019, https://www.newspapers.com/image/168522671/.

42 "Richmond," *The New York Age*, vol. 34 issue 21, February 12, 1921, 5, accessed
    12 December 2019, https://www.newspapers.com/image/39621367/.

Bibliography

Besonen, Julie. "Harlem of South Revived in Richmond." *The New York Times*, October
    30, 2011, accessed December 20, 2019. https://archive.nytimes.com/query.nytimes.
    com/gst/fullpage-9F04E1D6163AF933A05753C1A9679D8B63.html.

Bowen, J. W. E., ed. *The Voice of the Negro*, January 1904. New York: Negro Universities
    Press, reprinted 1969.

Bruce, Philip Alexander and William Glover Stanard. *The Virginia Magazine of History and Biography*, no. 1. (January 1, 1893).

Burrell, W. P. "History of the Business of Colored Richmond," in *The Voice of the Negro*, August 1904, ed. J. W. E. Bowen, 317–22. New York: Negro Universities Press, reprinted ed. 1969.

Burrell, W. P. and D. E. Johnson. *Twenty-five Years' History of the Grand Fountain of the United Order of True Reformers, 1881–1905*. Richmond: Grand Fountain, United Order of True Reformers, 1909.

"Chancery Bargain and Sale." *Richmond Times-Dispatch*, June 11, 1919, accessed December 15, 2019. https://www.newspapers.com/image/168582869/.

"Chancery Transfers." *Richmond Times-Dispatch*, October 24, 1917, accessed December 15, 2019. http://www.newspapers.com/image/168464878/.

Childers, Doug. "Elderslie Place." *Richmond Times-Dispatch*, August 2, 2014, accessed December 1, 2019. https://www.richmond.com/elderslie-place/article_c05d0379-cd32-5535-b8d6-432d102b8788.html.

Fahringer, Alyssa Toby. "Lora Effie Hotchkiss Ellyson (1848–1935)." *Dictionary of Virginia Biography*, Library of Virginia (1998–), published 2015, accessed November 8, 2019. http://www.lva.virginia.gov/public/dvb/bio.asp?b=Ellyson_Lora_Effie_Hotchkiss.

"Former Prominent Businessman Confederate Sailor and Soldier, Dead." *The Times-Dispatch*. December 21, 1911, accessed December 1 2019. https://virginiachronicle.com/?a=d&d=TD19111221&e=———-en-20-1-txt-txIN-%22maxwell+t.+clarke%22———-.

Foster, Lucy Ann Jackson. Notes relating to the work and clients of Fannie Criss. May 8, 1958. Valentine museum archives.

"Hotel Men In Florida Now in Their Glory." *The Freeman*. March 27, 1915, accessed December 15, 2019. https://news.google.com/newspapers?nid=FIkAGs9z2eEC&dat=19150327&printsec=frontpage&hl=en.

Luebke, Peter C. "James Taylor Ellyson (1847–1919)." *Dictionary of Virginia Biography*. Library of Virginia (1998–), published 2015, accessed November 5, 2019. http://www.lva.virginia.gov/public/dvb/bio.asp?b=Ellyson_James_Taylor.

Marquis, Albert Nelson. *Who's Who in America,1914–1915 VIII*. Chicago: A. N. Marquis & Company.

"Marriage, Money, & Minutes in Richmond, Virginia Society Irvine, Roberta Nolting. Archive Concerning Richmond and Big Stone Gap Virginia Society, Early 20th century." Kaaterskill Books, accessed December 15, 2019. https://www.kaaterskillbooks.com/pages/books/43868/roberta-nolting-irvine/archive-concerning-richmond-and-big-stone-gap-virginia-society-early-20th-century.

"Must Raise $68,346 for Hospital Today." *Richmond Times-Dispatch*. June 24, 1916, accessed December 15, 2019. https://www.newspapers.com/image/168522671/.

"A New Club and Cafe in Harlem." *The New York Age*, vol. 27 issue 7, November 13, 1913, accessed December 12, 2019. https://www.newspapers.com/image/33462304/.

Payne, Fannie C. Certificate and Record of Marriage. April 22, 1911. file no. 9929. New York State Department of Health. copy in possession of author.

"Personals and Briefs." *The Richmond Planet.* July 15, 1905, accessed December 15, 2019. http://www.newspapers.com/image/72193740/.

"Personals and Briefs." *The St. Luke Herald.* July 18, 1914, 4.

"Private Dwelling Sales." *The New York Times.* April 21, 1917: 18. ProQuest Historical Newspapers: The New York Times with Index.

"Property Transfers." *The Times-Dispatch.* October 2, 1903, accessed November 1, 2019 https://www.newspapers.com/image/145490141/.

"Richmond." *The New York Age*, vol. 34 issue 21, February 12, 1921, accessed December 12, 2019. https://www.newspapers.com/image/39621367/.

Richmond, Virginia City Directory, 1917 (Richmond: n.p. 1917).

Sydenstricker, Edgar and Ammen Lewis Burger. *School History of Virginia.* Lynchburg: Dulaney-Boatwright Company, 1914.

The Washington Bee. February 10, 1917.

United States Census. Madison, Cumberland County. Virginia, digital image, Ancestry. com: 1895 Index to Register of Marriages for the City of Richmond, Virginia, February 17, 1895, Virginia State Library: Vital Statistics, Marriages, City of Richmond 1878–1895, Microfilm Reel 68-9, February 17, 1895, Virginia State Library.

United States Federal Census, Year: 1870, Place: Madison, Cumberland, Virginia, Roll: M593_1642, 54A, Family History Library Film: 553141, accessed January 15, 2020. https://www.ancestry.com/imageviewer/collections/7163/images/4268495_00111?p Id=37138003.

United States Federal Census, Year: 1880; Place: Madison, Cumberland, Virginia, Enumeration District: 077, Roll: 1362, 53A, accessed December 15, 2020. https://www.ancestry.com/imageviewer/collections/6742/images/4244582-00112?pId=18710148.

United States Federal Census, Year: 1900, Place: Richmond, Jackson Ward, Richmond City, Virginia, Enumeration District: 0101, 17, FHL microfilm 1241739, accessed December 15, 2020. https://www.ancestry.com/imageviewer/collections/7602/image s/4117946_00237?pId=72833266.

United States Federal Census, Year: 1910, Place: Richmond Monroe Ward, Richmond (Independent City), Virginia, Enumeration District: 0142, Roll: T624_1645, 17B, FHL microfilm: 1375658, accessed January 15, 2020. https://www.ancestry.com/ imageviewer/collections/7884/images/4454411_00757?pId=176217133.

White, Fannie, Certificate of Death, October 15, 1867, no. 4637, New York State Department of Health, copy in possession of author.

Williams, Etta Rebecca. "Fannie Criss: Turn of the century dressmaker." *Richmond Literature and History Quarterly*, no. 4 (Spring 1982): 46–8.

5

Ruby Bailey: Making for Oneself, A Regional Fashion Designer Case Study

Joy Davis

Ruby Bailey represents the creative Black fervor of the early to mid-twentieth century from a perspective that has been underrepresented in both American history and fashion history. Based firmly in the Harlem neighborhood of New York City throughout her career, she was a creative stalwart, steadfast in her identity and her craft. Her career began in the visual and performing arts before she transitioned into fashion. A talented artist in many mediums, Bailey pioneered a unique artistic form during the 1960s that combined fashion and visual art. Her "cotton sculptures" or "manikins" referenced historical fashion dolls, but also served as an outlet for her fashion designs and represented important ideals of Black empowerment through aesthetic values championed by the Black Power and "Black is Beautiful" movements. Additionally, Bailey made connections throughout her life that put her at the center of the Harlem Renaissance and influential Harlem society. As a Black female artist, Bailey's work was often viewed through a lens of social prejudices. For example, throughout her career, the press frequently focused on her unmarried relationship status in their articles about her designs and achievements. Despite this, she maneuvered her way through Harlem society, making a name for herself. She used these connections to encourage other Black fashion professionals and artists and to advocate for arts education for Black children. Ruby Bailey did not have a traditional fashion career; however, she used fashion as a springboard for her creative expression and her art. This chapter examines Bailey's career and her impact by scrutinizing the contemporary press, as well as the archive of her work held in the collection of the Museum of the City of New York (MCNY).

Bailey was born around 1908 in Bermuda. After immigrating to the United States, circa 1912, Ruby, with her mother Louisa and her older sister Berel, settled in Harlem. Bailey's mother was an early and continual influence on her life. Louisa was an organist and seamstress by trade; the 1940 United States Census listed her as a dressmaker in their shared home.[1] In Bailey's unpublished autobiography, *I Did It My Way*, she only briefly mentions her mother and sister, despite the former being one of the first influences on her art practice. Yet Bailey consistently made clothing for her sister and designed all the clothes her mother wore.[2] Bailey considered her mother to be a top designer with an elite clientele and an inspiration for her fashion work.[3] She describes herself as being "'saturated' with high fashion since childhood," and from her days as a primary school student at Public School 119 in Harlem, she was determined that she would become a designer.[4]

The immigration of Bailey's family to the United States coincided with the start of the Great Migration in America that saw an influx of African Americans migrating from the southern areas of the country and the Caribbean to northern and western cities. This movement created a rush of people, ideas, and creativity to towns and cities already solidified as cultural hubs for Black people, including Chicago, Los Angeles, and, especially, New York City. The Great Migration of the 1910s birthed radical cultural and political moments, such as the Harlem Renaissance during the 1920s, and later, the Civil Rights Movement. These two major landmarks in American history helped to shape the Bailey's existence in America, and specifically in Harlem. Its influence on Bailey's life and art practice is evident in the history of Harlem that she includes in her autobiography. Although sporadic and disorganized, this two-page account starts with a remembrance of the poet Countee Cullen and the physician Dr. May E. Chinn and goes on to highlight a multitude of Black art, science, and business organizations, many of which she was a part. She also attributes the inspiration of the "Black is Beautiful" movement to beauty entrepreneur Madam C. J. Walker and references the Katherine Dunham Dancers, who were "adding a touch of exotica" to modern dance.[5] Growing up in this creative environment during the Harlem Renaissance—she was between the ages of seventeen and nineteen at the beginning of the movement—Bailey embraced both the visual and performing arts, participating in fashion shows, art exhibitions, and theatrical productions at prominent locales including St. Phillips Episcopal Church, the Savoy Ballroom, and the local nightclub Small's Paradise.[6] Her autobiography highlights—in the third person—both Bailey's career as an artist and her personal connections to her community, giving the reader a glimpse of both her prose and important moments in her life and career. Also evident is her benevolent impulse to work in her community, which could be attributed to a more general sense of civic duty honed in the United States during the years between the World Wars. This impulse would later lead Bailey to actively support the Civil Rights Movement.

Early Career in Performance and Theater Design

From a young age, Bailey began to develop her visual arts language, which later included her signature cotton sculptures. In 1920, she graduated from Public School 119 with an interest in painting and illustration that came from her supplemental education at multiple art schools and workshops, including time spent studying design at Hunter College.[7] As Bailey states in her autobiography, her painting and illustrating methods used unique techniques in pastel, tempera, watercolor, sepia, charcoal, and ink. By the 1930s, she was thriving in the art and performance scenes of Harlem and making a splash in modeling contests. While she also participated in theater and dance, performance was not her main focus. Dance, however, greatly influenced her later doll-making art practice; the gestures, poses, and bodies of dancers were imitated in the bodies she created. It was during this period that her visual art practice began to flourish. Painter, illustrator, milliner, doll-maker, and dressmaker: Bailey was a multi-focused artist. She took inspiration from many artistic and fashionable sources, including the "Black is Beautiful" movement, American *Vogue*, and stars of the Harlem Renaissance, such as dancers Katherine Dunham and Pearl Bailey. Her inspirations were not limited to either Black or white culture, Harlem or the larger New York City area, but drew from a wide range of American cultural references.

Both Bailey's autobiography and the contemporary press covering her career indicate that she also designed costumes for theaters throughout Manhattan and beyond. Housed in the fashion collection at the MCNY is a red, sleeveless dress, made from mesh or leno weave fabric with a repeated chain link design on the bodice and a bubble hem skirt. There is very little documentation accompanying the dress, which was brought into the MCNY's collection from the estate of Ruby Bailey. The dress was cataloged as a "cocktail dress in flocked scarlet leno-weave nylon;" however, its details indicate to both the author and MCNY's costume curator that it was likely used as a theater costume. The style of dress, including the high-waisted silhouette of the skirt, and the synthetic fabric, indicate that it dates to the early 1950s. The design of the dress allows for movement in a way that indicates its possible use as a dance garment. The size of the dress would have fit Bailey at the time, and she was still acting in small productions in Harlem during the early 1950s. The dress does not show signs of frequent wear, and it may be the only surviving material evidence of Bailey's connection to theater costume design. In addition, this dress represents the best example of Bailey's high-quality construction skills within the MCNY collection. The pattern cutting, seams, and hem finishing are of a higher quality than her other surviving garments. Given her professional experience, Bailey was well aware of the formal construction methods of the fashion industry. However, many of her extant garments held in the collection of MCNY are samples that show more improvisational work, made to execute her vision as quickly as possible. Much of the stitching was done quickly, in most cases hems and seams are unsecured. Bailey's design for theatrical performance during this period was varied. She was mentioned as a Barnum and Bailey costume designer in *The New York Age* newspaper in 1949, and in her autobiography she states that she created the nine-by-twelve-foot red velvet costume for Modoc, King of the Elephants.[8] In the Ringling Museum archival collection there is an illustration that depicts the elephant Modoc in a "Father Time" ensemble, which aligns with Bailey's press in the *The New York Age*.[9] The costume was made of a thick red fabric with fringed trim and was designed to drape over Modoc, reaching almost to the ground.

The Harlem Renaissance was a pivotal environment for Bailey's life and varied careers, and she was able to harness the energy of the cultural movement for both personal and community gain by partnering with multiple organizations and presenting her work to large audiences in New York. Along with being an active artist, she became a cultural socialite and was active in the social scenes of Harlem. The earliest press on Bailey as an artist occurred when she was still a student in 1926. The *New York Amsterdam News* reported on an "Open Air Extravaganza" put on by the YWCA, and Bailey was awarded a prize as an artist of the Beaux-Arts Club, though the press was unclear about the specifics of her piece.[10] For the rest of her life, Bailey supported organizations such as the Beaux-Arts Club. She advocated for educational leisure time with the Art Workshop for College and Industrial Women where she served on the board of the institution, and through the 1960s she supported Black women and children in the creative arts. For Bailey, her art practice was much more than producing objects that she fancied; she wanted to share the empowerment of creating art and help show that art to the world.

Bailey Takes the Plunge into Fashion and Doll-Making

In 1939, Bailey was a thirty-something, single seamstress working at a dress factory, while her sister Berel was a salesperson at a dress store.[11] At this time, Bailey had completed classes at the New York Academy of Design and the Barnard School of Design. Two years later, she appeared to be actively pursuing her career as a fashion designer in the New York fashion industry. In May

1941, she presented her work at the Renaissance Ballroom, where she showed her spring/summer fashion sketches. The *New York Amsterdam Star* reported that the collection is "giving millady individuality according to her color and type."[12] In August of the same year, she exhibited nineteen designs at the Alma Reed Galleries and her photograph was featured in the *New York Amsterdam Star News.*[13] This was one of the most prominent displays of her garments in an exhibition on record. She was described as a designer and fashion illustrator and as "the only Negro artist exhibiting."[14] Her designs were described as costumes for "exotic and conservative types."[15]

The extant fashion garments held in the collection of the MCNY show a range of Bailey's work, from simpler sportswear pieces to extravagant eveningwear and millinery design, all showcasing her eye for detail and unique embellishment. Within the Ruby Bailey collection there is an unlined, purple, woolen cape accessorized with an elegant brooch closure with a braided brass design and a faux gem at the center. Studying the cape tells the story of Bailey's design aesthetic beyond the fashion presentations covered in the press. Like many fashion designers of the 1940s, Bailey opted for a simple silhouette. The fabric is heavy and plush, and possibly made of alpaca. The cape has a high collar, structured shoulder, and a wraparound design. The silhouette dates this piece to the mid-decade, and it is an outerwear design that is in step with the rising popularity of sportswear in the United States, but with an added Harlem flair through the applied brooch.

Bailey's more opulent designs and ideas show a sensibility that can be compared to that of haute couturiers and high-profile dressmakers of the period. She had real talent for infusing whimsy and romance into her clothing designs. The "Tar Bush Hat"—the only hat that survives in Bailey's collection—is an opulent and fantastical design that also speaks to her technical skill. Bailey's hat has a twisted conical crown and a mushroom-shaped base with a beaded star or flower motif. The design resembles a mixture between the forms of snakes and Ottoman Empire headwear. The floral motifs are similar to those seen in carpets and paintings throughout the ancient Middle East. The hat has a beaded outline in a scalloped shape along the base. Thin, ruby, drop-shaped beads in a jagged pattern accent the base and the crown. A hood descends from the back of the hat and a second piece of fabric wraps around the front to conceal the wearer's face. The woolen blend hat has yet to be displayed by MCNY because of conservation concerns, made more complex by its intricate design.

One of Bailey's most prominent fashion designs is the *Bug* dress. Cataloged as the *Bug* evening dress in the MCNY collection, it is a tea-length strapless gown made of white linen with black trim and piqué details. The dress derives

Figure 5.1 Ruby Bailey, *Bug* evening dress, circa 1953–1956. Museum of the City of New York. Ruby Bailey. 2004.41.4A-D.

its title from its meandering scenes of bees, beetles, and spiders, all depicted in black, yellow, and translucent beading details. The spider sits at the top of the skirt. Yellow and black zigzag patterned trim is used to create the illusion of a web, capturing the bugs below it. Supporting the full skirt are three petticoats at above-knee length made of horsehair and flaring double-flounced crinolines. A photograph in MCNY's archive shows Ruby Bailey modeling the fantastical dress. Phyllis Magidson, Curator of Costumes and Textiles at MCNY, stated, "The only other designer I ever saw who had the audacity of putting a motif of that scale was [couturier Charles Frederick] Worth."[16]

Memorable designs such as these made Bailey a fixture in the Harlem fashion scene. According to fashion designer and textile artist Precious D. Lovell, who volunteered at MCNY and researched Bailey's work, "she allegedly won an award at the Savoy Ballroom" consistently between 1953 and 1957.[17] While there is little available evidence in the historic record of her work in the mainstream New York fashion industry, other than her own abridged autobiography and United States Census records, Ruby Bailey participated in a formalized Harlem fashion system along with other Black designers and dressmakers. This system operated outside of the mainstream New York fashion industry. Instead of keeping offices and showrooms on Seventh Avenue in the Garment District and hosting buyers and the press during Press Week as mainstream designers and manufacturers did, Harlem designers held fashion shows uptown in their own neighborhood venues which were covered by Black newspapers.[18] For example, during the summer and winter of 1954, Ruby modeled her own designs at the Savoy Ballroom and the Audubon Ballroom, respectively.[19] In 1958, Bailey took to the Dreamland Ballroom to model her own designs for the National Association of Fashion and Accessory Designers (NAFAD). Bailey's participation in the NAFAD event speaks to her vital role in the Harlem fashion scene during the mid-century. Founded in 1949 by Civil Rights activist and educator Mary McLeod Bethune, NAFAD was one of the most significant organizations created for Black fashion and accessory designers in the country. Bailey's growing prominence in fashion was recognized by Bethune early on; in 1949, she invited Bailey to attend a conference in Harlem's Hotel Theresa sponsored by the National Council of Negro Women. This meeting was one of NAFAD's first events and was aimed at organizing and supporting Black designers across the United States and connecting them with the mainstream industry.[20]

Bailey experienced a career peak in 1951, showing her work throughout New York, and garnering her largest number of press pieces. In January, for example, *The New York Age* reported on the culmination of work done by NAFAD members from across the country. Bailey was among the many designers featured, which also included Zelda Wynn Valdes.[21] Valdes was one of Harlem's most respected designers. She counted Ella Fitzgerald, Mae West, Eartha Kitt, and Josephine Baker as clients, and served as a leader in the NAFAD organization.[22] The event was held for an audience of manufacturers, buyers, suppliers, and others in order to promote Black fashion professionals and forge industry relationships. After 1958 there are fewer references to Bailey's work in newspapers, but she continued to design clothing, keeping up with evolving trends. One dress of note created after her period of prominent press is a dashiki cape dress dated between 1963 and 1966. The dress has a vibrant orange background with colorful floral patterns. There is loose stitching throughout the garment which can be attributed to Bailey's quick hand, though the edges of the attached cape are tightly stitched at the hem. Inside a paisley-filled circular design at the center of the dress there are floral, oval shaped, coral-colored elements encircled by turquoise, sapphire, and agate stones. Additionally, fringed raffia with plastic coating decorates the hem.

Bailey also created a doll-sized version of the cape dress for a corresponding cotton sculpture. She called both pieces *Africa Speaks*, making her an early fashion adopter of African-inspired styles championed by the Black Power and "Black is Beautiful" movements that would culminate during the late 1960s and 1970s. The aesthetic outlets of both movements continued the legacy of the larger Civil Rights Movement. While Black Power was more militant in both action and aesthetics, it was intertwined with "Black is Beautiful," which rejected direct and indirect white or mainstream aesthetic aspirations, including the wearing of business suits and the straightening of Black hair. Instead, the movements championed "natural" hair and styles that affirmed "Black people's racial beauty."[23] For example, in 1968, a news story featuring Kathleen Cleaver, a leading woman on the front lines of the Black Panthers, discusses the power of her afro and the "Black is Beautiful" movement, connecting natural hair to "a new awareness among Black people that their own natural ... appearance is beautiful ... for so many, many years we were told that only white people were beautiful ... but this has changed because Black people are aware."[24] Some of Ruby Bailey's cotton sculptures feature natural hair. The most notable in MCNY's collection are dolls cataloged as wearing, "turquoise-patterned harem pant and midriff top," and a "striped caftan jumpsuit." Bailey sourced hair materials for her cotton sculptures at barbershops in Harlem.

Figure 5.2 Ruby Bailey, *Africa Speaks* caftan, circa 1965. Museum of the City of New York. Ruby Bailey. 2004.41.6.

Figure 5.3 Ruby Bailey, cotton sculpture wearing turquoise-patterned harem pant and midriff top, circa 1965. Museum of the City of New York. Ruby Bailey. 2004.41.29.

Bailey used her cotton sculptures to advocate for the natural hair movement, which saw its early incarnations in the natural hair traditions that persisted throughout the United States and the Caribbean during the period of the Great Migration. Her estate collection also includes photographs of dolls wearing headwraps and turbans, which she created to match their garments. Along with Black hair, the headwraps that Bailey included in her art pieces engage in a dialog that was extremely relevant to Black beauty and cultural tradition during the 1960s. Helen Bradley Foster, in her chapter "Crowning the Person" in *New Raiments of Self*, discusses the African American sartorial politics of the headwrap, including Zora Neale Hurston's reflections on how "Blacks in the Northeast" saw it as a monument to enslaved ancestors, or the Uncle Tom narrative. Hurston saw the headwrap as representative of identity politics within the Black community. Foster further cites historian John Roberts's observation that women of the rural South held on to the tradition of headwraps into the 1960s.[25]

The genesis of Bailey's doll work were Barbie dolls. Barbie fashion dolls were launched in March 1959 by the American toy company, Mattel, Inc. Ruth Handler used a German doll called Bild Lilli as her inspiration and is credited with the original design.[26] Bailey started using Barbies as a readily available blank canvas, much like a fashion designer uses a dress form. She then began to manipulate the Barbie dolls from their original form. Many of her original dolls, held in her estate's collection, were manipulations of Barbies. Her modifications included cutting off the original hair and replacing it with sourced hair, which she might style, painting the skin of the dolls, and using the original shape of the dolls' arms and legs to build upon with gesso, a material used to build and prepare surfaces in painting and sculpture. She soon moved on from Barbies and started to create her own dolls from scratch. Bailey described the cotton sculptures as "integrated fashion manikins," and thought of her work as ingenious, stating, "cotton has never been used as an art medium in this form, emerging hard as a rock."[27] The conservator who cared for the cotton sculptures estimates that Bailey achieved this form by adding adhesive to the cotton and heating it over a stove to create an end product that would harden. Bailey describes the materials and her process: "The materials involved are not compatible, with no harmony in relationships, which was an added impetus for experimentation. Her inner vision has elevated cotton to the status of great art … indeed a phenomenon."[28] She states that she created the manikins for adult enjoyment and defines her dolls as cotton sculptures to separate them from children's dolls or toys, elevating them to a higher art form.

In her autobiography and related press, Bailey uses the word "manikins" to describe the cotton sculptures that modeled her "exclusive designs," shedding light on how she used the dolls in her art practice and their deep connection to her fashion design.[29] The most obvious connection is that Bailey made full-sized fashion garments that replicated the designs on the dolls. This chapter would also argue that once she decided to stop displaying her fashion illustrations, the dolls acted as both samples and as a new way of articulating her vision. Ruby Bailey's cotton sculptures fit into a long lineage of miniaturized fashion figures that were used to communicate fashion culture and information. Fashion dolls were created by dressmakers serving the French aristocracy during the seventeenth and eighteenth centuries and disseminated by the Parisian fashion system.[30] The dolls were intended for consumption by adult women as representations of the latest styles and silhouettes. In the simplest way, the fashion doll acted as an advertising tool for a growing fashion system that continues to dominate the Western world. Early twentieth-century couturier Paul Poiret, who opened his Parisian fashion house in 1905, reimagined the idea of the fashion doll during the 1910s by dressing porcelain dolls with his creations.[31] He showcased these dolls through advertisements, one of the many ways he marketed his work in the Euro-American market.

One of the most famous uses of fashion dolls to promote, not only fashion information but also diplomacy and cultural value, was the tour of the Théâtre de la Mode. In 1944, toward the end of World War Two, the French fashion system was fractured and disorganized due to Paris's occupation by the Nazis throughout the war. In an effort to fight the perception that the Parisian fashion industry was dead and to market post-war styles, the *Chambre syndicale de la haute couture*, the French fashion regulating commission, created the Théâtre de la Mode, a replication of Poiret's fashion doll tour.[32] With a selection of dolls dressed by Parisian couturiers, the tour was also created to reconnect with the American fashion press, including publications such as American *Vogue*. According to fashion scholar Adam Geczy, twentieth-century Catalonian sculptor Joan Rebull created the approximately two hundred and forty dolls, with bodies made of wire and heads made of plaster. The dolls toured the United States until 1946.[33]

Fashion dolls could also be used by fashion consumers. Peggy Hamilton, for example, was a costume designer, socialite, and fashion writer in Los Angeles, who carried dolls wearing outfits that matched her own as accessories.[34] The *Los Angeles Times* published a profile on Hamilton in 1923, and she was seen as eccentric at best for carrying her dolls around town.[35] The reporter states,

"Miss Hamilton appeared carrying one of these little travesties in the lobby of the [Ambassador] hotel and was immediately surrounded by scores of women who wished to know where the 'cunning' little thing came from."[36] For Hamilton, they were accessories and symbols of wealth, fashion literacy, and culture: "It appears now that the doll fad is scheduled to replace all other fads for moons to come."[37] Bailey and Hamilton shared a love of whimsy and fashion, manifested through fashion dolls, but their articulations of that love were very different. For Ruby Bailey, fashion dolls were a vital component of her art practice based on her impulse to create whimsical, alternative worlds and companions to her fashion designs, as well as an expression of Black cultural pride and support for progressive Black social and political movements.

Within this wider historical context, Bailey created a new concept for fashion dolls, and she shifted her focus to her cotton sculptures after 1962. In 1971 they were described by writer Sara Slack as a "unique hobby," and she recognized Bailey as one of the first Black artists who glorified the figure of the Black woman.[38] The skin color of the dolls varied depending on the theme or ethos of the doll and the companion ensemble. Most of the dolls started out as white Barbies, but Bailey's collections gradually grew to include predominantly brown skin tones. Her sculptures, arranged in tableaus, often focused on Black culture, but she also reveled in creating statement dolls that celebrated the United States' participation in the space race. In 1978 Bailey was featured as an artist in an event held by the Hatch-Billops Collection, a visual and literary archive documenting the output of contemporary Black artists. Fellow recognized artists included Romare Bearden, Richard Hunt, Jacob Lawrence, Mel Edwards, and Alma Thomas.[39] Bailey herself notes that she showed her designs at the Waldorf Astoria Hotel and that the MCNY requested a presentation of her dolls during the 1980s.

Conclusion

Much to the chagrin and disappointment of Ruby Bailey, most Black creatives of her era were not able to capitalize on their creative skills or sustain their legacies beyond their lifetimes. Working outside the mainstream industry and circles of influence, there was not as much money or recognition in fashion design and visual art during the mid-twentieth century for Black makers. Although organizations such as the Hatch-Billops Collection and the Alma Reed Gallery engaged with Bailey and artists like her, this did not translate into ongoing support for the artists to maintain sustainable careers. Despite these constraints, Bailey, in many ways, thrived in Harlem's creative circles, producing the work she wanted to produce and showcasing it for decades. She was also a confident member of many African American cultural, social, political organizations and movements who did not bow to convention. Bailey never discussed her reasons for not marrying, despite the press's attention on her marital status. The contemporary newspapers' focus on the glamorous figure she cut, despite not having a man, dismissed the interconnected legacy she crafted throughout her life in Harlem. She was steadfast in her mission. Her estate holder remembers her as "a loner," stating that Bailey used to say, "I have no use for other people."[40] Yet her impact touches many. Artists who have brought together fashion and sculpture, as well as other art mediums, such as Precious D. Lovell, Betye Saar, Yinka Shinobare, and Virgil Abloh, have all followed in her footsteps. Like Bailey, they have benefited from being multi-disciplined and multifaceted in their approach to fashion. Ruby Bailey did not benefit from the publicity that later Black artists could command, yet she persevered in her art practice despite her humble following and lack of mainstream attention. Furthermore, her art practice was a seamless representation of self.

In some ways, Bailey was ahead of her time. Her art practice was intertwined with fashion and was deeply rooted in Harlem as a site of creativity, as well as in the evolving Black experience of the twentieth century. That connectedness did not waiver until her death in 2003 at the age of ninety-seven. Although Bailey did not have a traditional fashion career, her story and archive helps reframe the narrative of Black designers and Black visual artists of the twentieth century, artists who were educated and empowered by the Harlem Renaissance and helped to visualize new Black American identities during the Civil Rights era. Examining her many inspirations, it can be understood that Bailey sought to push the boundaries of fashion and her own artistic work.

Notes

1 "United States Census, Year: 1940, Place: New York, New York County," Enumeration District: 31–1537, roll: m-t0627-02660, 18A, 1940 Census, published online, accessed March 1, 2019, https://1940census.archives.gov/search/?search. result_type=image&search.state=NY&search.enumeration_district=31-1537#filena me=m-t0627-02660-00926.tif&name=31-1537&type=image&state=NY&index=18 &pages=48&bm_all_text=Bookmark.

2   "Marva Louis Tea Hostess: Holders of Patrons," *New York Amsterdam Star*, May 3, 1941, 1.

3   Ruby Bailey, *I Did It My Way* (New York: Self-Published, 1980), 1, in the collection of the Museum of the City of New York.

4   Ibid.

5   Ibid.

6   Ibid.

7   Ibid., 2.

8   Ibid., 2.

9   Miles White, *Father Time Elephant Blanket,* 1949 (paint and ink on paper costume rendering), The Ringling Museum online collections, accessed March 28, 2019, https://emuseum.ringling.org/emuseum/objects/738/father-time-elephant-blanket?ctx=e1dae1b9-5240-45eb-98cd-a42932864455&idx=1.

10 "Fashion Hints: Chiffon Tunic," *New York Amsterdam News*, June 16, 1926, 10.

11 "United States Census, Year: 1940."

12 "Marva Louis Tea Hostess," 1.

13 "19 Designs on Exhibit," *New York Amsterdam Star News*, August 16, 1941, 6.

14 Ibid.

15 Ibid.

16 Steffie Nelson, "A Closetful of Genius," *The New York Times*, February 13, 2005, accessed March 1, 2019, https://www.nytimes.com/2005/02/13/nyregion/thecity/a-closetful-of-genius.html,

17 Precious D. Lovell, "Reintroducing Ruby Bailey!," *Museum of the City of New York Blog: New York Stories*, January 5, 2016, March 28, 2019, https://blog.mcny.org/2016/01/05/reintroducing-ruby-bailey/.

18 "Consumer Fashions," *New York Amsterdam News*, July 17, 1954, 10; "Winggs Sponsor Colorful Style Show," *The New York Age*, vol. * issue *, December 4, 1954, 14.

19 ""Consumer Fashions," 10; "Winggs Sponsor Colorful Style Show," 14.

20 Nancy Deihl, "Zelda Wynn Valdes: Uptown Modiste," in *The Hidden History of American Fashion: Rediscovering 20th-Century Women Designers*, ed. by Nancy Deihl (London: Bloomsbury Academic, 2018): 223–36, 231–2.

21 "Fashion Designers Plan Breath-Taking Display at Tavern," *The New York Age*, vol. 71 issue 46, January 20, 1951, 7.

22 Deihl, "Zelda Wynn Valdes," 232.

23 Stephanie M. H. Camp, "Black is Beautiful: An American History," *The Journal of Southern History* 81, no. 3 (August 2015): 675–90, 686.

24 "Kathleen Cleaver and Natural Hair," video file, 0:57, YouTube, posted by Larry D Bluford Jr, undated, accessed March 29, 2019,https://www.youtube.com/watch?v=M-TXqu2vBcg.

25 Helen Bradley Foster, *New Raiments of Self: African American Clothing in the Antebellum South* (Oxford: Berg Publishers, 1997), 272–315. *Bloomsbury*

Fashion Central, accessed March 28, 2019, http://dx.doi.org.i.ezproxy.nypl. org/10.2752/9781847888808/NEWRAIM0009.

26 Robin Gerber, *Barbie and Ruth: The Story of the World's Most Famous Doll and the Woman Who Created Her* (New York: Harper Business, 2010), 12–17.

27 Bailey, *I Did It My Way*, 2.

28 Ibid.

29 Ibid.

30 Valerie Steele, *Fifty Years of Fashion: New Look to Now* (New Haven: Yale University Press, 2000), 39.

31 "Society Captivated By Dolls: Times Fashion Editor Their Sponsor," *Los Angeles Times*, February 13, 1923, 119.

32 Adam Geczy, *The Artificial Body in Fashion and Art: Marionettes, Models, and Mannequins* (London: Bloomsbury Academic, 2018), 89–106.

33 Ibid.

34 Michelle Tolini Finamore, *Hollywood Before Glamour: Fashion in American Silent Film* (London: Palgrave, 2013), 141–67.

35 Ibid.

36 "Society Captivated By Dolls," 119.

37 Ibid.

38 Sara Slack, "Sara Speaking," *New York Amsterdam News*, May 29, 1971, 5.

39 Howard Thompson, "Going Out Guide: Images," *The New York Times*, April 19, 1978, C21.

40 Nelson, "A Closetful of Genius."

Bibliography

Collections
The Museum of the City of New York
The Ringling Museum Online Collections

"19 Designs on Exhibit." *New York Amsterdam Star News*, August 16, 1941, 6.

Bailey, Ruby. *I Did It My Way*. New York: Self-Published, 1980, in the collection of the Museum of the City of New York.

Camp, Stephanie M. H. "Black is Beautiful: An American History," *The Journal of Southern History* 81, no. 3 (August 2015): 675–90.

"Consumer Fashions." *New York Amsterdam News*, July 17, 1954, 10.

Deihl, Nancy. "Zelda Wynn Valdes: Uptown Modiste," in *The Hidden History of American Fashion: Rediscovering 20th-Century Women Designers*, ed. Nancy Deihl, 223–36. London: Bloomsbury Academic, 2018.

"Fashion Designers Plan Breath-Taking Display at Tavern." *The New York Age*, vol. 71 issue 46, January 20, 1951: 7.

"Fashion Hints: Chiffon Tunic." *New York Amsterdam News*, June 16, 1926: 10.

Finamore, Michelle Tolini. *Hollywood Before Glamour: Fashion in American Silent Film*. London: Palgrave, 2013.

Foster, Helen Bradley. *New Raiments of Self: African American Clothing in the Antebellum South*. Oxford: Berg Publishers, 1997. *Bloomsbury Fashion Central*, March 28, 2019. http://dx.doi.org.i.ezproxy.nypl.org/10.2752/9781847888808/ NEWRAIM0009.

Geczy, Adam. *The Artificial Body in Fashion and Art: Marionettes, Models, and Mannequins*. London: Bloomsbury Academic, 2018.

Gerber, Robin. *Barbie and Ruth: The Story of the World's Most Famous Doll and the Woman Who Created Her*. New York: Harper Business, 2010.

"Kathleen Cleaver and Natural Hair (1968)." Video file, 0:57, YouTube. Posted by Larry D. Bluford Jr., undated, accessed March 29, 2019 https://www.youtube.com/ watch?v=M-TXqu2vBcg.

Lovell, Precious D. "Reintroducing Ruby Bailey!" *Museum of the City of New York Blog: New York Stories*, January 5, 2016, accessed March 28, 2019. https://blog.mcny. org/2016/01/05/reintroducing-ruby-bailey/.

"Marva Louis Tea Hostess: Holders of Patrons." *New York Amsterdam Star*, May 3, 1941: 1, 17.

Nelson, Steffie. "A Closetful of Genius." *The New York Times*, February 13, 2005, accessed March 1, 2019. https://www.nytimes.com/2005/02/13/nyregion/thecity/a-closetful-of-genius.html.

Slack, Sara. "Sara Speaking." *New York Amsterdam News*, May 29, 1971: 5.

"Society Captivated By Dolls: Times Fashion Editor Their Sponsor." *Los Angeles Times*, February 13, 1923.

Steele, Valerie. *Fifty Years of Fashion: New Look to Now*. New Haven: Yale University Press, 2000.

Thompson, Howard. "Going Out Guide: Images." *The New York Times*, April 19, 1978: C21.

"United States Census, Year: 1940, Place: New York, New York County," Enumeration District: 31-1537, roll: m-t0627-02660, 18A, 1940 Census, accessed March 1, 2019. https://1940census.archives.gov/search/?search.result_type=image&search. state=NY&search.enumeration_district=31-1537#filename=m-t0627-02660-00926. tif&name=31-1537&type=image&state=NY&index=18&pages=48&bm_all_ text=Bookmark.

"Winggs Sponsor Colorful Style Show." *The New York Age*, December 4, 1954, 14.

6

Arthur George "Art" Smith: An Artist About Form, A Man About Substance

Kristen J. Owens

Arthur George "Art" Smith was a queer, Afro-Caribbean modernist jewelry designer based in New York during the mid-twentieth century. For over thirty-five years his avant-garde jewelry designs traveled the world in international exhibitions, sold steadily to the local clients of his Greenwich Village shop, and adorned the bodies of Black jazz musicians, writers, and professional dancers. Smith's designs reflected his continual use of the body as his point of reference, as well as his sensibility as a jazz enthusiast—he was a member of the Duke Ellington Society for ten years. The smooth, sensuous, and organic forms of his jewelry evoke movement and sound, "reflecting both the lines of the body and its capacity for movement," as stated by *Craft Horizons* in 1970.[1] His triple finger rings made with large semi-precious stones, copper chest plate necklaces, and silver mobile earrings that recalled the influential work of kinetic sculptor Alexander Calder emboldened their wearers and created an air of intrigue around their identities. Although Smith was working during a period when there were significantly fewer opportunities available for a Black, queer immigrant, his designs stand strong within the canon of mid-twentieth century modern jewelry and express the momentous change occurring within American society and fashion at this time. His political upbringing, unique creative process, and strong social and cultural views have created space for a new interpretation of his jewelry design in relation to Afrofuturism.

Both fashion and Afrofuturism offer creative methods for either reflecting or rejecting a time period's social, cultural, and political ideals, as well as opportunities to re-imagine the possibilities of Black identity. As exemplified by Afrofuturist musicians like Grace Jones and movies such as *Black Panther* (2018), fashion can be used as a medium through which Afrofuturist ideologies are explored. This includes, but is not limited to, self-governance, ownership

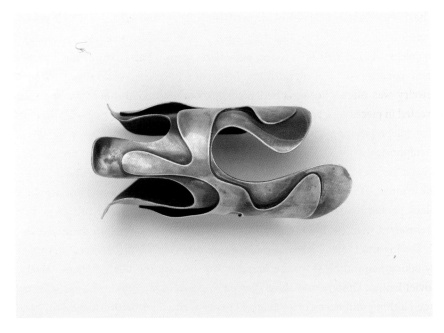

Figure 6.1 Art Smith, silver *Lava Bracelet*, circa 1946. Brooklyn Museum, Gift of Charles L. Russell, 2007.61.16. Creative Commons-BY (Photo: Brooklyn Museum, 2007.61.16_PS2.jpg).

over one's body or its relationship to the environment, social injustice, and ideals related to beauty or social status. Smith's *Lava Bracelet,* made in 1946, exemplifies not only some of Smith's signature design techniques as a modernist jeweler, but also lends itself to an Afrofuturist interpretation. The *Lava Bracelet* is made of silver and consists of organic and abstract forms, overlaid and patinated to give definition and contrast to the overlapping layer. Surrealism, abstraction, and biomorphism—artistic design elements based on naturally occurring patterns or shapes reminiscent of nature and living organisms—were popular design techniques used by modernist jewelers, as was the use of metals such as copper and silver. Although designed in ways that work with and not against the natural design of the human body, this piece takes up a considerable amount of space in comparison to the portion of the body it is designed to fit. On the one hand, it resembles a piece of body armor, and on the other, it evokes images of traditional African tribal jewelry reserved for someone of significant rank.

Although the techniques and materials used by Smith take inspiration and influence from the past and his contemporary moment, they also, especially when modeled on a Black body, express Black beauty and futuristic technology.

The 1960s "Black is Beautiful" movement rejected the idea that Black people were less attractive or desirable than white people. Black people were encouraged to celebrate their rich skin tones, wear their natural hair texture, and increase their consciousness by consuming Black literature, art, and fashion. Smith's jewelry was often photographed on Black bodies, and the negative space he created in pieces such as *Lava Bracelet* interacted with the models' bodies in ways that celebrated the natural form of the Black body. Interpreted as physical and metaphorical armor, as well as high status adornment, the bracelet protects the wearer's expression of self and creates space for imagining the Black body within the context of ancient and/or future African diasporic royalty. How would a Black person living in a Wakanda-esque utopia in which Black people govern themselves, their communities, and their natural resources adorn themselves?[2]

During the 1960s, high and mainstream fashion also engaged with futurism by taking inspiration from the "space race" between the United States and the Soviet Union. Designers such as Pierre Cardin in France, created lines of Space Age clothing and accessories that conveyed technology and futurism through streamlined shapes, bold color blocking and cut-outs, and metallic colors and embellishment. Within this context, in 1962, Smith created the *Galaxy Necklace*. This silver, "wreath-like, asymmetrical necklace composed of a semi-circular neck piece that is open at the front," literally forms a galaxy of "short, crescent-shaped flattened wires that terminate in small spheres of varying size."[3]

Art Smith's ability to take raw materials like sheet metal and wire and intuitively sculpt them into breathtaking three-dimensional forms inspired by movements such as surrealism and biomorphism and African tribal jewelry, speaks to what scholar Ytasha Womack considers to be one of the central tenets of Afrofuturism: imagination, "a way of looking at the future, and alternate realities through a Black cultural lens."[4] Coined in 1993 by white writer and cultural critic Mark Derry, Afrofuturism is the "expression of blackness, black struggles and black ideas, through the imagining of new, hopeful and advanced futures or worlds."[5] Writer, community organizer, and artist Alisha Acquaye further expounds, "With the use of magical realism, Afrocentricity, African traditions and aesthetics, intertwined with technology, sci-fi, and social awareness, Afrofuturism narrates a parallel or distant reality that is empowering and effervescent."[6] As an international aesthetic movement, philosophy of science, and philosophy of history, Afrofuturism allowed artists, musicians, writers, and designers to reclaim their Black intersectional identities decades prior to the coining of the phrase, as eloquently summarized by Lisa Yaszek in her essay, "An Afrofuturist Reading of Ralph Ellison's *Invisible Man*,"

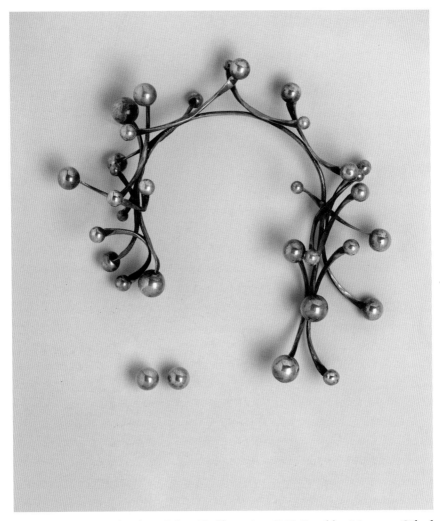

Figure 6.2 Art Smith, silver *Galaxy Necklace*, circa 1962. Brooklyn Museum, Gift of Charles L. Russell, 2007.61.8. Creative Commons-BY (Photo: 2007.61.8_2007.61.20a-b_PS2.jpg).

Although there have been relatively few book-length studies of Afrofuturism to date, scholars generally agree that the movement began in the late 1950s with jazz musicians such as Sun Ra and Lee "Scratch" Perry who presented themselves as alien visitors from other worlds. In the 1960s, Black Arts Movement authors including Ishmael Reed and Amiri Baraka also began telling stories about fantastic Black people who travelled freely through time and space. By blending science fictional motifs with more conventional modes of Black cultural expression these artists insisted on the right of Afrodiasporic subjects to fully participate in the dawning space age. After all, their stories suggested, if Black men and women could imagine themselves travelling to other worlds and other times, what right did anyone have to prevent them from staking their claims on the future since it was actually unfolding in the present?[7]

Although Smith's jewelry designs are not explicitly recorded as being influenced by time travel, science fiction, or Space Age fantasies, his practice did evolve in tandem with technologies and processes in craft design, as well as the Space Age fashion aesthetic. As a member of the modernist jewelry movement, he used craft as a means of communicating his post-war social, cultural, and political values, rebelling against the country's push toward mass consumerism by placing value on jewelry that demonstrated the hand of an artist. By blending his influences of biomorphism, surrealism, and constructivism, with global elements such as traditional African jewelry from a range of African cultures, Smith insisted on the acknowledgment of the rich history of design across the African Diaspora. His free form, body-conscious design techniques and lifelong collaboration with Black jazz musicians, artists, dancers, and writers, are indicative of Afrofuturism's celebration of Black cultural expression and use of the Black radical imagination as a methodology to reclaim the history of the past and the history of the future.

From Representational to Three-Dimensional Forms

Art Smith leaves behind an impressive exhibition history, mesmerizing designs, and a legacy as a self-made jewelry artist. However, the most fascinating parts of his story are those that spark mystery. Articles and oral interviews in special collections at the Brooklyn Museum of Art, the Museum of Arts and Design, and the Archives of American Art, all in New York City, map Smith's overall trajectory from a student growing up in Brooklyn to a shop owner in Greenwich Village. Yet, as archival information is discovered and analyzed, gaps appear in his personal and professional journey, such as missing or conflicting details about his birthdate and place, the years he attended the Cooper Union school and met his mentor Winifred Mason, and the date that he opened his own jewelry shop. This may partly be the result of Smith's own lack of timekeeping. During an oral history interview with Paul Cummings for the Archives of American Art in 1971, Smith repeatedly dismisses Cummings's inquiries about specific time frames and dates. Smith tries his best to give estimates and finally admits midway through the interview, "I'm very bad with time."[8]

In *Art as Adornment: The Life and Work of Arthur George Smith*, Charles Russell, Smith's partner of eight years, reveals that although Smith's Jamaican mother became a naturalized United States citizen in 1947, Smith himself never went through the formalization of becoming a naturalized citizen. In a post-Second World War society, this caused him a lot of anxiety, and so he began to lie about his age. He began to tell others that he was born in Brooklyn in 1923, but the truth was that he was born in Cuba to his Jamaican parents, James and Mary Smith around 1917. The family immigrated to Brooklyn, New York around 1920.[9] Smith's father was a "Garveyite," a devotee of the Jamaican political activist Marcus Garvey. Garvey was founder the Universal Negro Improvement Association and African Communities League—a Black nationalist and Pan-Africanist organization—on a campaign to unite all of Africa and its diaspora. James Smith's involvement in the movement undoubtedly impacted Art Smith's understanding of his position in the world, instilling in him a sense of awareness and resilience that would come in handy in his older years as an art student and shop owner. In elementary school, Smith began to show an interest in the arts. He won several poster contests, including one for The American Society for the Prevention of Cruelty to Animals. His interest in drawing grew while he was a student at Alexander Hamilton High School in Brooklyn. He took a painting elective twice a week, and as his affinity grew for portraits and landscapes, his painting continued outside of the classroom: at home, on field trips, and at some of his favorite parks. Although his parents did not keep Smith from following his creative tendencies—he was also enrolled in piano lessons and was beginning to develop a deep interest in jazz—they hoped he would pursue a career as a tailor, doctor, or lawyer. In one of these professions he would be stable, able to work consistently, and provide for himself and his community. Despite his parents' wishes for him, Smith applied for a full scholarship to the Cooper Union for the Advancement of Science and Art. Out of the two hundred aspiring students that took the exam, he was one of the sixty who were accepted and one of a handful that were Black. During his beginnings as a student at Cooper Union, Smith would experience several significant moments that would steer his path toward working with three-dimensional forms and eventually jewelry design. As an incoming student he was required to take a course in architecture, a course he dreaded because of his struggles with math. The New York World's Fair Corporation came to New York in 1939 and included Cooper Union in a contest for best architectural design. Smith's design was voted best of his class. His architecture instructor and the Assistant Dean of Cooper Union Esmund Shaw suggested that Smith focus his studies on architecture because, as a Black man, it would be easier for him to get a job in the civil service sector. Smith refused, however, and continued to take other foundational courses such as design, economics, and painting.

In his painting class, Smith was assessed by his professor, who was again influenced by his race. In this case, he found himself in an altercation with his painting professor, Peppino Mangrovite. After disagreeing about Smith's preference to mixing his colors on the canvas instead of on his palette, the professor called him difficult and compared him unfavorably to another, "colored boy in his evening class that gave him no trouble."[10] The professor refused to critique his work from then on, and Smith, unamused by what he considered the superficiality of painting, became more interested in working with his hands to create things that were, in his opinion, "tangible not just an illusion."[11] He shifted his course work to sculpture, three-dimensional design, and material study and also took courses on decorative design and color, both of which remained influential to his jewelry-making practice.

Smith's transition into three-dimensional forms resulted in his rejection of the limitations presented by the representational elements of painting, as well as the limitations projected onto him by the prejudice of his professors. By rejecting the future that these professors envisioned for him, he was able to begin exploring the processes of craft design and technologies to free himself from these past narratives and imagine new futures. According to Yaszek, "As its name implies, Afrofuturism is not just about reclaiming the history of the past, but about reclaiming the history of the future as well."[12] This includes her connection to Kodwo Eshun's theory "that our most culturally pervasive visions of tomorrow are generated by a 'futures industry' that weaves together technoscientific findings, mass media storytelling practices, and economic prediction to make sense of its own movements," and, "More often than not, the futures industry conflates blackness with catastrophe."[13] Yet Yaszek's exemplifies how Afrofuturist artists, such as science fiction author Octavia Butler, used specific tropes to demonstrate, "the Afrodiasporic subject's cognitive dissent … from those visions of tomorrow that are generated by the futures industry."[14] Yaszek equates this dissent with W. E. B. Du Bois's theory of Black people's "double consciousness." Smith's transition into three-dimensional design also rejected the futures industry's conflation of Blackness with catastrophe as he crafted his own future, literally with his hands.

While finishing his studies, Smith landed a part-time job teaching in the crafts department of Junior Achievement in Harlem, an organization devoted to helping teenagers find employment. At Junior Achievement he was introduced to jewelry design through his fellow instructor, Winifred Mason. Mason is recorded as the first African American professional jewelry designer known by name.[15] When Smith met her, she was creating handmade jewelry and running her business out of her home. Mason spent a significant amount of time in Haiti, and this was reflected heavily in her designs. Her work introduced Smith to the possibility of utilizing metals such as copper and brass, which she would dramatically arrange, burnish, and stamp. Mason's style is exemplified by a copper and brass cuff bracelet with dangling orbs in the collection of the National Museum of African American History and Culture (NMAAHC). The bracelet consists of a curved band of hammered copper with an opening so that it can be adjusted to the size of its wearer. As detailed in the catalog description, "suspended from the band are circular brass and copper orbs in a pattern of small brass circle, small copper circle, large brass circle with overlaid smaller copper circle."[16] Although the date range spans 1938–1993, the overlaid arrangement, hammered treatment, and signature stamp "Chenet/ d'Haiti" are similar to her designs from the 1940s and 1950s. Mason's copper and brass diamond-design cuff, also held by NMAAHC, was created around 1945 and is a stunning example of her use of brass, as well as how her research in Haiti influenced her designs. The criss-cross diamond design was inspired by Haitian peg drums, an influence that recurs often in her work. In 1945 she received a Rosenwald Fellowship grant—a fund established in 1917 by Julius Rosenwald, part owner of Sears, Roebuck and Company—that allowed her to study the art and culture of Haiti. During her time in Haiti, Mason gathered folk materials and basic art patterns by West Indian artisans and used them as inspiration to express similar feelings in jewelry.[17] It was during her time in Haiti that she is also assumed to have met her husband, Jean Chenet. Her signature, "Chenet" or "Chenet d'Haiti," appears on her jewelry from around this time. The influence of Mason's work would have a profound impact on Smith's jewelry design process.

Smith's childhood love of jazz was resurrected during the final years of his studies. He frequented jazz clubs in Harlem and Greenwich Village and on one occasion met Talley Beatty, an African American dancer in the Katherine Dunham Dance Company. Katherine Dunham was a choreographer, dancer, and anthropologist known as a founder of the anthropological dance movement. Dunham received her undergraduate, graduate, and doctorate degrees in anthropology and, as with Mason, received a Rosenwald Foundation grant to study dance in the Caribbean. This included studies in Trinidad, Jamaica, and Haiti. In 1945 she opened the famous Dunham School in New York City.

Figure 6.3 Winifred Mason Chenet, copper and brass diamond-design cuff, circa 1945. Collection of the Smithsonian National Museum of African American History and Culture, 2016.173.3.

Soon after she founded the Katherine Dunham Dance group, which eventually became the Katherine Dunham Dance Company, devoted to Afro-Caribbean dance. It is no wonder then that Smith's encounter with Dunham's dancer Talley Beatty became the start of a lifelong friendship and collaboration. They became involved in the same musical and social circles, including shared relationships with Dunham and Mason.

Smith graduated from Cooper Union around 1940. He escaped the draft into World War Two due to his heart murmur and was able to secure a full-time job at the National Youth Administration Bureau of the Works Progress Administration designing graphic arts—painting and illustration—for the Harlem YMCA. There he met Perry Watkins, a well-known set designer for Broadway productions and subsequently entered into a year and a half apprenticeship with him. This experience of designing sets, among other factors, such as his growing love for jazz, would influence his dramatic yet sensuous jewelry designs. Around 1943 he transitioned from working at the Harlem YMCA back to Junior Achievement in Harlem full-time, teaching teenagers how to create objects for everyday use from sheet metal.

During this period at Junior Achievement, Smith began taking jewelry-making classes at New York University and also developed his leading design concept: the "human body is 'armature' for the sculpture (jewelry) and the jewelry must be in harmony with the body it was created for."[18] His relationship with Winifred Mason was growing closer and she became his mentor. Smith would work with her a couple of times a week in her home shop, and when she expressed her desire to open a shop in Greenwich Village with his assistance, he agreed.[19] During the mid to late 1940s, Mason opened her shop, Haitian Bazaar, at 133 West Third Street. Smith virtually ran the shop—he opened and closed and managed maintenance, all while fabricating Mason's designs in copper and brass—and she focused on the business aspects. While working in her shop and growing familiar with the types of designs that appealed to Mason's customers, Smith engrossed himself in the study of jewelry design, reading books and building his own collection of clippings from the New York Public Library filled with images of Egyptian and Nubian jewelry for inspiration.[20]

Smith's interest in Egyptian and Nubian jewelry could have been tangentially inspired by the pieces he created for Mason's customers that were based on her influences from diasporic culture through Black West Indian folk art and design. His interest also could have stemmed from the images and philosophies instilled in him as a child by his father's Black nationalist and Pan-Africanist following of Marcus Garvey. This exposure to a particular Black consciousness rooted in the solidarity of Black people across the African Diaspora may have influenced Smith's gravitation toward those images. During the mid-twentieth century, Greenwich Village was known for being a melting pot of races, ethnicities, and creative talents. Since the 1930s, it was the center of bohemian life in New York City, attracting a range of artists working in modernist painting, music, sculpture, and literature. It was also one of the few areas of the city in which interracial and same sex couples could express themselves with more freedom. Shops became informal salons where artists and customers discussed liberal ideas about art, politics, and social issues. Smith moved from Brooklyn to Bank Street in Greenwich Village and became part of the "Neal Salon," an informal group that met in the apartment of Beatty's friend from the Katherine Dunham Dance Company, Frank Neal. The salon served as a space for Black gay artists to not only discuss ideas for creative projects, but to safely share their frustration with racial, gender, and sexual orientation discrimination. It was through these salons and his close relationship with Beatty that Smith was introduced to a number of Black musicians, writers, artists, and dancers such as James Baldwin, Lena Horne, Harry Belafonte, Brock Peters, and Charles Sebree.

After about two years of working alongside Mason in her shop, Smith decided it was time to move on and strike out on his own. He opened his first shop on Cornelia Street in Little Italy in lower Manhattan and stayed there for approximately four years by his own estimate. During his time on Cornelia Street he experienced a series of racially motivated attacks against him, his shop, and his shop assistants. The Italians who made up most of the area's population disliked that Smith, a Black queer man, was operating his shop in the neighborhood and made their dissatisfaction known. A group of men attempted to run him over with a car, shattered his shop windows, and constantly harassed his assistants. The racial tension eventually drove Smith out. He opened a second shop at 140 West Fourth Street in Greenwich Village and operated it until his health declined in 1978.

Art Smith: Messenger of Modernism

Greenwich Village was New York City's center for craft production during the mid-century. Modernist jewelry artists such as Paul LaBelle, Sam Kramer, and Frank Rebajes were running successful shops and studios in the neighborhood. Smith soon became one of the most sought-after jewelry designers of the era. As stated by Toni Greenbaum in *Messengers of Modernism: American Studio Jewelry 1940–1960*, "Beginning in 1940, a revolutionary jewelry movement began to emerge in the US, and this was then spurred on by the devastation of WW2, the trauma of the holocaust, the fear of the bomb, the politics of prejudice, the sterility of industrialization and the crassness of commercialism."[21] Modernist jewelry artists, among many other artists during this time, used their craft as a means of communicating their post-war social, cultural, and political values. Studio jewelry was part of a movement that was largely college-oriented and led by young liberals as a rebellion against conformity. These art pieces became a part of the wardrobe of the American middle-class liberal and intellectual. Art historian Blanche Brown, for example, expressed the appeal of modernist studio art jewelry,

> About 1947 I went to Ed Weiner's shop and bought one of his silver square-spiral pins … because it looked great, I could afford it, and it identified me with the group of my choice—aesthetically aware, intellectually inclined and politically progressive. That pin … was our badge and we wore it proudly. It celebrated the hand of the artist rather than the market value of the material. Diamonds were the badge of a philistine."[22]

Indulging in excess or incredibly expensive jewels thus translated as unethical. According to fashion historians Daniel Cole and Nancy Deihl, "The 1940s presented a study in contrast: a contrast between war and peace, and between the patriotic austerity of the war years and the joyful opulence of the post-war period. Within these ten years, fashion offered opposing images of women— exemplified by masculine 'utility' fashions and the buoyant femininity of the "New Look.""[23] However, former Decorative Arts Curator at the Brooklyn Museum and curator of the exhibition *From the Village to Vogue: The Modernist Jewelry of Art Smith*, Barry R. Harwood also draws the connection between the appeal of modernist jewelry to a sect of middle-class liberals and their rebellion against the post-war push toward mass consumerism, "In the postwar era, the new jewelry especially appealed to liberal, educated middle-class consumers. At a time where prosperity and burgeoning consumerism went hand in hand with feelings of alienation and fear of nuclear annihilation, modernist jewelry became a symbol of the rejection of the past and a belief in the power of creativity and newness."[24] Jewelry became a perfect medium for demonstrating the value of intimacy and human connection, resulting in "a new kind of person to person object, made by one individual for the enjoyment of the other."[25] Most of the jewelry designers working within the modernist movement were familiar with each other's work and shared very similar influences. As stated by Harwood, "they eschewed traditional materials such as gold, platinum and precious stones—diamonds, rubies and emeralds—in favor of lesser materials such as copper, brass, aluminum, silver, ceramics, and glass and hard stones—quartz, opal and agate."[26] Each artist cultivated and maintained their own distinct design language while sharing similar inspiration from movements such as surrealism, cubism, constructivism, Dadaism, and abstract expressionism. Jewelry was an ornamental representation of contemporary art that integrated an awareness of human form and wearability.[27]

Much like those of his contemporaries, Smith's influences included biomorphism, surrealism, constructivism, and global elements, particularly in his case, traditional African jewelry from a range of African cultures. The most central aspects of his designs were his deep understanding of the human body and his vision of the jewelry being molded to the human form. As stated by Harwood, Smith applied "a sculptor's sensitivity to the human form and the power of negative space."[28] In the 1969 catalog for Harwood's exhibition at the Museum of Contemporary Craft—now the Museum of Arts and Design—Smith is quoted,

> A piece of jewelry is in a sense an object that is not complete in itself. Jewelry is a "what is it?" until you relate it to the body. The body is a component in design just as air and space are. Like line, form, and color, the body is a material to work with. It is one of the basic inspirations of creating form.[29]

During the 1950s when the revealing and body-conscious styles of the next decade were years away, Smith anticipated fashion's embrace of the body through his jewelry designs. Most of Smith's designs were created in free form, working with sheet metal and wire and occasionally incorporating stones. His use of line and space were carefully considered, both in relation to the desired design elements and in terms of economics—the amount of materials he could afford. He states in his interview with Cummings that he originally worked more often with larger sheets of metal, but as he transitioned "largely out of brass and copper into silver those big massive shapes would have been prohibited in silver. So instead of using any expensive metal, I would define an area by two wires and create a more positive mass that way."[30]

In most cases, Smith's design process involved working with the material first and drawing or illustrating later. He might draw out an idea and abandon it and begin fabricating a piece directly from his imagination. A drawing might be created afterwards as a documentation. Or, in other cases he might sketch something very minimal and use that as a guide for the creation of a more elaborate piece. For example, for the promotion of the 1969 traveling crafts exhibition, *Objects USA*, Smith was asked to carry out a demonstration at the Craft Students League, a program provided by the YWCA of the City of New York. The YWCA was founded as the Young Women's Christian Association in New York City in 1858 and centered on advocacy for young women's leadership and civil rights. After abandoning a previous idea, he took along a bare sketch for a piece he could create with two pieces of wire and formed it onto the model's neck live in front of the audience. Of this presentation he said, "it was effective and I could hammer it and show detail techniques. The other reaction, the other procedure that I find happening in the creative process is that ideas recur, literally in the self-conscious ... I don't have preferences, I don't have a great direction that I insist on following. And to me that's very rewarding."[31]

Throughout the 1950s, 1960s, and 1970s, Smith designed pieces for a wide variety of clients from interested tourists who knew very little about modernist jewelry to collectors. In his shop he sold pieces on commission and general sale. Most buyers, museums, and galleries discovered his work through word of mouth, but he also paid for advertisements and campaigns. During the 1950s Smith's jewelry was featured in a number of publications including *Life* magazine,

Vogue, Harper's Bazaar, and *The New Yorker*'s shopper guide, "On the Avenue." Despite the number of articles and photographs from later in the twentieth century, preserved in the Art Smith Collection at the Brooklyn Museum, that show Black female models wearing his designs, the models photographed in these publications were often white. They were dressed elegantly in plain black turtleneck or crew neck sweaters with their hair styled away from their faces and behind their ears. During the 1950s, this simple, monochromatic look—a black sweater, usually worn with black pants and ballet flats—became synonymous with what is now recognized as the "Beat Generation." With its beginnings as a New York-based literary movement consisting of a small group of writers and poets who used their work to express their discontent with conservative American life, the influence of the "Beatnik" message began to spread across America to cities such as San Francisco. A core element in this subculture's philosophy was uncensored self-expression and spontaneity. Free form jazz, particularly bebop played by artists such as Dizzy Gillepsie and Charlie Parker, and African American Beat poets such as LeRoi "Amiri Baraka" Jones and Ted Joans, were popular among artists in Greenwich Village.[32] During the late 1940s and into the 1950s and 1960s, Smith became a steady figure in the Greenwich Village intellectual, art, and music scene.

Like LeRoi "Amiri Baraka" Jones and Dizzy Gillepsie, Smith pulled from his experiences as a Black man and chose an unrestricted form of creative expression that aligned with his socio-political philosophies. His choice to combine a creative technique specific to a particular Black cultural expressive tradition with the tools and philosophies of modernist jewelry design are in and of itself radical and Afrofuturist. However, Smith's designs could also appeal to more mainstream tastes. In some editorial images of his work, the models wear silhouettes that reflect Christian Dior's ultra-feminine New Look. These styles fall more in line with mainstream, post-war, conservative American values that a portion of his clientele and possibly even Smith himself rejected. Although contradictory, this universal appeal kept his designs appreciated by many across cultures, space, and time.

In the Smith Archives at the Brooklyn Museum there are a range of images from white models reminiscent of Audrey Hepburn in black turtlenecks or scoop-neck tops wearing asymmetrical necklaces that lay flat on the chest, to Black women with short natural hair textures or pressed hairstyles wearing printed tube tops or elegant one-shoulder dresses modeling Smith's oversized choker necklaces or cuff bracelets. Throughout his career, his jewelry appealed to a range of consumers. This range would include Black women from Harlem

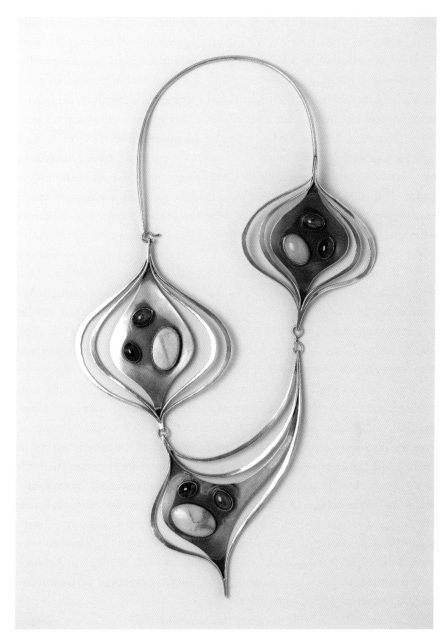

Figure 6.4 Art Smith, silver, amethyst, chrysoprase, rhodonite, and green quartz *Ellington Necklace*, circa 1962. Brooklyn Museum, Gift of Charles L. Russell, 2007.61.4. Creative Commons-BY (Photo: Brooklyn Museum, 2007.61.4_PS2.jpg).

who loved and admired his work, artists and intellectuals already familiar with modernist design, as well as tourists visiting the Village and his shop for the very first time. Smith's designs were sold in stores located all over the United States, including boutiques such as Milton Heffling in Manhattan, and others in Boston, San Francisco, and Chicago, and department stores such as Bloomingdale's. He started designing pieces out of silver more prominently during the 1960s, resulting in growing requests for custom designs. Commissions also came from his artistic social circles and through his friendship with Beatty. Smith designed for several avant-garde Black dance companies and for dancers, Pearl Primus and Claude Marchant. Aside from jewelry, Smith also designed costumes and sets for dance performances. These projects challenged his design ingenuity; he had to create pieces that fit into the narrative of the choreography and were wearable and easy to move in for the dancers, while maintaining his bold, eye-catching, and theatrical style. Coming full circle to his love of jazz music, the composer, pianist, and bandleader Duke Ellington also commissioned Smith to design a pair of cufflinks that incorporated the first notes of Ellington's famous 1930 song, "Mood Indigo." Additionally, Smith was asked to create a brooch for Eleanor Roosevelt that was presented to her by the Peekskill, New York chapter of the National Association for the Advancement of Colored People (NAACP).

Throughout the mid to late twentieth century and into the twenty-first, Smith's designs have been exhibited at institutions such as the Museum of Arts and Design, the Gansevoort Gallery, the Brooklyn Museum, Jamaica Arts Center, and galleries on university campuses across the country. His work has been included in renowned traveling exhibitions, including *Objects USA,* and displayed at NMAAHC in Washington, DC. During and after his career, Smith's jewelry was coveted and preserved in personal collections. During the 1960s Smith suffered a heart attack and his health subsequently declined during the 1970s, forcing him to close his shop in 1978. Smith's *Last Necklace,* "an asymmetrical necklace composed of a curved wire neck piece, open at front and terminating in small, silver-clad black spherical stones, from which attach larger, pivoting wire members that are bent and flattened into angular forms," was completed in 1979.[33] A beautiful combination of his signature design elements—asymmetry and biomorphism—this necklace's overall design evokes futurism. Its curved neck provides a smooth beginning toward sharp, sporadic gestures that complete a bittersweet end. Smith passed away in 1982 due to a subsequent heart attack and his collection was left to his sister, and eventually ended up in the care of his partner, Charles Russell.

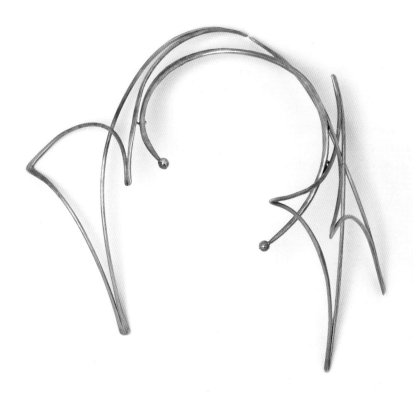

Figure 6.5 Art Smith, silver and stone *Last Necklace*, 1979. Brooklyn Museum, Gift of Charles L. Russell, 2007.61.11. Creative Commons-BY (Photo: Brooklyn Museum, 2007.61.11_PS2.jpg).

Conclusion: Modernist Jewelry, Afrofutures

According to Yaszek, "As a popular aesthetic movement centred on seemingly fantastic tropes such as 'the encounter with the alien other' and 'travel through time and space,' Afrofuturism holds the potential to bring the Afrodiasporic experience to life in new ways."[34] Art Smith's jewelry designs are timeless and have a wide-ranging appeal. Aside from raw sheet metal and wire, Smith literally used space as a material for imagining the possibilities of form.[35] His intersectional identities—Black, immigrant, queer, and Caribbean—were met with prejudice and racial violence from the time he was a student at Cooper Union through and beyond the opening of his first jewelry shop on Cornelia Street in Little Italy during the 1940s. However, Smith never allowed external sources to limit him or his design practice. Smith's jewelry designs empowered the wearer to take ownership of one's body and express one's true identity despite the limitations projected onto them by the outside world.[36] The challenging conditions in which he practiced his art forced him into the realm of three-dimensional forms and the abstraction in his new work allowed him to gesture toward speculative futures.

Fashion, along with music and literature, has long been used as a medium to grapple with contemporary issues of race, gender, and ethnicity. Within the realm of Afrofuturism it has been used to do the same, celebrating traditional African aesthetics while also, "reimagining the possibilities of black identity and governance over our own bodies and minds."[37] Afrofuturism is a means of using the past to conjure up an ideal present or future, and it fully embraces the idea that an individual's vision of self can shift with what they wear. Arthur George "Art" Smith's free form creativity, resilience, ingenuity, and involvement in artistic and social movements that not only addressed inequalities, but also produced art that reimagined the possibilities of autonomy, have created space for a new interpretation of his jewelry design in relation to Afrofuturism. For, Afrofuturism is "an artistic aesthetic, but it is also a method of self-liberation or self-healing."[38]

Notes

1 "The Jewelry of Art Smith," *Craft Horizons* 30, no. 1 (January/February 1970): 20–3, 21.

2 Wakanda is the fictional African country defined by advanced technology and modern interpretations of pan-African traditional culture that serves as the main setting of the film, *Black Panther* (directed by Ryan Coogler, Marvel Studios, 2018). This film, part of the Marvel action movie franchise, is based on the comic book character Black Panther, first introduced by Marvel Comics in 1966. The connection of the 2018 film with the time period of the "Black is Beautiful" and other African American political movements of the 1960s, its stunning costume and set design, and its wild box office success, especially among African diasporic audiences, make it a particularly powerful and popular cultural touchstone for Afrofuturism.

3   *Galaxy Necklace*, The Brooklyn Museum, open collection, accessed March 23, 2020, https://www.brooklynmuseum.org/opencollection/objects/179133.

4   Ytasha Womack, "Afrofuturism Imagination and Humanity (at the Sonic Arts Festival)," video file, 25:11, YouTube, posted by Sonic Acts, June 14, 2017, accessed February 20, 2020, https://www.youtube.com/watch?v=xlF90sXVfKk.

5   Alisha Acquaye, "Black to the Future: OkayAfrica's Introduction to Afrofuturism," *OkayAfrica*, July 10, 2017, accessed October 5, 2019, https://www.okayafrica.com/african-future-okayafrica-introduction-afrofuturism/.

6   Ibid.

7   Lisa Yaszek, "An Afrofuturist Reading of Ralph Ellison's *Invisible Man*," *Rethinking History* 9, no. 2/3 (June/September 2005): 300.

8   Oral history interview with Art Smith, August 24–31,1971. Archives of American Art, Smithsonian Institution.

9   Charles L. Russell, *Art As Adornment: The Life and Work of Arthur George Smith* (Denver: Outskirts Press, 2015), 39.

10 Oral history interview with Art Smith.

11 Ibid.

12 Yaszek, "An Afrofuturist Reading of Ralph Ellison's Invisible Man," 300.

13 Ibid.

14 Ibid., 301.

15 Jacqueline M. Atkins and Pat Kirkham, *Women Designers in the USA, 1900–2000 Diversity and Difference* (New Haven: Yale University Press, 2000), 135.

16 "Cuff bracelet with dangling orbs designed by Winifred Mason Chenet," National Museum of African American history and Culture online collections, accessed March 23, 2020, https://nmaahc.si.edu/object/nmaahc_2018.4.1?destination=edan-search/collection_search%3Fedan_q%3Dcopper%252C%2520brass%2520bracelet%26edan_local%3D1%26op%3DSearch/.

17 Atkins and Kirkham, *Women Designers in the USA*, 135.

18 Russell, *Art As Adornment*, 39.

19 Oral history interview with Art Smith.

20 Russell, *Art As Adornment*, 40.

21 Toni Greenbaum, *Messengers of Modernism: American Studio Jewelry 1940–1950* (Montreal: Montreal Museum of Decorative Arts 1996), 15.

22 Ibid., 20.

23 Daniel Cole and Nancy Deihl, *The History of Modern Fashion From 1850* (London: Laurence King Publishing, 2015), 193.

24 Barry R. Harwood, *From Village to Vogue: The Modernist Jewelry of Art Smith* (Brooklyn: the Brooklyn Museum, 2008), 1–2.

25 Brooklyn Museum Library. Special Collections, Arthur Smith Papers: Art Smith Jewelry Press Release. 1948–1990. Record number: b782304.

26   Harwood, *From Village to Vogue*, 2.

27   Ibid.

28   Ibid.

29   Ibid., 3.

30   Oral history interview with Art Smith.

31   Ibid.

32   Linda Welters, "The Beat Generation: Subcultural Style," in *Twentieth-Century American Fashion*, ed. by Linda Welters and Patricia A. Cunningham (New York: Berg Publishers, 2005), 149.

33   *Last Necklace*, The Brooklyn Museum, open collection, accessed March 23, 2020, https://www.brooklynmuseum.org/opencollection/objects/179136

34   Yaszek, "An Afrofuturist Reading of Ralph Ellison's *Invisible Man*," 299.

35   Oral history interview with Art Smith.

36   Ibid.

37   Shayna Watson, "How Afrofuturism Progressed From Sci-fi Literature to Fashion," *The Root*, August 28, 2016, accessed February 20, 2020, https://www.theroot.com/how-afrofuturism-progressed-from-sci-fi-literature-to-f-1790856546.

38   Womack, "Afrofuturism Imagination and Humanity."

Bibliography

Acquaye, Alisha. "Black to the Future: OkayAfrica's Introduction to Afrofuturism." *OkayAfrica*, July 10, 2017, accessed October 5, 2019, https://www.okayafrica.com/african-future-okayafrica-introduction-afrofuturism/.

Arthur Smith Papers, Brooklyn Museum Library, Special Collections, SCR SC03.

Atkins, Jacqueline M. and Kirkham, Pat. *Women Designers in the USA, 1900–200 Diversity and Difference*. New Haven: Yale University Press, 2000.

Cole, Daniel and Deihl, Nancy. *The History of Modern Fashion From 1850*. London: Laurence King Publishing, 2015.

Greenbaum, Toni. *Messengers of Modernism: American Studio Jewelry 1940–1950*. Montreal: Montreal Museum of Decorative Arts, 1996.

Harwood, Barry R. *From Village to Vogue: The Modernist Jewelry of Art Smith*. Brooklyn: The Brooklyn Museum, 2008.

"The Jewelry of Art Smith," *Craft Horizons* 30, no. 1 (January/February 1970): 20–3.

Oral history interview with Art Smith, August 24–31, 1971. Archives of American Art, Smithsonian Institution.

Russell, Charles. L. *Art As Adornment: The Life and Work of Arthur George Smith*. Denver: Outskirts Press, 2015.

Watson, Shayna. "How Afrofuturism Progressed from Sci-fi Literature to Fashion," *The Root*, August 28, 2016, accessed February 20, 2020. https://www.theroot.com/how-afrofuturism-progressed-from-sci-fi-literature-to-f-1790856546.

Welters, Linda. "The Beat Generation: Subcultural Style," in *Twentieth-Century American Fashion*, ed. Linda Welters and Patricia A. Cunningham, 145–68. New York: Berg Publishers, 2005.

Womack, Ytasha. "Afrofuturism Imagination and Humanity at the Sonic Arts Festival." Video file, 25: 11. YouTube.com. Posted by Sonic Acts, June 14, 2017, accessed February 20, 2020. https://www.youtube.com/watch?v=xlF90sXVfKk.

Yaszek, Lisa. "An Afrofuturist Reading of Ralph Ellison's *Invisible Man*," *Rethinking History* 9, no. 2/3 (June/September 2005): 297–313.

Section 3

Into the Mainstream: Seventh Avenue and Beyond

7

Wesley Tann: The Glamour and the Guts

Nancy Deihl

In 1973 an article in *Women's Wear Daily* featured the work of seven Black designers under the title, "The American Spirit of '73." The important fashion periodical stated that "It all began in 1961 with Wesley Tann's better ready to wear." One of the young designers profiled, Scott Barrie, further acknowledged Tann's significance, saying, "I have enormous respect for that man. He taught us all so much–technically–and cared that we do things right."[1] Throughout his long career, both in fashion and later in related industries, Tann was repeatedly lauded as a pioneer and a groundbreaker. His work has frequently been considered among the milestones of Black fashion. In 1999 retailer J. C. Penney included Tann in a full-page salute to prominent Black Americans that appeared in several publications.[2] In 2004 he was honored in New York by The Fashion & Arts Xchange (FAX) for "pioneering contributions" to fashion, along with model agency founder Ophelia DeVore and journalist Teri Agins, among others.[3] A 2007 article in *Ebony* cited Tann as, "Among the first Blacks to have a successful and visible clothing business in the country's fashion center on Seventh Avenue in New York."[4] Further recognition came with inclusion in two notable museum exhibitions, *Black Style Now*, at the Museum of the City of New York (September 9, 2006 to February 19, 2007), and *Black Fashion Designers* at The Museum at the Fashion Institute of Technology (December 6, 2016 to May 16, 2017).

Tann's career in the 1960s coincided with the burgeoning recognition of Black talent in the creative industries. While often identified in the press specifically as a "Negro designer," in the parlance of the time, Tann was not pigeonholed in terms of aesthetic or clientele. His clothes were described as "timeless" and "refined," appealing to women of all ethnicities who were willing to pay for the distinctive fabrics and details that he built his reputation on. Late in his life, Tann told a reporter for the Newark newspaper, *Star-Ledger*, that at one time his race had made it difficult to procure fabric for his designs.[5] But in a 1962 profile in the *Baltimore Afro-American*, Tann claimed, "my color has helped me rather than hurt me … If I had a good garment to offer and others had the same, I stood out because I was black. This gave me more attention and thus more attention was directed to my garment and its workmanship."[6]

John Wesley Tann, Jr. was born on July 17, 1928 in Rich Square, North Carolina, the child of John Wesley Tann and Abbie (Mitchell) Tann. His father "was a farmer on his own plot of ground,"[7] and his mother was a dressmaker who taught Wesley Jr. to sew. At age thirteen, after the death of his mother, Wesley Jr. left home and went to Washington, DC where he initially and briefly lived at the YMCA. By his own account, he "appealed to Rep. Adam Clayton Powell to help him find a place with a more homelike atmosphere. The Congressman put him in touch with Mr. and Mrs. Belford Lawson, a husband and wife legal team."[8] Tann graduated from a high school in the city and completed a bachelor's degree at Howard University. The exposure to the affluent African American social set of Washington, DC was foundational; Tann later said of his time there, "Most of my future life was based on that experience."[9] He lived in Washington, DC until 1947, then moved to briefly to Newark, New Jersey, where he lived with his sister, Mabel. After Newark, Tann went to Hartford, Connecticut, where he attended the Hartford Art School of Fashion while he held several jobs including one at an aircraft factory and in dressmaking companies.[10] In Hartford, Tann was active in local theater and community groups, designing costumes for performances and the décor for special events. He was noted as the treasurer and chair of the social committee of a Young Adult Club in 1952, a social organization for young singles.[11] Although Vi Velasco, an actress who was Diahann Carroll's understudy in the 1962 Broadway play *No Strings*, was named as Tann's fiancée in at least one press source, he never married.[12] By 1954 he had moved to New York City. He attended the Mayer School of Fashion, took night classes at the Fashion Institute of Technology,[13] and worked for a number of manufacturers, "always as the assistant."[14] His numerous jobs reflected the range of merchandise produced by the American fashion industry during the 1950s, with great variety in quality and price. He "worked for companies that made lingerie, $3.98 daytime dresses, cocktail dresses, bridal gowns" and in better sportswear and dresses.[15] In 1960, Tann was employed at Mister Vee, a firm that produced private label clothing—clothes that were sold in its own specialty shops. *Women's Wear Daily* (*WWD*) praised Tann's "bold ideas" rendered with "careful workmanship, 'boutique' styling and unusual fabrics." The article also noted that all pieces were completely lined, a detail that characterized Tann's output through his career.[16] He designed for the company but not all of his work found its way into the line; he was allowed to sell his original designs to other manufacturers and "this gave him the confidence that led to his establishing his own company in February 1961."[17]

News of Tann's new enterprise, Wesley Tann, Inc., was enthusiastically received in the fashion industry; he quickly had orders from department and specialty stores and enjoyed supportive press coverage. In February 1962 *WWD* labeled Tann a "Young Individualist" in a short piece that included three sketches of dresses and a photo of the designer. They asserted that "buyers from leading specialty stores are already beating a path to this off-beat studio" and praised Tann's simple shapes, color sense, and craftsmanship.[18] In March 1962 a reporter described Tann's studio on West 27th Street in Manhattan's flower district as a hive of creativity—"a loft just larger than the size of a large closet"—with a small staff. Tann was portrayed as "a perfectionist, a man so aware of the details of workmanship that his garments look almost entirely handmade."[19] Prices were high, ranging from $90 to $225 for daywear and up to $450 for evening looks.[20] Even at that early point in his career, his clothes were available at a wide selection of retailers: in New York at Lord & Taylor and Henri Bendel; through Pauline Brooks's salon in Baltimore; in Chicago at Bramson's; at Neiman-Marcus in Dallas; and I. Magnin and Joseph Magnin in California.

However, working on the fringes of the industry had its challenges. Less than two years after opening his business, Tann organized a group of young designers, all New York City-based but outside the main industry center on Seventh Avenue, to promote their work and "stage coordinated preview showings twice a year."[21] Members included other dress designers, sweater and sportswear firms, as well as costume jewelry and novelty companies. Although widely dispersed in terms of location, Tann described their common strength as merchandise "just below couture prices."[22] They considered their individuality an asset, "To be truly creative, they believe, one must be able to work without the multiple restrictions a Seventh Avenue concern imposes."[23] With a plan to present their collections in the evening to avoid conflict with Seventh Avenue showings, the group intended to increase promotion and production. It was a propitious moment to capitalize on changes in retail; specialty shops and boutiques had begun to exert pressure on traditional selling environments and even large department stores were experimenting with in-store boutiques.

Tann's choice of fabrics was fundamental to his aesthetic. He used a wide range of fine textiles, mostly natural fibers. Many of his designs were based on elegant, classic fabrics such as khadi silk-linen blends, ribbed silks, georgette, wool crêpe and jersey, and refined wool tweeds. But he was also inspired by

Figure 7.1 Wesley Tann and his staff in the studio on West 27th Street, New York City, in 1962. Courtesy of The Detroit News.

"off-beat" choices. For example, for fall 1962, he said he had acquired Peruvian rugs, "made jackets and coats out of them," and that they were selling well.[24] In 1963 he used upholstery fabric for luxurious coats. One style, a theater coat in a brocade patterned with falling leaves, available at Bergdorf Goodman and Neiman-Marcus, was pictured in *Town & Country*.[25] A similar style was featured in a fashion show in New Canaan, Connecticut that was covered by *The New York Times*.[26] The show was sponsored by the Gallery Shop, a boutique with branches in New Canaan and Greenwich, founded by Joan Toulouse and Marilyn Driscoll who declared that their mission was to bring fashion-forward styles to an area known for its conservative style, targeting younger, "more daring" customers.[27] Tann created exclusive designs for the store, one of the young designers promoted by the Gallery Shop, who "banded together and set out to storm the rock walls and split fences of suburbia."[28]

In 1962, the fashion world experienced a brief infatuation with silk saris, inspired by Jacqueline Kennedy's trip to Pakistan and India where she purchased several to have made into dresses. Designers and manufacturers offered styles based on saris at all price levels, ranging from twenty-five-dollar rayon sari-printed dresses in junior sizes at Gimbels, to custom evening gowns that cost more than ten times that figure. Tann used sari fabric for several styles. A Chanel-style suit in turquoise and gold silk employed the borders as pocket trim and at the hems and was priced at $275. He also created a two-piece dress in red and gold with a sleeveless bateau-neck tunic over a straight skirt. Priced at $200, it featured the silk's opulent border as hems on tunic and skirt, and on the side seams and as a narrow waist tie. Both were featured in *The New York Times* and were available at Henri Bendel.[29] The Philadelphia store Joseph Horne Co. carried several of Tann's sari-inspired designs, and displayed one that resembled an Indian original in its window, eliciting great interest from the public, especially those attuned to novel, "exotic" influences.[30]

Tann's clothes were praised for fine details; a reporter noted that the designer liked to "turn his dresses inside out to show off the linings and the neatly finished seams, tucks and armholes."[31] Commenting on his commitment to superb construction in 2007, on the occasion of the *Black Style Now* exhibition at the Museum of the City of New York, Tann said, "'When we did clothes, the clothes floated on the body,' the 78-year-old Tann says proudly. 'I learned to set a sleeve the way Coco Chanel did so when you raised your arm, the jacket didn't jump out from the side.'"[32] His preoccupation with linings was well-known. According to Tann, "A black dress should never have a black lining. When a client slips her arm into a garment it must give her that certain feeling."[33] Many of his garments were lined with contrasting fabric, in bold patterns, or surprising colors, but always offering the sensation of quality that the designer strove for: "China silk always makes me feel like a king."[34]

Tann once asserted, "I design apparel for 'that particular woman'"[35] who preferred clothes that were unique without being obvious. His customers were drawn to Tann's simple shapes; he repeatedly called them "background clothes" and said that "when a woman has to be concerned about what she is wearing the clothes aren't right for her."[36] Tann's clientele extended from well-heeled suburbanites to well-known entertainers. In 1966 he designed gowns for opera stars Leontyne Price, Renata Tebaldi, and Régine Crespin for a performance closing the Metropolitan Opera's season. He dressed Price in peacock chiffon,

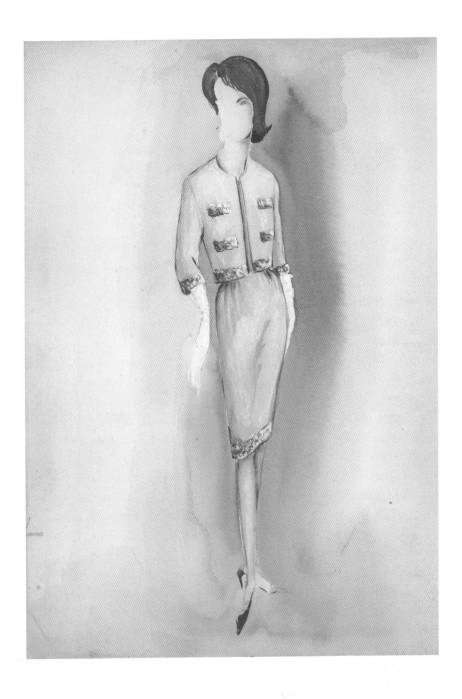

Figure 7.2 and 7.3 Tann's 1962 collections included several styles inspired by Indian saris. Courtesy of Mabel Blair and the Amuh Family.

Figure 7.4 A black wool coat lined with boldly patterned black and white silk exemplifies Tann's approach to unique, luxurious design and construction. Wesley Tann, late 1950s. Gift of Audrey Smaltz. © The Museum at FIT.

Tebaldi in jade green chiffon, and Crespin in magenta matte jersey.[37] In 1962 Henri Bendel asked him to design maternity clothes, "for the woman who usually pays $100 or more for a dress when she's not pregnant."[38] And when Jacqueline Kennedy announced her pregnancy in 1963, *WWD* asked several popular designers to suggest styles for the First Lady, knowing that, "her wardrobe [was] bound to have a tremendous impact on maternity design, regardless of whether she wears maternity clothes per se."[39] Tann sketched a simple, sleeveless full-length dress in Nile green wool crêpe, with a raised waistline and fullness at the front provided by a hidden godet. He also proposed doing a short version of the dress.[40] One of his devoted clients Jackie Wellington, a model and an instructor at the Ophelia DeVore School of Charm, was named to the *New York Amsterdam News*' Best Dressed list in 1963. In an interview about the honor, Miss Wellington, an advocate of simplicity in dress, stated her allegiance to Tann.[41] For her marriage one year later, she wore a white brocade dress and jacket designed by Tann.[42]

Throughout his career, Tann participated in fashion shows. Unlike the expensive, theatrical runway presentations of the twenty-first century, these were well staged, but relatively accessible events, often open to the public through the purchase of tickets. Many were sponsored by retailers, press groups, and civic organizations, sometimes put together by fashion professionals who "packaged" the events and circulated them to various venues. "Fashion and All That Jazz" was sponsored by the Fashion Group of Philadelphia in May 1962 and included Tann, described as creating "young intellectual daytime and evening clothes," among other adventurous designers ranging from small Greenwich Village entrepreneurs to the California-based Rudi Gernreich, renowned for his daring aesthetic.[43] A show of tennis fashions held at the West Side Tennis Club in Forest Hills, New York, during the National Championships in 1962, garnered enthusiastic press coverage. Organized by Louise McGann and Edith Berke, a duo known professionally as the Fashion Coordinators, the show featured specially commissioned tennis outfits from a group of designers including Vera Maxwell, Ellen Brooke, and Oleg Cassini. Tann showed a short white tennis dress with decorative saddle stitching.[44] Tann also supported the efforts of the National Association of Fashion and Accessory Designers, an organization of Black designers popularly known as the NAFADs, showing his work in their benefit fashion shows and appearing as a speaker and panelist at their conferences.[45] He was included in at least two Ebony Fashion Fairs, an annual fashion event organized by Eunice Johnson of the Chicago-based Johnson Publishing Company—the publishers of *Ebony* and *Jet* magazines—that was of particular importance to the Black community. Each year the Fair toured the United States, presented as a charity benefit at each location. Tann also had a long association with the Northside Center for Child Development in New York City, served on its sponsoring board, and participated in numerous fashion shows for the non-profit organization.

Wesley Tann Inc. enjoyed a rapid rise to prominence. One year after its founding, the designer declared he was turning a profit.[46] The abundance of press coverage of his collections, and its remarkably supportive tone, offers evidence of industry-wide respect for the designer. Articles and interviews repeatedly stressed Tann's specialty-store focus, emphasizing that he had no aspirations to become a mainstream brand. Tann's aesthetic straddled the sophistication of the 1950s and the more youthful focus of the 1960s. While his pared-down silhouettes were in line with the prevailing simplicity of fashion, architectural details and crispness lent elegance and distinction. In a market increasingly based on trendy fashions and low-cost materials, his chosen niche of youthful, but elegantly crafted dresses at a high price point represented a potentially risky position. His sister Mabel Tann Blair also remarked that during the late 1960s it was often difficult for Black Americans to obtain business financing.[47] It is then perhaps not surprising that the business closed in 1965, after only four years.

Despite the short lifespan of his label, aspects of Wesley Tann's career pointed to the future of fashion. Although he upheld high-quality construction, he was consistently identified with youthful energy and innovation. A column in *WWD* compared the impact of Tann and several of his contemporaries to the Bossa Nova, an exciting new rhythm in popular music, praising the "Off-Seventh Avenue group" as "young and yeasty," "fusing elements of native genius, imagination, acquired skills, hard work, and daring."[48] In 1964 Tann participated in an experiment with a new technology that hinted at novel possibilities in communication. He and a model used a Picturephone in New York's Grand Central Terminal to call the Picturephone center in Washington, DC. On the other end, an attendant tested the quality of the image by attempting to describe the outfits being modeled. Aside from a bit of trouble conveying the actual textures of the clothes, Tann felt the experiment was a success. "'What we could always do, of course, is to send swatches to buyers before calling them on this thing,' he said. 'That way, there's no guess work about color or fabric. As far as the lines and the seaming are concerned, we could have a commentator work with the model, much the same as in a fashion show.'"[49]

Tann was dedicated to the next generation of American designers and served on the advisory board of the High School for Fashion Industries in Manhattan.

Figure 7.5 Jacquelyn Mayer, Miss America 1963, wearing a dress and coat by Wesley Tann. Hagley Museum and Library, Joseph Bancroft & Sons Company/Miss America Collection.

In an interview about the school and its relationship to the industry, Tann called for professional development for faculty, more up-to-date equipment, and an increase in participation from Seventh Avenue. He said, "manufacturers should donate scholarship monies so that more students will be able to continue their formal education." He also added that most of the students were either Black or Puerto Rican and that, "they must be shown the advisability of going ahead with their studies. 'Just my being there helps sometimes,' said Mr. Tann … 'A lot of those kids feel that if I made it, maybe they can also.'"[50] His involvement with education continued at the Harlem Institute of Fashion. The brainchild of Lois K. Alexander, the Institute opened in September 1966 on West 125th Street to train African Americans in fashion-related skills. Alexander, a lifelong advocate for recognition of Black contributions to the fashion industry, said the aim of the school was "not to make Cardins out of these people, but to teach them how things are done on Seventh Avenue so doors will open to them."[51] The non-profit school was funded by a group of donors and opened with donated sewing machines and fabrics. Although Tann had closed his wholesale business, he was still running a studio and signed on as a volunteer instructor, teaching the basics of dressmaking. "'I have a selfish motive, though,' he said. 'I'm hoping I can hire two or three of my students to go to work for me.'"[52] In addition to classes, the Institute also sponsored events. Mrs. Alexander organized the 1967 Fashion Promenade on 125th Street for which Tann served as a judge, along with designer, Pauline Trigère; Mildred Finger, a buyer for Bergdorf Goodman; Derrill Horton, a fashion merchandiser; and Cathy Aldridge, fashion reporter for the *New York Amsterdam News*. In a decision that reflected changing beauty standards, the panel judged Miss Ollie Williams, a young woman with a natural hairdo, Fashion's Best Example of Good Grooming.[53] At that time, Harlem's image as a fashion site was further enhanced by several new shops. Votre Boutique on Amsterdam Avenue opened in 1967, established by jazz pianist Mary Lou Williams and restaurateur Mrs. Joseph "Ann" Wells. The tiny storefront boutique featured pink walls, red carpeting, and a piano and promoted original designs by Black designers, including Tann.

After closing his business Tann worked for other prominent fashion firms. He served as vice-president of the Jeremy Originals division of the large Jerry Silverman Company,[54] and later worked at Bobbie Brooks, another major womenswear label.[55] He continued to participate in charity fashion shows and was often called upon to speak on career panels. He was also a valued advisor to younger designers. In 1969 Scott Barrie said Tann, who called Barrie and others his "children," visited his studio, offering hints for cutting and "the

Figure 7.6 In 2008, Tann proposed a simple high-waisted sheath dress for First Lady Michelle Obama's Inauguration wardrobe. Courtesy of Mabel Blair and the Amuh Family.

right way to put in a zipper."[56] In 1974 Tann moved to Newark where his sister still resided. He purchased a large house "with 22 'little rooms' which he turned into two apartments."[57] There, he worked as an event planner and started an interior design firm, Wesley Tann and Associates Interiors. He also began an impressive, almost career-level engagement with issues of historic preservation, neighborhood renewal, and education. As the long-time president of the Osborne Terrace Block Association, he advocated for physical upgrades to the area but also celebrated its history. His beautiful garden was the scene for parties and benefits for a variety of causes.[58] In the early 2000s, as an impeccably dressed octogenarian, he gave classes in etiquette and home decorating through Newark's Department of Neighborhood and Recreational Services,[59] but continued to be called upon for fashion advice. After Barack Obama was elected President of the United States in November 2008, designers vied for a chance to dress the charismatic new First Lady, Michelle Obama. Competition was especially keen among American designers. By that time considered an "elder statesman" of fashion, Tann offered a sketch of a "sophisticated sheath" with a low-cut back for her to wear to the inaugural ball.[60]

John Wesley Tann Jr. died on November 23, 2012. A street-sign tribute, "J. Wesley Tann Jr. Way," was installed in 2014 in Newark's South Ward, at the corner of Clinton Avenue and Osborne Terrace, where Tann lived and "made civic virtue his calling card as president of the block association."[61] As a further tribute to Tann's investment in gracious living, Cory Booker, at that time the mayor of Newark and a frequent guest at Tann's events, called him "the eternal first gentleman of the city."[62] As his long-time friend Audrey Smaltz said of Tann, "Wesley had a savoir-faire that was all his own."[63] Throughout his life, Wesley Tann embodied a commitment to elegance, specifically *accessible* elegance. His work within the fashion industry, his efforts to train young people at the Harlem Institute of Fashion, his mentorship of Black designers, and his dedication to personal uplift and neighborhood beautification can be seen as a coherent trajectory in support of excellence.

Notes

1 Ki Hackney and Keitha McLean, "The American Spirit of '73." *Women's Wear Daily*, June 21, 1973, 5.
2 "JC Penney Salutes a Remarkable Color in the Fashion World. Black." *Philadelphia Tribune*, February 12, 1999, A5.

3   Renee Minus White, "FAX Celebrates 10th Year of Excellence." *New York Amsterdam News*, February 11, 2004, 17.

4   Michael Henry Adams, "How Black Style Became Beautiful." *Ebony*, September 1, 2007, 75.

5   Liza Irizarry, "I am New Jersey – Wesley Tann Jr. Bon Vivant." *The Star-Ledger*, January 18, 2009, 7.

6   "Male Designers Hits in Fashion World." *Baltimore Afro-American*, April 28, 1962, 8.

7   Ibid.

8   Ibid.

9   Irizarry, "I am New Jersey," 7.

10 "Male Designers Hits in Fashion World," 8.

11 "Miss Foote Heads North End Center Young Adult Club." *The Hartford Courant*, October 1, 1952, 21.

12 "Fashion Should be Fun; Clothes Should Bear Mileage Says Tann." *Baltimore Afro-American*, September 29, 1962, 6.

13 Charlotte Curtis, "Designer Thrives Away from Crowd." *The New York Times*, March 31, 1962, 15.

14 "Male Designers Hits in Fashion World," 8.

15 Curtis, "Designer Thrives Away from Crowd," 15.

16 "New Firm Stresses Workmanship, Fine Fabrics in Play Fashions." *Women's Wear Daily*, January 9, 1961, 19.

17 "Male Designers Hits in Fashion World," 8.

18 "Young Individualist," *Women's Wear Daily*, February 21, 1962, 33.

19 Curtis, "Designer Thrives Away from Crowd," 15.

20 Ibid.

21 Mort Sheinman, "Off-7th Ave. Previews Set By Young Designers Group." *Women's Wear Daily*, November 9, 1962, 19.

22 Ibid.

23 Charlotte Curtis, "Fashion Individualism Pays Off for Designers." *The New York Times*, April 9, 1963, 74.

24 Theresa Fambro, "Designer Spurns Seventh Ave. for Loft: Wesley Tann Finds Success in Tiny Space." *Chicago Daily Defender*, September 4, 1962, 15.

25 "Close-Ups." *Town & Country*, October 1963, 75.

26 Marylin Bender, "Seven Individualists Band Together to Show Their Fashions in Suburbia." *The New York Times*, June 1, 1963, 37.

27 Etta Froio and Peter Davis Dibble, "New York – Who Needs It?" *Women's Wear Daily*, March 13, 1963, 5.

28 Bender, "Seven Individualists," 37.

29 Charlotte Curtis, "Indian Sari Fashioned into a Plethora of Styles." *The New York Times*, July 17, 1962, 28.

30 "Who's Sari Now? Not Joseph Horne with Fashion 'Beat.'" *Women's Wear Daily*, June 20, 1962, 39.

31 Curtis, "Designer Thrives Away from Crowd," 15.

32 Liza Irizarry, "Basic Black–African-American Style-Makers, From High Society to Hip-Hop Fashion Today." *The Star-Ledger*, January 22, 2007, 25.

33 "Fashion Should Be Fun," 6.

34 "New Firm," 19.

35 Fambro, "Designer Spurns Seventh Ave. for Loft," 15.

36 "Fashion Should Be Fun," 6.

37 "Eye: More on the Met's Closing." *Women's Wear Daily*, April 13, 1966, 49.

38 "Wesley Tann." *Women's Wear Daily*, March 27, 1962, 4.

39 "New Ideas are Born." *Women's Wear Daily*, April 23, 1963, 39.

40 While he has been credited in some sources with designing maternity wear for Jacqueline Kennedy, it is unclear whether she actually ordered anything from Tann.

41 Thomasina Norford, "Mrs. Javits on Best Dressed Women's List," *New York Amsterdam News*, February 16, 1963, 1.

42 "Surprise Wedding." *New York Amsterdam News*, November 7, 1964, 1.

43 "'Kooky' Fashions to Get Sendoff at Showing Here." *The Philadelphia Inquirer*, May 4, 1962, 21.

44 "Designers Turn Talents to Tennis Dresses." *Women's Wear Daily*, September 6, 1962, 28.

45 "Designer, Experts at NAFAD Confab." *New York Amsterdam News*, July 18, 1964, 29.

46 "Wesley Tann," 4.

47 Mabel Tann Blair in discussion with the author, March 13, 2020.

48 Caroline McCall, "Minding the Store." *Women's Wear Daily*, November 20, 1962, 6.

49 Mort Sheinman, "Eye of the Needle." *Women's Wear Daily*, September 1, 1964, 15.

50 Mort Sheinman, "Help Wanted: The Glamour and the Guts." *Women's Wear Daily*, July 17, 1964, 22.

51 Judy Klemesrud, "School's Design: Jobs for Negroes in Fashion." *The New York Times*, September 17, 1966, 14.

52 Ibid.

53 Cathy Aldridge, "Natural Coiffed Miss Wins Fashion Prize." *New York Amsterdam News*, April 29, 1967, 11.

54 Bill Cunningham, "Black Fashion Designers …" *Chicago Tribune*, August 25, 1969, B3.

55 Barbara Kukla, "Designer Throws Elegant Benefit for United Negro College Fund–Inner City Garden Hosts Social-Event of Year." *The Star-Ledger*, September 23, 1999, 2.

56 Cunningham, "Black Fashion Designers," B3.

57 Reginald Roberts, "Neighborhood to Celebrate 100 Years of History on Osborne Terrace; Residents Hope Renovations Can Turn Old 'Doctors' Row' around." *The Star-Ledger*, March 19, 1998, 1.

58 Barbara Kukla, "'Midnight in the Garden' Spells Dawn for Students' Aspirations." *The Star-Ledger*, September 14, 2000, 4.

59 Katie Wang, "5-Star Etiquette Class–Manners are on the Menu, Courtesy of the City of Newark." *The Star-Ledger*, June 23, 2008, 1.

60 Renee Minus White, "Inaugural Dress Ideas for Mrs. Obama." *New York Amsterdam News*, 25 December 2008, 16.

61 Barry Carter, "In This Community, There Are Signs That Point to Lives Well Lived." *The Star-Ledger*, 21 October 2014, 15.

62 Irizarry, "I am New Jersey," 7.

63 Audrey Smaltz, fashion commentator, editor, and founder of the Ground Crew, in discussion with the author, March 9, 2020.

Bibliography

Aldridge, Cathy. "Natural Coiffed Miss Wins Fashion Prize." *New York Amsterdam News*, April 29, 1967, 11.

Bender, Marylin. "Seven Individualists Band Together to Show Their Fashions in Suburbia." *The New York Times*, June 1, 1963, 37.

"Canine Couture." *New York Amsterdam News*, November 7, 1964, 14.

Carter, Barry. "In This Community, There Are Signs That Point to Lives Well Lived." *The Star-Ledger*, October 21, 2014: 15.

"Close-Ups." *Town & Country*, October 1963, 75.

Cunningham, Bill. "Black Fashion Designers … " *Chicago Tribune*, August 25, 1969, B3.

Curtis, Charlotte. "Designer Thrives away from Crowd." *The New York Times*, March 31, 1962: 15.

Curtis, Charlotte. "Fashion Individualism Pays Off for Designers." *The New York Times*, April 9, 1963: 74.

Curtis, Charlotte. "Indian Sari Fashioned into a Plethora of Styles." *The New York Times*, July 17, 1962: 28.

"Designer, Experts at NAFAD Confab." *New York Amsterdam News*, July 18, 1964, 29.

"Designers Turn Talents to Tennis Dresses." *Women's Wear Daily*, September 6, 1962, 28.

"Eye: More on the Met's Closing." *Women's Wear Daily*, April 13, 1966, 49.

Fambro, Theresa. "Designer Spurns Seventh Ave. for Loft: Wesley Tann Finds Success In Tiny Space." *Chicago Daily Defender*, September 4, 1962, 15.

"Fashion Should be Fun; Clothes Should Bear Mileage Says Tann." *Baltimore Afro-American*, September 29, 1962: 6.

Froio, Etta and Peter Davis Dibble. "New York – Who Needs It?" *Women's Wear Daily*, March 13, 1963, 4–5.

Hackney, Ki and Keitha McLean. "The American Spirit of '73." *Women's Wear Daily*, June 21, 1973, 4–5.

Irizarry, Liza. "Basic Black – African-American style-makers, from High Society to Hip-Hop Fashion Today." *The Star-Ledger*, January 22, 2007, 25.

Irizarry, Liza. "I am New Jersey – Wesley Tann Jr. Bon Vivant." *The Star-Ledger*, January 18, 2009, 7.

"J. Wesley Tann II – NYC Fashion Designer Praised by Cory Booker, 84." *The Star-Ledger*, November 29, 2012, 32

Klemesrud, Judy. "School's Design: Jobs for Negroes in Fashion." *The New York Times*, September 17, 1966, 14.

"'Kooky' Fashions to Get Sendoff at Showing Here." *The Philadelphia Inquirer*, May 4, 1962, 21.

Kukla, Barbara. "'Midnight in the Garden' Spells Dawn for Students' Aspirations." *The Star-Ledger*, September 14, 2000, 4.

"Male Designers Hits in Fashion World." *Baltimore Afro-American*, April 28, 1962, 8.

McCall, Caroline. "Minding the Store." *Women's Wear Daily*, November 20, 1962: 6.

"Miss Foote Heads North End Center Young Adult Club." *The Hartford Courant*, October 1, 1952, 21.

"New Firm Stresses Workmanship, Fine Fabrics in Play Fashions." *Women's Wear Daily*, January 9, 1961, 19.

"New Ideas are Born." *Women's Wear Daily*, April 23, 1963, 39.

Norford, Thomasina. "Mrs. Javits on Best Dressed Women's List." *New York Amsterdam News*, February 16, 1963, 1.

Roberts, Reginald. "Neighborhood to Celebrate 100 Years of History on Osborne Terrace; Residents Hope Renovations Can Turn Old 'Doctors' Row' Around." *The Star-Ledger*, March 19, 1998, 1.

Sheinman, Mort. "Eye of the Needle." *Women's Wear Daily*, September 1, 1964, 15.

Sheinman, Mort. "Help Wanted: The Glamour and the Guts." *Women's Wear Daily*, July 17, 1964, 22.

Sheinman, Mort. "Off-7th Ave. Previews Set By Young Designers Group." *Women's Wear Daily*, November 9, 1962, 19.

"Surprise Wedding." *New York Amsterdam News*, November 7, 1964, 1.

Wang, Katie. "5-Star Etiquette Class – Manners are on the Menu, Courtesy of the City of Newark." *The Star-Ledger*, June 23, 2008, 1.

"Wesley Tann." *Women's Wear Daily*, March 27, 1962, 4–5.

White, Renee Minus. "FAX celebrates 10th Year of Excellence." *New York Amsterdam News*, February 11, 2004, 17.

White, Renee Minus. "Inaugural Dress Ideas for Mrs. Obama." *New York Amsterdam News*. December 25, 2008, 16.

"Who's Sari Now? Not Joseph Horne with Fashion 'Beat'." *Women's Wear Daily*, June 20, 1962, 39.

"Young Individualist," *Women's Wear Daily*. February 21, 1962, 33.

8

Jay Jaxon: An Unsung Couturier

Darnell-Jamal Lisby

Many designers have risen to become heralded figures within the history of fashion as arbiters of the art of haute couture, from Christian Dior to Ralph Rucci. Of these canonized designers, there has been little-to-no documentation of those of African descent. African American designers of ready-to-wear, such as Stephen Burrows and Scott Barrie garnered significant press during the late 1960s and 1970s in New York. In comparison, the couturier Jay Jaxon had a more modestly documented career. However, it was still influential. Jaxon established a distinguished reputation among New York's Seventh Avenue designers, and then in a groundbreaking move, went on to become one of the first African Americans to work in a high-profile position in the Parisian fashion industry. As the head designer of Jean-Louis Scherrer, the press hailed him as "le premier couturier noir de Paris" or the first Black couturier in the city of Paris.[1] Despite this recognition as one of the only American designers during the twentieth century to accomplish such a feat, little is known of Jaxon's career. His visibility paved the way for the succeeding generation of American designers, including Patrick Kelly, to find success in Paris. This chapter attempts to document, clarify, and characterize some of Jaxon's career, interpreting his creative process and forming a better understanding and appreciation of his work.

Born in 1941 in Queens, New York as Eugene Jackson, Jaxon pursued a variety of unrelated jobs, as well as attending law school, before realizing that his talent lay in fashion design. After selling several decadent, custom-made dresses to the Bonwit Teller and Henri Bendel department stores, Jaxon moved to Paris in 1967, where he briefly apprenticed under Yves Saint Laurent and worked under Marc Bohan at Christian Dior. One his most notable positions, as mentioned, was serving as the artistic manager of Jean-Louis Scherrer from 1969 to 1970, arguably making him the first Black designer to work in a visible and leading role for a Parisian couture house.[2] After a six-year tenure in Paris, Jaxon moved back to the United States in 1973, continuing to design under several luxury fashion companies and wholesalers, such as Benson & Partners and Pierre Cardin-New York. He also worked as a costume designer for several televised productions, primarily during the 1980s and afterward. By the 1990s, Jaxon's visibility in the fashion industry had declined; however, the design aesthetic he developed throughout his career contributed to a crucial period of change and modernization in both Paris and New York. His designs incorporated a myriad of influences, including the elements of dress from a variety of Asian cultures; distinct American sportswear, luxurious Parisian styles, and the combination of functionality and high fashion aesthetics. Many of his collections harkened back to the elongated, draped, and high-waisted A-line silhouettes of the 1930s, emphasizing plunging necklines and pronounced shoulders. Jaxon's designs were sensuous, yet elegant, building an aesthetic legacy for his contemporaries and successors to follow. Despite being an unsung figure in fashion, Jaxon quietly blazed a path for diverse designers beginning in the late 1960s. The foundation of style he established during his career is undeniably present in contemporary fashion.

Jaxon recounted his introduction to fashion design in an interview with the *Orlando Evening Star* before his first haute couture runway presentation for Jean-Louis Scherrer in January 1970. He said that as a student at New York University, he worked as the law librarian and dated a young lady who was a seamstress.[3] This young woman attempted to produce a dress for herself to wear for a party and was unsuccessful. Jaxon ended up making the dress for her and at the event attendees lauded the dress. He dropped out of law school immediately and began a costume design program after realizing his talents.[4] This education would inform the costume design work he executed toward the latter part of his career. Jaxon's transition, especially into a creative field, and his supplemental employment as a banker, illustrates the tenacious spirit that proved beneficial to his career. He frequently executed multiple projects simultaneously and spent short periods at various fashion companies. This career trajectory was typical for designers in the fashion industry during the late twentieth century, especially African American designers such as Willi Smith and Arthur McGee. Yet history and the industry frequently overlook the design careers built from varied experiences in favor of the much rarer career path of long-term employment at a single or small number of design houses. Jaxon's story is, therefore, a vital narrative to emphasize in the history of fashion and helps create a more holistic view of the industry.

A significant boost to Jaxon's reputation as a luxury fashion designer came when he designed six dresses inspired by kimonos for the specialty stores Bonwit

Figure 8.1 Jaxon's designs were featured in national magazines such as *Glamour* in 1967, around the time he moved to Paris. Photo by William Connors/Condé Nast via Getty Images.

Teller and Henri Bendel.[5] The dresses made their first appearance in a fabric preview and fashion show luncheon at the Philharmonic Hall (Lincoln Center) in June 1967. The garments integrated textiles designed by Julian Tomchin, who was the luncheon's host and Coty award-winning print designer for the manufacturer Chardon Marche.[6]

The author of the *Women's Wear Daily* article reviewing this collection noted that Jaxon's design ingeniously showcased innovative ways to fashion new fabrics for the following year. *Vogue's* September 1967 monthly editorial, "Vogue's Own Boutique," featured one of the styles that Jaxon sold at Bonwit Teller. It was a striped, silk satin twill kimono—the silhouette with its oversized bell-shaped sleeves, narrow ankle-length skirt, and obi-like sash, unequivocally romanticized the traditional Japanese garment.[7] Jaxon's inclusion in the Tomchin fashion show marked him as an ascending insider in the New York fashion industry, yet he still sought more significant opportunities to influence fashion. Shortly after this presentation, he moved to Paris. As Western fashion evolved throughout the 1960s, transitioning from the "New Look" hour-glass silhouette to the A-line silhouette, a liminal space opened up within fashion that allowed for new ideas and contributions. Growing youth movements and political unrest spurred these changes and calls for social justice from anti-war protesters, students, women, and people of color, especially African Americans. Within this dynamic context of bridging cultures together, Jaxon, along with other young designers, experimented with international sources of inspiration and silhouettes, as seen in his kimono designs.

When Jaxon arrived in Paris in 1967, he came to a fashion city in transition. The haute couture industry was declining in its position of power within the international fashion industry. It was being challenged by designer ready-to-wear, much of it inspired by youth cultures. Valerie Steele states in *Fifty Years of Fashion*, "In the 1960s, as *Women's Wear Daily* observed, 'The old guard no longer sets fashion … The mood is youth-youth-youth.'"[8] Instead of adapting with the course of fashion during the late 1950s, the hegemonic couture houses used excommunication and fear as a means to consolidate power. The governing body of haute couture, the *Chambre syndicale de la haute couture*, for example, briefly revoked Pierre Cardin's membership in 1959 after he launched his ready-to-wear line.[9] Yves Saint Laurent, who mentored Jaxon, later opened his famous Rive Gauche boutique in 1966, making him another early couturier to recognize the importance of ready-to-wear and to sell it under his name. With the growing acceptance of ready-to-wear by the mid-1960s, Saint Laurent retained his status as a member of the *Chambre syndicale*. Saint Laurent also designed several

Figure 8.2 Jaxon's silk satin twill kimono in *Vogue*'s "Vogue's Own Boutique" in the magazine's September 1967 issue. Jack Robinson, Vogue © Condé Nast.

thematic collections at this period in his career that incorporated elements from global diasporas, including his Spring 1967 collection, which was based on various African cultures. Jaxon was very fond of mixing cultural references within his designs, forming a stylistic bond with the famed couturier and reflecting the young fashion zeitgeist.

According to a June 14, 1973 *Women's Wear Daily* column discussing Jaxon's return to the United States, he also designed for Givenchy and various Left Bank boutiques, most likely after leaving Jean-Louis Scherrer around 1970.[10] Within the tight-knit community of designers working in haute couture, many bounced from one house to another and overlapped with future competitors in a system that trained through apprenticeship. Yves Saint Laurent and Jean-Louis Scherrer, for example, both worked under Christian Dior before the designer died in 1957. Jay Jaxon's development and growth as a designer was, therefore, profoundly entangled in the couture apprenticeship system with roots going back to Dior's atelier and through it, further back into Parisian couture history. In addition to their shared aptitude for working with techniques such as heavy embroidery and luxurious fabrics, Saint Laurent and Scherrer both tended to form collections inspired by a variety of global cultures. Perhaps due to their shared training at Dior, both designers also returned to a distinctive silhouette throughout their careers, one that emphasized a narrow waist and incorporated a voluminous skirt or bottom half of an ensemble. Jaxon also emphasized this silhouette in his designs, as evidenced by the work he produced when he returned to the United States. However, he reinterpreted the more decadent, extreme variations shown in Paris with restraint for the American market.

Jaxon began as the artistic manager of Scherrer in late 1969. His first collection was for the spring 1970 ready-to-wear season.[11] Jean-Louis Scherrer was born in 1935; he was a formally trained couturier, receiving his diploma from the *École de la chambre syndicale de la couture parisienne* before working for Christian Dior beginning in 1956. In 1962, Scherrer opened his couture house with initial success before spinning into legal troubles.[12] Jean-Louis Scherrer's backer, Parures et Creations, which was led by Standard Oil heir Francis Francis, began making unapproved ready-to-wear collections under the Jean-Louis Scherrer name in 1968.[13] Scherrer left the company to fight his financial backers and attempt to take back control of the couture house. Designer Serge Matta was chosen by the financial backers to design in Scherrer's absence at the end of 1968. Jaxon was then appointed to the position of artistic manager, likely in the latter half of 1969. It is unclear if there was any overlap between Matta's and Jaxon's tenures as designers at the house. Fashion journalists' reviews of the Scherrer collections designed from the end of 1969 into 1970 support the possibility that Jaxon had complete design autonomy over the house at that time. Invitations sent to the press to attend the Jean-Louis Scherrer 1970 spring/summer ready-to-wear presentation in November 1969 also confirm that Jaxon was at the head of the fashion house during the latter half of that year.[14]

The reviews of the next collection were mixed. *Women's Wear Daily's* "Paris Eye" column, from January 27, 1970, reported, "Jay Jaxon is the new designer at Jean-Louis Scherrer these days, and Monday he came up with a collection that would have looked right in deluxe rtw [ready-to-wear] three winters ago. It wasn't couture. It wasn't summer. It was proper and you can't fault Jaxon's taste."[15] Jaxon's conservative aesthetic did not impress the reporter, and it cannot be ruled out that racial bias could have played a part in these reviews from the prestigious publication. Conversely, placing his collection at the center of fashion, the *Daily Dayton News* of Dayton, Ohio, noted in the article, "Paris Hems Go Midcalf," that the lengths of the skirts at Scherrer were lower, a trend seen in the collections of many of haute couture houses such as Philippe Venet and Molyneux.[16] Jaxon stated that his goal was to create elegant fashions, and this collection aligned his style with the work of other couturiers, reinforcing his vision as compelling.[17] The lengthening of the skirt was a break from the mini-skirt trend made fashionable by the Youthquake movement, and one that aimed to revert fashion to a period of mature sophistication.[18] Although *Women's Wear Daily* expressed the view that the collection was dated, the article also stated that his collection exuded the traditional luxury and elegance of the Jean-Louis Scherrer house. It also praised Jaxon, saying, "He's got a good color sense which shows best in those beautifully printed rounded shawls he puts over late-day dresses."[19] The same article noted that Jaxon presented wedding gowns in the middle of the runway presentation, throwing off the expectations of the audience who took this to mean the show was ending. The insinuation was that Jaxon did not understand fashion show protocol; it was more likely that Jaxon attempted a new way of presenting his haute couture collection, deviating from the tradition of showing wedding ensembles last. His experience working in Paris haute couture and New York ready-to-wear fashion makes an accidental mis-ordering of garments improbable; Jaxon purposefully changed the sequence of the runway presentation. Although this first haute couture collection seemed to be in line with the established aesthetic of the Scherrer house, perhaps this presentation alteration marked a small act of Jaxon's independence as a designer. The *Orlando Evening Star* published three sketches of Jaxon's designs, presumably styles produced for the spring 1970 Scherrer haute couture collection. Two sketches utilized the same silhouette, which comprised sleeveless tunic tops with bows and styled with wide-leg bell-bottom trousers. One ensemble had a distinctive polka dot print.[20] On one hand, these sketches appear to be an extension of Jaxon's earlier aesthetic focused on the billowing silhouettes popular in East Asian traditional dress that allow the fabric to drape freely. On the other, these designs exemplify the general transition in fashion to the longer, bell-shaped, A-line silhouettes that became popular during the 1970s.

It is also important to note that except for *Women's Wear Daily*, most of the press reviews gave much more attention to Jaxon's racial identity than to the design of the clothing, publicizing his remarkable position in the international fashion industry and as an influencer of taste. Objectively, this angle of coverage had a long-term effect of helping to make Black fashion professionals more visible and eventually normalizing their roles in the industry. Victories such as the feat that Jaxon accomplished by rising to the head of a Parisian couture house challenged the fashion hegemony's perception of the capabilities of Black designers in participating in the highest realms of the fashion system. Through the first two decades of the twenty-first century, there has not been another African American designer at the helm of an haute couture house. Yet after Jaxon's success was Patrick Kelly's 1988 induction into the *Chambre syndicale du prêt-à-porter* as the first American member of the ready-to-wear organization (see Chapter 12 by Eric Darnell Pritchard). Subsequently, Black individuals from the broader African Diaspora have reached heights in the industry, including British tailor Ozwald Boateng who was appointed the head of Givenchy's menswear in 2003. French designer Olivier Rousteing became the creative director of Balmain in 2011, and in 2019, the largest luxury conglomerate in the world, LVMH Moët Hennessy Louis Vuitton, wholly funded and launched Fenty, the fashion house of multi-talented Barbadian entertainer Robyn Rihanna Fenty. Virgil Abloh became the creative director of menswear at Louis Vuitton in 2018, the only Black American who has visibly ascended to a leading role in Paris fashion since Patrick Kelly.

In July 1970 Jean-Louis Scherrer won his case against Parures et Creations and was able to take back control of his atelier with the help of his new financial backer, Jean D'Albray-Orlane Cosmetics & Co. Upon the terms of their conditions, Scherrer would continue producing his haute couture and ready-to-wear collections and create a new cosmetics line.[21] After Jaxon's exit from Scherrer, the press covered his work in Paris and his return to the United States. In 1971 the *Honolulu Star-Bulletin* featured Jaxon's menswear design in an article reviewing the spring 1972 fashion shows and the trends trickling down from

Paris into American fashion. These designs included a shrunken-fit, cap-sleeve, wool sweater, and leather jacket.[22] The fitted sweater styled over a shirt with an immense collar shown in the editorial emphasized the exaggerated silhouette, reflecting the extreme accentuation of the details of men's fashion during the "Peacock Revolution." Jaxon was known for womenswear, but designing menswear highlighted his expansive design abilities. A 1972 *Women's Wear Daily* article praised an ensemble designed by Jaxon, a duffle coat over a pair of black trousers. Again, the boxy shape of the coat, in conjunction with the bell-bottom trousers, illustrated the extreme silhouette juxtaposition that was fashionable in various designers' collections and quotidian style throughout the decade. The article noted that the American department stores Saks Fifth Avenue and Henri Bendel were clamoring to sell the look, highlighting how well Jaxon's taste resonated with American consumers.[23] It was during this period that Jaxon created designs for Left Bank boutiques and the haute couture house Givenchy.[24] Even though his time in haute couture was relatively brief, Jaxon's presence created new visibility for Black designers in the Parisian fashion landscape, creating opportunities for the (still very few) Black designers who followed him.

Jaxon returned to New York in 1973 to open arms. His friend and collaborator Julian Tomchin threw Jaxon a party, well attended by the New York fashion industry, including peers such as Stephen Burrows.[25] This warm reception extended beyond his initial return home. While his career continued to flourish in New York, Jaxon's aesthetic persisted in the same vein of haute couture-level elegance that he firmly established during his time in Paris. He brought his refined taste to American ready-to-wear fashion. The following year, Jaxon was named the new designer for the Seventh Avenue fashion manufacturer Benson & Partners.[26] For his first collection, he produced sixty garments for the holiday season, describing the collection as "a classy look rather than a classic look."[27] One of the designs from this collection included a plunging neckline blouson top and a matching pair of wide-leg pajama trousers. This ensemble referenced the 1970s resurgence of 1930s neoclassical style. During the 1930s many designers and couturiers such as Madeleine Vionnet and Madame Grès looked to ancient Greece and Rome as sources of inspiration for their intricately draped silhouettes. During the 1970s and early 1980s, designers like Jaxon revived these soft, liquid silhouettes, moving away from the more rigid styles of the 1960s. Jaxon's blouson hangs effortlessly upon the model's body, creating a majestic yet sensual silhouette, a look for a modern Aphrodite. This ensemble is an illustrative example of the fluid 1970s high style also commonly seen in the designs of Jaxon's peers, such as Scott Barrie and Halston. Additionally, this design showed Jaxon embracing the still-controversial inclusion of trouser ensembles in womenswear for office and formal settings.[28] The silhouette and fabrication of this set make it suitable for a semi-formal occasion.

The December 1974 issue of *Vogue* showed a belted white jersey dress with another plunging neckline from the spring 1975 collection for Benson & Partners.[29] This is another dress design that showcases Jaxon's aesthetic during the decade. The lightweight material of the dress ideally suited the Hawaiian vacation-themed editorial, while the silhouette and materials projected a subtle luxuriousness. Despite Jaxon's successful collections at Benson & Partners, the company would close down after the 1974 holiday season, and Jaxon left the company before this occurrence.[30] By 1976 Jaxon's name appeared in the press as the designer for Pierre Cardin-New York.[31] Gunther Oppenheim and Sanford Smith, entrepreneurs and owners of the fashion firm Modelia, licensed the Cardin name and formed the company in 1969, four years before they went on to partner with Anne Klein.[32]

Jaxon's success in the mainstream inspired pride in African American communities. In a 1976 editorial spread in *Essence* magazine entitled, "First Peoples Designers," Jaxon was featured alongside peers such as Scott Barrie, Stephen Burrows, Willi Smith, and several other Black designers.[33] Since its inception by Essence Communications Inc. in 1970, *Essence* magazine positioned itself as the premier lifestyle and fashion guide for African American women.[34] This editorial celebrated the multitude of emerging and innovative Black designers that were currently active in the highest realms of the fashion and garment industries. The section on Jaxon featured an ensemble he had produced for Pierre Cardin-New York. It consisted of a silk blouse with a detachable tie, a high-cut double watch-pocket vest, and corduroy jodhpurs (riding pants). Named after the Indian city of Jodhpur, this trouser evolved from the traditional churidar trouser and salwar-kameez pant-and-tunic ensemble. This blended style points back to Jaxon's interest in the histories of global cultures as a source of design inspiration. Additionally, the voluminous silhouette created by the jodhpurs and the blouse contrasted with the cinched waistline of the vest, creating a romantic silhouette. These androgynous elements again spoke to the sensuality and sexual freedom of the decade. They exuded a sense of gender neutrality that was popular in youth and subcultural fashion during the late 1960s and adopted by mainstream fashion during the 1970s. With the growing acceptance of elements such as pants, jumpsuits, and pointed-collar and button-front shirts in women's fashion, the gender separation between men's and women's clothing decreased at this time.[35] Pierre Cardin was a trailblazer in championing this movement with his Space Age-inspired, gender-neutral ensembles that sought to democratize fashion. Jaxon continued this legacy through his menswear-inspired designs for the licensed brand.

After designing for Pierre Cardin-New York, Jaxon became the designer for the sportswear company Muney Designs in 1977.[36] By the turn of the 1980s, Jaxon was also designing sportswear for Pliers Inc. A 1980 advertisement for the brand stated, "STYLES: slim, sensuous, smashing … FIT: flattering, feminine, fabulous … QUALITY: quiet."[37] Besides the text, four models were pictured wearing Jaxon's designs, which included chunky, cable knit sweater-and-trouser ensembles, and a heavy knit dress. This elevated, yet casual, sportswear marked a significant change from the sophisticated styles he produced in Paris and during the early 1970s in New York. Expanding the range of fashion he could design, this transition further represents his adaptability across the industry. The American industry emphasized functionality and mobility significantly more than the fashion industry in Paris, and Jaxon created a space for himself that allowed him to express the myriad of design concepts that he honed throughout his career in a range of styles.

During the 1980s and 1990s, Jaxon designed costumes for several television productions, which drew on his earliest training in clothing design. His obituary noted his costume design work; however, little information is available about the programs he worked on as a costume designer.[38] One verified credit is his work as the costume designer for the 1983 *Motown 25* television production, though the extent of his designs for the program is unclear.[39] He may have designed costumes for the leading performers, which included Michael Jackson and the Jackson 5 and Diana Ross, or he may have designed the clothing of the band and backup dancers. The fact that he worked on a television program of this caliber and significance—this show was a historical event during which Michael Jackson performed the Moonwalk for the very first time—spoke to the respect he garnered in the fashion and costume design worlds. Before *Motown 25*, he was the lead costume designer of the 1972 film, *L'Odeurs des Fauves*, directed by Richard Balducci. Although there is much more to uncover about Jaxon's costume work, his designs were seen nationally and internationally in the television programs *Ally McBeal* and *The Division*, as well as the 2005 film, *Mr. and Mrs. Smith*.

Jay Jaxon made a significant contribution to the tradition of luxury fashion by working as an haute couture designer. He also added his vision to the changing and modernizing fashion culture of the late 1960s and early 1970s in both Paris and New York. Even though he was not documented in the press to the same extent as his white peers and even some of his Black peers such as Willi Smith and Stephen Burrows, Jaxon was an enormously important trailblazer in fashion. He was the first visible Black designer to penetrate the hierarchical haute couture system, becoming the first Black couturier in Paris. Yves Saint Laurent mentored him, and his time in Paris only amplified his natural talents and exquisite capabilities. Jaxon believed that elegance was an essential quality of his designs, and he returned to New York to produce sensual yet accessible fashions that melded his haute couture sensibilities with the ease of American sportswear. Jaxon died in 2006. His legacy remains his very presence. He helped normalize Black professionals in the Eurocentric fashion system, opening the door for later Black couturiers such as Olivier Rousteing at Balmain. Jaxon showed that Black designers were talented, capable, and true arbiters of taste. Although he was an unsung couturier, his legacy is immense.

Notes

1   Yvette de la Fontaine, "American (Designer) In Paris—A Real First—He's Black." *Orlando Evening Star,* January 23, 1970, 17.
2   In 1968 Hylan Booker, an African American designer from Detroit, was appointed the head of the House of Worth. Charles Frederick Worth is generally noted as the first haute couturier, and he established his house in Paris in 1858. However, after closing in 1952, the House of Worth was revived and relocated to London during the late 1960s. April Calahan and Cassidy Zachary, hosts, "Founding Father of Haute Couture: Charles Frederick Worth," Dressed: The History of Fashion (podcast), February 27, 2018, accessed December 1, 2019, http://costumesociety.org.uk/blog/post/dressed-the-history-of-fashion-podcast-review.
3   De la Fontaine, "American (Designer) In Paris,"17.
4   Ibid.
5   Ibid.
6   "In June, England Turns its Thoughts to the Outdoor Sporting Fixtures." *Women's Wear Daily Bureau London*, June 23, 1967, 1, accessed December 1, 2019, https://libproxy.fitsuny.edu:2818/docview/1523620848?accountid=27253.
7   "Vogue's Own Boutique," *Vogue*, September 1, 1967, 326,. accessed December 1, 2019. https://libproxy.fitsuny.edu:2818/docview/911868322?accountid=27253/.
8   Valerie Steele, *Fifty Years of Fashion: From New Look to Now* (New Haven: Yale University Press, 1997), 50.
9   Myra Walker, "Cardin, Pierre," in *The Berg Companion to Fashion*, ed. by Valerie Steele (Oxford: Bloomsbury Academic, 2010), accessed January 10, 2020, http://dx.doi.org/10.5040/9781474264716.0002743.

10 "Eye." *Women's Wear Daily*, June 14, 1973, 8, accessed December 1, 2019, https://libproxy.fitsuny.edu:2818/docview/1627612325?accountid=27253.

11 "Advertisement (Jean-Louis Scherrer)," *Women's Wear Daily*, October 8, 1969, 40, accessed December 1, 2019, https://libproxy.fitsuny.edu:2818/docview/1523580467?accountid=27253.

12 "Eye," *Women's Wear Daily*, June 25, 1969, 8, accessed December 1, 2019, https://libproxy.fitsuny.edu:2818/docview/1523620056?accountid=27253.

13 "Scherrer Wins $45,000 in Suit on Former Backers," *Women's Wear Daily*, December 24, 1969, 22, accessed December 1, 2019, https://libproxy.fitsuny.edu:2818/docview/1523637126?accountid=27253.

14 "Advertisement (Jean-Louis Scherrer)," *Women's Wear Daily,* October 8, 1969, 40.

15 "Paris Eye." *Women's Wear Daily*, January 27, 1970, 16, accessed December 1, 2019, https://libproxy.fitsuny.edu:2818/docview/1564939035?accountid=27253.

16 "American Jaxon's Debut: Paris Hems Go Midcalf." *Dayton Daily News,* January 27, 1970, 27.

17 Ibid.

18 Ibid.

19 "Paris Eye," 16.

20 Yvette de la Fontaine, "American (Designer) in Paris," 1-B.

21 "The Features: Jean D'Albray-Orlane Backs Scherrer Couture." *Women's Wear Daily*, November 30, 1970, 8, accessed December 1, 2019, https://libproxy.fitsuny.edu:2818/docview/1523630443?accountid=27253; "Eye." *Women's Wear Daily*, July 16, 1970, 8, accessed December 1, 2019, https://libproxy.fitsuny.edu:2818/docview/1523551330?accountid=27253.

22 "Dame Fashion Comes Down with a Case of the Uglies." *Honolulu Star-Bulletin,* November 3, 1971, 56.

23 "Eye." *Women's Wear Daily*, April 14, 1972, 6, accessed December 1, 2019, https://libproxy.fitsuny.edu:2818/docview/1523587479?accountid=27253.

24 "Eye." *Women's Wear Daily*, June 14, 1973, 8, accessed December 1, 2019, https://libproxy.fitsuny.edu:2818/docview/1627612325?accountid=27253.

25 Ibid.

26 "Sportswear Briefs," *Women's Wear Daily*, June 5, 1974, 39, accessed December 1, 2019, https://libproxy.fitsuny.edu:2818/docview/1627434298?accountid=27253.

27 "Plunging in." *Women's Wear Daily*, August 14, 1974, 1, accessed December 1, 2019, https://libproxy.fitsuny.edu:2818/docview/1627463859?accountid=27253.

28 Ibid.

29 "Fashion: Hawaii-Adventures in Sundressing." *Vogue*, December 1, 1974, 180, accessed December 1, 2019, https://libproxy.fitsuny.edu:2818/docview/904341800?accountid=27253.

30 "In Brief: Benson & Partners to Shut Down." *Women's Wear Daily*, November 15, 1974, 8, accessed December 1, 2019, https://libproxy.fitsuny.edu:2818/docview/1627463663?accountid=27253.

31   Marian McEvoy, "Some Designers Cool to Interstoff Fabrics." *Women's Wear Daily*,
       May 21, 1976, 1, accessed December 1, 2019, https://libproxy.fitsuny.edu:2818/docv
       iew/1627227136?accountid=27253.

32   Tom McDermott, "Focus: Cardin-New York has a Winner: Cardin-New York has
       Big Winner on S.A." *Women's Wear Daily*, October 24, 1969, 1, accessed December
       1, 2019, https://libproxy.fitsuny.edu:2818/docview/1540343947?accountid=27253.

33   "First Peoples Designers." *Essence*, November 11, 1976, 64, accessed December 1,
       2019, https://libproxy.fitsuny.edu:2818/docview/1818428432?accountid=27253.

34   "The ESSENCE Brand—Where Black Women Come First." *Essence* magazine
       online, accessed June 2, 2019, https://www.essence.com/about/.

35   Karina Ready, "1970–1979." *Fashion History Timeline*, October 11, 2019, accessed
       December 1, 2019, https://fashionhistory.fitnyc.edu/1970-1979/.

36   "Sportswear Briefs." *Women's Wear Daily*, February 1, 1977, 16, accessed December 1,
       2019, https://libproxy.fitsuny.edu:2818/docview/1699971209?accountid=27253.

37   "Advertisement (Pliers, Inc.)." *Women's Wear Daily*, March 2, 1980, 59, accessed
       December 1, 2019, https://libproxy.fitsuny.edu:2818/docview/1498751370?account
       id=27253.

38   "Paid Notice: Deaths Jaxon, Jay Jason." *The New York Times,* August 17, 2006,
       accessed December 1, 2019, https://www.nytimes.com/2006/08/17/classified/paid-
       notice-deaths-jaxon-jay-jason.html.

39   "Jay Jaxon." *Internet Movie Database* (IMDb), accessed January 1, 2020, https://
       www.imdb.com/name/nm3058239/.

Bibliography

"Advertisement (Jean-Louis Scherrer)." *Women's Wear Daily*, October 8, 1969, 40,
       accessed December 1, 2019. https://libproxy.fitsuny.edu:2818/docview/1523580467?
       accountid=27253.

"Advertisement (Pliers, Inc.)." *Women's Wear Daily*, March 26, 1980, accessed December
       1, 2019. https://libproxy.fitsuny.edu:2818/docview/1498751370?accountid=27253.

"American Jaxon's Debut: Paris Hems Go Midcalf." *Dayton Daily News*, January 27,
       1970, 27.

Calahan, April and Cassidy Zachary, hosts. "Founding Father of Haute Couture:
       Charles Frederick Worth."

"Dame Fashion Comes Down with a Case of the Uglies." *Honolulu Star-Bulletin*,
       November 3, 1971, 56.

De la Fontaine, Yvette. "American (Designer) In Paris—A Real First—He's Black."
       Orlando Evening Star, January 23, 1970, 1–B.

Dressed: The History of Fashion (podcast), February 27, 2018, accessed December 1,
       2019. http://costumesociety.org.uk/blog/post/dressed-the-history-of-fashion-
       podcast-review.

"Eye." *Women's Wear Daily*, June 25, 1969, accessed December 1, 2019. https://libproxy. fitsuny.edu:2818/docview/1523620056?accountid=27253.

"Eye." *Women's Wear Daily*, July 16, 1970, accessed December 1, 2019.

"Eye." *Women's Wear Daily*, April 14, 1972, accessed December 1, 2019. https://libproxy. fitsuny.edu:2818/docview/1523587479?accountid=27253.

"Eye." *Women's Wear Daily*, June 14, 1973, accessed December 1, 2019. https://libproxy. fitsuny.edu:2818/docview/1627612325?accountid=27253.

"The ESSENCE Brand—Where Black Women Come First." *Essence* magazine online, accessed June 2, 2019. https://www.essence.com/about/.

"Fashion: Hawaii-Adventures in Sundressing." *Vogue*, December 1, 1974, accessed December 1, 2019. https://libproxy.fitsuny.edu:2818/docview/904341800?account id=27253.

"The Features: Jean D'Albray-Orlane Backs Scherrer Couture." *Women's Wear Daily*, November 30, 1970, accessed December 1, 2019. https://libproxy.fitsuny.edu:2818/do cview/1523551330?accountid=27253.

"First Peoples Designers." *Essence*, November 11, 1976, accessed December 1, 2019. https://libproxy.fitsuny.edu:2818/docview/1818428432?accountid=27253.

"In Brief: Benson & Partners to Shut Down." *Women's Wear Daily*, November 15, 1974, accessed December 1, 2019. https://libproxy.fitsuny.edu:2818/docview/1627463663? accountid=27253.

"In June, England Turns its Thoughts to the Outdoor Sporting Fixtures." *Women's Wear Daily Bureau London*, June 23, 1967, accessed 1 December 2019. https://libproxy. fitsuny.edu:2818/docview/1523620848?accountid=27253.

"Jay Jaxon," *Internet Movie Database* (IMDb), accessed January 1, 2020. https://www. imdb.com/name/nm3058239/.

McDermott, Tom "Focus: Cardin-New York has a Winner: Cardin-New York has Big Winner on S.A." *Women's Wear Daily*, October 24, 1969, accessed December 1, 2019. https://libproxy.fitsuny.edu:2818/docview/1540343947?accou ntid=27253.

McEvoy, Marian. "Some Designers Cool to Interstoff Fabrics." *Women's Wear Daily*, May 21 1976, accessed December 1, 2019. https://libproxy.fitsuny.edu:2818/docview/ 1627227136?accountid=27253.

Musée Yves Saint Laurent Paris. "1966 Saint Laurent Rive Gauche," accessed December 22, 2019. https://museeyslparis.com/en/biography/saint-laurent-rive-gauche.

"Paid Notice: Deaths Jaxon, Jay Jason." *The New York Times*, August 17, 2006, accessed December 1, 2019. https://www.nytimes.com/2006/08/17/classified/paid-notice-deaths-jaxon-jay-jason.html.

"Paris Eye." *Women's Wear Daily*, January 27, 1970, accessed December 1, 2019. https:// libproxy.fitsuny.edu:2818/docview/1564939035?accountid=27253.

"Plunging in." *Women's Wear Daily*, August 14, 1974, accessed December 1, 2019. https://libproxy.fitsuny.edu:2818/docview/1627463859?accountid=27253.

Ready, Karina. "1970–1979." Fashion History Timeline, October 11, 2019, accessed December 1, 2019, https://fashionhistory.fitnyc.edu/1970-1979/.

"Scherrer Wins $45,000 in Suit on Former Backers." *Women's Wear Daily*, December 24, 1969, accessed December 1, 2019. https://libproxy.fitsuny.edu:2818/docview/1523637126?accountid=27253.

"Sportswear Briefs." *Women's Wear Daily*, June 5, 1974, accessed December 1, 2019. https://libproxy.fitsuny.edu:2818/docview/1627434298?accountid=27253.

"Sportswear Briefs." *Women's Wear Daily*, February 1 1977, accessed 1 December 2019. https://libproxy.fitsuny.edu:2818/docview/1699971209?accountid=27253.

Steele, Valerie. *Fifty Years of Fashion: From New Look to Now*. New Haven: Yale University Press, 1997. https://libproxy.fitsuny.edu:2818/docview/1523630443?accountid=27253

"Vogue's Own Boutique." *Vogue*, September 1, 1967, 326–329, accessed December 1, 2019. https://libproxy.fitsuny.edu:2818/docview/911868322?accountid=27253

Walker, Myra. "Cardin, Pierre," in The Berg Companion to Fashion, ed. Valerie Steele. Oxford: Bloomsbury Academic, 2010, accessed January 10, 2020. http://dx.doi.org/10.5040/9781474264716.0002743.

9

Dapper Dan: The Original Streetwear Designer and Influencer

Ariele Elia

Until 2017, Daniel R. Day, professionally known as Dapper Dan, was largely unknown within mainstream fashion, although he is a legend in the New York hip hop community.[1] Day's designs combine the power of luxury brand logos with the street styles worn in Harlem. His undeniable influence is seen in the early twenty-first-century fully monogrammed looks on designer runways and more recently in the rise of drop culture (or limited releases) perfected by streetwear brands. Despite his impact within fashion history, his career has been overlooked by scholars. This is partially attributed to Day going underground for twenty-five years following lawsuits from Louis Vuitton, Gucci, MCM, and Fendi. This chapter aims to investigate his design process and to position his work within fashion history prior to his 2017 collaboration with Gucci. Although he designed in New York City, his work exists outside of the established fashion industry. This case study focuses on an alternative point of view on the history of fashion, broadening the idea of who creates fashion, what is considered fashion, and where fashion occurs.

Day approaches design through personal experiences and uses clothing as a sartorial language. He explains how his previous careers have influenced his work,

> Dress and appearance ha[ve] allowed me to adjust to the role I want to play in society. It has evolved because the roles I've played in society have evolved. Each level of my life required a different look. My looks always had to conform with how to best influence the people. When I was a gambler, I had to be appealing, guys had to want to win money from me or to break me. I wore suits, ties, and carried a big wad of money when I was gambling because it enticed the players. I would wear more pimpy looking clothes as a dice player. As a gambler, I had to be boisterous, braggadocious because everybody wants to beat a guy like

Figure 9.1 Dapper Dan wearing his own design for Gucci at the Metropolitan Museum of Art's gala, 2019. Photo by Neilson Barnard/Getty Images.

that. That's not who I am, but that's what it called for. When working in the checks and credit card business, I had to be eloquent and polite with a sense of humbleness to be credible. I had more of a Wall Street look, a more cultured and refined look.[2]

Day did not set out to be a fashion designer. Before opening his boutique in 1982, he had a successful career as a street hustler running dice and numbers games in Harlem, along with manufacturing fake credit cards. He discovered loopholes in the various systems and exploited them to make a profit. In Harlem, Day recognized an opportunity to cater to hustlers and drug dealers, explaining, "All I knew was there was a demand among the drug dealers in the community and it made business sense to open a store of some kind to supply the demand."[3] His foray into fashion began by selling furs in Harlem. It was a way out of the "street" lifestyle, akin to rap music being a means of breaking out of poverty for professional rap artists who go on to enjoy financial and economic success. Day notes, "Harlem had a fashion history rich with fur coats. When you look at old photographs of Harlem, that's what you see people wearing … fur was an important status symbol, part of what folks would call 'ghetto fabulous.'"[4] As he had in his other careers, Day educated himself on the industry through library books and combined that knowledge with his hustler's mentality, resulting in a unique business venture. Day notes, "I don't remember hearing anyone in the fur industry going to school, they learned it through family members who worked in the industry."[5] He identified and visited three other Black furriers, one in New York and two in Chicago, where he learned from their experiences in the fur business. His friendship with New York-based Jewish tailor Irving Chaiken afforded him the opportunity to further study various manufacturing techniques, working with different types of furs from chinchilla to fox.[6] As Day himself became more knowledgeable about the business, he realized two major issues: fur was seasonal and the products supplied were of an inferior quality, which he described as "chitlins."[7] Day discovered a New Jersey wholesaler, Fred the Furrier, who had access to superior furs. Fred's brother persuaded Day to expand into selling leather goods and connected him with his nephew's brand, Andrew Marc.[8] The Dapper Dan of Harlem boutique had a short stint selling Andrew Marc leather coats until the retailer A. J. Lester complained that they were being undercut by Day.[9] To placate their larger client, Andrew Marc stopped selling coats to Day, but agreed to sell him the jackets without the label inside.

Acquiring skilled Black pattern makers and seamstresses to execute Day's ideas was difficult and posed a problem for his new business. As noted in his memoir, "Our community did not have access to the means of production or manufacturing necessary for high-end fashion. There weren't many black students in fashion school or black-owned luxury goods factories where I could just take my furs and leather skins and ask them to create my designs."[10] The Harlem Institute of Fashion, founded by Lois K. Alexander in 1966, was located in heart of Harlem at 155 West 126th street. It served as one of the few educational resources that catered to aspiring Black designers, offering courses in dressmaking, tailoring, and millinery.[11] An older generation of Harlem men ordered their custom suits from the neighborhood tailoring shop owned by Orie Walls and located next to the Apollo Theater. Walls was known for creating suits in a traditional Harlem style, complete with nineteen-inch cuffs, pleats, and back flap pockets.[12] After the closure of Walls's business, men ordered suits from a local department store on 125th Street. This presented a business opportunity for Day to design custom suits and accessories for a modern clientele.[13]

The foundation for Day's brand was established a couple of decades earlier during his initial trips to West Africa. He reflects on his experience, "Seeing all those skilled artists and tailors in all those different countries [Nigeria, Kenya, Uganda, Ethiopia, Egypt, and Tanzania] making beautiful things with their hands, had a permanent impact on me. Looking back, I realized that was what really changed me and my whole concept of fashion. It went deeper than I'd ever realized."[14] During his second trip to Africa, he met a Fulani tailor named Ahmed in Monrovia, Liberia, who created custom suits based on Day's fabric selection and design ideas.[15] They collaborated on "Dapper Dan originals," mixing African fabrics with American cuts and silhouettes.[16] Decades later, as Day was looking for tailors, he recalled his experience working with Ahmed. Coincidently, he came across a Senegalese street vendor in Harlem and mentioned his need of an African tailor. A week later, Sekou (Big Sek) arrived at his boutique and would become the first of twenty-four Senegalese tailors to work under Day.[17] He enthusiastically remarks, "Their sewing was amazing, they learned how to sew from their elders. But if they needed a job and didn't know how to sew, I still hired them and had one of the guys … teach them how to sew."[18] Historical documentation tracing the origins and practice of African tailoring is rare, but Shantrelle P. Lewis provides a background of the craft in her book, *Dandy Lion: The Black Dandy and Street Style.*

> Africans were some of the first, if not the first, groups of humans to sew, and over time, tailoring became an art form in Africa. African cloth—its textures and colors and prints—bore sacred and spiritual meanings; cloth also reflected wealth and status and was significant at all levels of society.

So, when African tailors first came in contact with European fashions, they blended styles and cultures with centuries' worth of refined African tailoring and aesthetics behind them.[19]

Most tailors are accustomed to working with wool, silk, and cotton fabrics, but Day was interested in creating custom leather suits. He shared his knowledge of leather working, the various qualities, hides, and characteristics with his tailors.[20] Day is often referred to as a tailor, but as he notes, "I can't sew at all. I'm not a tailor; I'm an observer and a people person. Big Sek would take a client's measurements as I made conversation, gathering information about who they were and what they wanted."[21] French couturiers Jean Patou and Lucien Lelong played similar roles as stylists of their fashion houses. Through magazines, tradeshows, and careful research, Day built a robust visual vocabulary to describe the details that went into a custom suit. This was used to translate the client's desires and Day's design ideas to the tailor. He approaches fashion from a sociological, psychological, and business perspective, in a similar way as other self-taught designers such as Rei Kawakubo and Miuccia Prada. His designs have the power to transform the wearer's identity, exuding an aura of confidence and cool as they walked down the streets of Harlem. These creations are noted for their ability to challenge the traditional ideals of fashion, beauty, and socio-economic structures. Most fashion companies are divided between the head designer who manages the creative vision, and a business partner who oversees finances. Rarely, does an individual have the talent or time to successfully excel at both. Day's previous careers allowed him to master the concepts he needed to run a successful fashion business: supply and demand, investment, margins, and growth.

In 1982 at age thirty-seven he opened his first boutique at 43 East 125th Street. The shop was the size of a small grocery store, and he started with three tailors working on sewing machines in the backroom. For ten years, his store remained open for twenty-four hours a day, and he often slept in a makeshift apartment created in the back. Most of his clientele came in after leaving clubs in the middle of the night, and the entrance, a half-drawn security gate, was manned with a guard. Later, he expanded to a larger space at 41 East 125th Street. Like a couturier, Day worked with each client individually, customizing the silhouette, fit, fabric, and color selection. On occasion clients requested a twenty-four-hour turnaround time on orders. The introduction of luxury logos into Dapper Dan designs came when a customer's girlfriend walked into the boutique carrying her new Louis Vuitton clutch. Everyone in the store gathered to view her authentic Louis Vuitton bag. Day notes this was the first time he had seen one in person.

He arrogantly said to the boyfriend, "You excited about a little bag? Imagine if you had a whole jacket ... I can do that."[22] After the client left, a feeling of panic set in, realizing he promised the client an idea that he did not know how to execute. His initial thought was to purchase an item from Louis Vuitton and use the monogram fabric to make the jacket.[23] Upon entering the Louis Vuitton store on Madison Avenue, he was shocked to only see the LV monogram on small accessories or large steamer trunks. The stiff, coated canvas was not an ideal fabric for apparel. Day's next stop was Gucci, a few doors down. After scouring the store for any hint of a monogrammed fabric—while being followed around the store—he discovered a garment bag with the signature Double G intarsia logo. Although not what he originally planned, he developed an alternative design idea, noting, "The garment bag didn't provide enough material. I could only do accents with them, not a whole outfit, and people wanted a whole outfit."[24] It is interesting to note that his first monogrammed piece was made from authentic Gucci fabric. Solving the problem of procuring large quantities of monogrammed fabric served as the basis for developing Dapper Dan's signature looks. Day began thinking of techniques to print on a more supple, flexible material, such as his hallmark leathers. He began by creating a stencil which was later screen-printed onto cotton, then leather. To develop the stencil, he cut out luxury brand logos from catalogs and taped them together, creating a pattern. In his memoir he recalls the various challenges endured in the development of his monogram silkscreens, such as the tedious process of aligning the logos and piecing them together.[25] An early example of his stencil was featured in the Museum of Modern Art's 2017 exhibition, *Items: Is Fashion Modern?* To print on larger pieces of leather, Day photographed the small stencil sample and enlarged it to a five-foot scale. Another challenge was bonding the ink to the leather. As he notes, the chemicals he used at the time are now banned in the United States. In a 1989 interview with *New York Magazine*, he claimed that his monogrammed fabrics were imported from Korea, but later admitted this was said to protect his silkscreen process in the Harlem studio.[26] He purchased a three-story building at 38 East 125th Street to make room for his latest production process. The first floor was an apartment, the mezzanine served as a space for his tailors and new machines purchased at auction, the top floor was the screen-printing studio, and the subbasement became fur storage.[27] Day's son Danny Jr. taught him how to use Corel Draw, an early vector-based design software, which allowed him create larger, more precise screens. This shifted his practice from manually setting the logos to building them digitally. Eventually, sublimation printing and computerized embroidery machines replaced silkscreen printing. He

Figure 9.2 Dapper Dan, custom silk screen (on wall) and Louis Vuitton and Gucci monogrammed jackets in the *Items: Is Fashion Modern?* exhibition, Museum of Modern Art, 2018. Photo by Laura Walton, @lauraewalton.

began experimenting with SawGrass printers, which were limited to one color at a time, requiring multiple passes, and later used various models of Epson sublimation printers with varying success. This technology was cutting edge at the time and only used by large production companies. Sublimation allows the ink to transform from a solid to a gas. When heat and pressure are applied, the ink permanently imbeds into the fabric's substrate. During the late 1980s, he purchased a Japanese Barudan computerized embroidery machine for $57,000, which allowed him to use seven colors at a time.[28]

The 1980s is largely recognized as the era of what is now called "logomania." However, the origins of monogrammed apparel fabric began during the 1960s. As the European luxury model shifted away from couture to licensing and ready-to-wear, garments featuring designer monograms were increasingly incorporated into collections. In 1968, the house of Christian Dior created a silk, red and blue, knee-length dress with the monogram, "Miss Dior" printed throughout. Fashion curator Colleen Hill explains, "This early example of branding speaks to the importance of a consumer's ability to 'buy in' to a luxury brand at relatively little cost – a concept that would become more fully developed during the next decade and beyond."[29] That same year, Gucci debuted their first ready-to-wear collection showcasing the "Double G" logo created earlier in the decade.[30] They presented monogrammed head-to-toe ensembles, including a mini dress and gogo boots, along with men's pants, shirts, and hats. Roberto Lunghi credited the transformation to a young woman working in Gucci's Florence office. He recalled that her "sole task [was] to think up new ways to adorn the Gucci goods with the GG initials and the Gucci colours."[31] By the early 1970s, the creative direction of the company shifted and monogrammed garments faded from shelves.

The 1980s ushered in an era of great opulence and extravagance in fashion. Women moved into executive corporate roles, giving them more disposable income. Power suits consisting of broad shoulders and pencil skirts became the uniform for these women to assert their power within the business world. *Vogue* was filled with advertisements for designer suits in bright colors, stacks of gold bracelets, and lavish furs with large shoulder pads. It was also an era of postmodern fashion, defined by the mixing of trends from the past with eccentric elements to make them relevant for the time. Fashion historian Dana Thomas provides context to another important change, the corporate takeover of luxury brands,

> Corporate tycoons and financiers saw the potential. They bought—or took over—luxury companies from elderly founders and incompetent heirs, turned the houses into brands, and homogenized everything: the stores, the uniforms, the products, even the coffee cups in the meetings. Then they turned their sights on a new target audience: the middle market, that broad socioeconomic demographic that includes everyone from teachers and sales executives to high-tech entrepreneurs, McMansion suburbanites, the ghetto fabulous, even the criminally wealthy. The idea, luxury executives explained, was to "democratize" luxury to make luxury "accessible."[32]

When Day started his business during the early 1980s, fashion brands were not designing garments that appealed to his clientele. He notes, "I moved the heritage brand aesthetic away from the Madison Avenue look and gave it that distinct uptown flavor. I was taking the logos to places the brands never would and making it look good on us."[33] The looser-fitting silhouettes of baggy pants, bomber jackets, and tracksuits represented a rebellion against the mainstream styles sold in luxury stores. It was a unique style created by the hustlers, rappers, b-boys and b-girls on the streets of Harlem, Brooklyn, Queens, and the Bronx. Kim Hastreiter, editor of *Paper* magazine, provides insight into the styles seen in 1984, writing,

> Long before the days of luxe hip-ification, Gucci, Louis Vuitton, and Dior were conservative brands, churning out little ladylike pocketbooks for the wealthy and white. In those days, the kids in Harlem and the Bronx who were birthing the hip-hop scene had little money to buy luxury labels, so they invented a smart and rad new style that turned status upside down in the face of white establishment. They began to turn up on the street and at rap concerts decked out in bootleg luxury logos … they plastered these all over their casual sports clothes … Fast-forward 10 years, when Tom Ford took the design helm at Gucci and Marc Jacobs did the same at Louis Vuitton. The first thing that they did to these labels was pay homage to the street culture that had embraced brand names so outrageously during the previous decade.[34]

Day catered to his clients' taste by creating ostentatious custom ensembles to match their unique personalities. His earliest clients were hustlers and gangsters who continued the tradition of ordering tailor-made suits with unique colors and details. His prior career running dice games gave him insight, as Day explains, "Early on I knew the personality that my customers wanted to portray on the streets. I knew that flamboyance played a big role in their life. Their intentions are to impress people, it is pretty much the same as dice players, just with a different outcome."[35] Systematic racism and discrimination ensured that luxury brands would not welcome anyone with the appearance of a hustler or gangster into their stores. The stores often locked their doors to Black consumers, despite the fact that they had money to purchase goods. Luxury brands did not want their monogram associated with Day's clientele, fearful of how it would represent them and the reaction of their conservative clients. At the same time, luxury brands did not carry clothing that appealed to Day's clientele. The combination of these elements provided the perfect opportunity for the Dapper Dan of Harlem boutique to find success. Hip hop artists and groups, such as Boogie Down Productions, Big Daddy Kane, and LL Cool J became customers of Dapper Dan of Harlem when they achieved the success that afforded a custom piece. Hip hop artists commonly incorporate the names of luxury brands in their lyrics as a status symbol—Schoolly D, for example, released the single, "Gucci Time" in 1986.[36] Hip hop artists' desire to emulate the style of gangsters and hustlers, including their accessories such as gold dookie chains, further recommended Dapper Dan because he could create the complete look.[37] Athletes of the era, such as boxer Mike Tyson, also frequented the boutique. Day notes, "I knew none of them would be caught dead in a knockoff, so I had to convince them that, while it had the high-end material and craftsmanship of a luxury item, it was something new and different. They had to see that I had taken these brands and pushed them into new territory. I knocked them up, I didn't knock them off. I blackenized them."[38] Luxury brands of the 1980s did not consider creating utilitarian garments such as snorkel coats; however, Day specifically designed them to meet the needs of his gangster clientele. His three-quarter length, nylon quilted, bullet-proof, zip-up parka included two large front pockets. To prove its durability, he allowed customers to test the Kevlar lining before tailoring the Gucci, Polo, MCM, or Fendi fabric into parkas and matching hats.[39] In 1985 the ensemble would cost a client $2,500.[40] Despite the heat of the summer months, customers continued to wear their parkas for protection. Fendi was the one of the only brands to catch on to this trend and feature their Zucca (double F) logo—designed by creative director Karl Lagerfeld—on pants and coats during the early 1990s and 2000s.[41] Fendi's spring and fall 2018 collections later paid homage to these monogrammed designs. Everything from mink bomber jackets to trench coats, dresses, boots, and baby strollers were festooned with the Zucca monogram.[42]

Jackets were a staple of the Dapper Dan of Harlem boutique, which was driven by Day's recognition of the importance of nightlife and showing off. He notes, "The fly guys in Harlem, they live behind the reputation of their cars, but when they go into a club, they can't drive their car in."[43] In reference to the Alfa Romeo, a popular car during the late 1980s, he designed a white leather bomber jacket with a large leather Alfa Romeo logo patch on the center back. The side of each sleeve had a circular patch with an "A" and "R." This jacket signaled to women in the club that the wearer had money and the car to match. The Fat Boys, a Brooklyn hip hop trio, were often photographed in different Dapper Dan jackets. The album cover of *Falling in Love* (1987) showcases Mark "Prince Markie Dee" Morales and Damon "Kool Rock-Ski" Wimbley in Louis Vuitton bomber jackets. They flank Darren "Buff Love" Robinson (a.k.a. "the Human Beatbox") in a blue leather jacket trimmed with a monogrammed Gucci lapel and cuffs. The Louis Vuitton monogram was a mainstay in Day's work. One of his most remarkable jackets was created for Olympic gold medal winner, Diane Dixon. The jacket had eccentric leg-o-mutton sleeves, on-trend during the 1980s, with a brown mink body. A fitted, cotton Louis Vuitton ensemble designed for the famed rapper Roxanne Shante shows a similarly feminine style of Day's work. Surprisingly, he also dressed Roxanne Shante's impersonator The Real Roxanne in a Louis Vuitton monogrammed kufi, cropped jacket, and skirt suit, trimmed with curved sections of brown suede. The two engaged in a one-year rap battle known as The Roxanne Wars.

Day realized the power and potential of placing monograms on apparel decades ahead of Louis Vuitton. The first Louis Vuitton ready-to-wear collection would not hit the runway for another twenty years during the spring 2000 season, under the creative direction of Marc Jacobs. The show featured coats, cropped jackets, skirts, hats, and umbrellas in Louis Vuitton's monogrammed fabric. Marc Jacobs also understood the power of the Louis Vuitton logo during

copyright © Steve Friedman 2019

Figure 9.3 The Fat Boys wearing Dapper Dan custom leather jackets and caps, 1987. Photo: Steve Friedman © 2020.

Figure 9.4 Rapper Roxanne Shante wearing a Dapper Dan ensemble, circa 1989. Photo by Michael Ochs Archives/Getty Images.

this later wave of logomania, noting: "When you look at [Louis Vuitton], you see it is mass-produced luxury, Vuitton is a status symbol. It's not about hiding the logo. It's about being a bit of a show-off."[44] Hip hop artist Lil' Kim often wore Louis Vuitton among other luxury brands. She became close friends with Marc Jacobs, noting he was one of the first designers to embrace her and listen to her music.[45] As their relationship developed, Kim would have lunch with him at the studio while he took her through his design process. Kim notes that she constantly saw Day's designs on the streets of New York City. It's plausible that this may have influenced Jacob's Spring 2000 collection.

During the late 1980s, MCM (Modern Creations Munich) was famous for its monogrammed luxury bags and luggage, which embodied an aura of jet set travel. This is illustrated in a 1987 ad in *Vogue*, featuring a luggage cart stacked with nine pieces of luggage.[46] At the time MCM was only known as a luggage company, but Day transformed the company into a lifestyle brand. He designed an MCM monogram-printed leather jacket resembling a 1920s gangster suit for the notorious drug dealer and gangster, Alberto "Alpo" Martinez. The front was double-breasted with a shawl collar and the back featured a looser-fitting bomber style. Day said, "I wanted to give it a rich look. I didn't want it to look like anything that anybody else had. I wanted it to look like street tuxedo look."[47] Female rap duo Finesse & Synquis wore yellow and teal MCM-logo fitted suits on their album cover, *Soul Sister* (1988). Their names were centered within hearts in block letters on the back of their cropped jackets. MCM would later launch a ready-to-wear collection in spring 2006 featuring monogrammed looks. Misa Hylton has worked as the brand's global creative partner since 2018. She began her career as a stylist for Missy Elliot, Lil' Kim, and other hip hop artists. In an interview with Complex, she notes her designs were influenced by the foundation Day created during the 1980s.[48]

In 1988 Day expanded his customization to automobiles, fully upholstering his red jeep with MCM monogrammed seats, side door panels, roll bars, convertible top, and spare wheel cover.[49] In total, the printing and installation took one week. Day went on to apply different luxury labels to automotive design, creating a Gucci convertible rooftop cover for rapper Rakim and a Gucci wheel cover for his partner Eric B.'s jeep with his name in gold letters. Day's brown Mercedes was upholstered in beige and brown monograms and burgundy Gucci fabric, including the wheel cover. This was not the first luxury branded car—a decade earlier in 1978 Sammy Davis Jr. purchased a Gucci limited-edition Cadillac Seville for $29,900.[50] The car featured a twenty-four-carat gold-plated inlaid

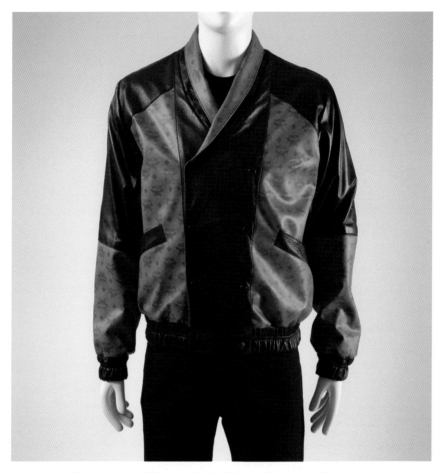

Figure 9.5 Dapper Dan of Harlem, High-Tek double-breasted leather jacket originally created for Alberto "Alpo" Martinez, 1987. Gift of Dapper Dan of Harlem. © The Museum at FIT.

hood and wheel covers, horse bit decorated fenders, monogrammed roof, and a dashboard with Gucci's green-red-green stripe.[51]

B-boys and b-girls—break boys and girls—originated a form of break dancing in the Bronx starting in the 1970s. Their name derives from hip hop moves performed during the break of a song. They were known for setting various fashion trends, including the tracksuit—often by Adidas—and sneakers with fat laces. Day took the idea of the tracksuit and made a dressier version using luxury brand logos and adding his own design elements. Rappers wore the tracksuits on album covers, during performances, and at night clubs. Artists Eric B. and Rakim worked with Day early in their careers to create matching

Figure 9.6 Dapper Dan's monogrammed jeep, 1988. Photo by Michael Schwartz/ New York Post Archives/© NYP Holdings, Inc. via Getty Images.

gold and black Gucci tracksuits for their 1988 album cover, *Follow the Leader*. The sleeves had gold Gucci monograms and the name of the album was featured down the front. Each of their names were written in large gold block letters with the monograms in the background. Eric B. also had a large double G on the center back of his jacket, while Rakim's featured a Nation of Islam logo. A gold V-shaped accent filled with the Gucci monogram ran down the side leg of the pants connecting to a stripe ending with a Double G logo at the knee. Day recalls people visiting Gucci stores asking for tracksuits, like the ones they had seen in the music videos and quickly realizing they did not sell them.[52] Yet during the early 1990s Gucci was making a comeback into fashion relevancy. Creative director Dawn Mello emphasized the quality and craftsmanship of their leather goods, placing the monogram on the interior of some products. Their most popular items were small structured handbags and leather loafers with the horse bit emblem.[53]

Dapper Dan's influence reached across the Atlantic. A 1988 brown Gucci tracksuit, closely resembling the ones created for Eric B. and Rakim, was featured in the Victoria & Albert Museum's 1994 exhibition, *Street Style: From Sidewalk to Catwalk*. The exhibition labeled it a British b-boy ensemble and described its context, "Brand consciousness and relentless competition amongst hip hoppers, in the mid to late 1980s, eventually led to individual customization. Tailors, the most famous being Dapper Dan in Harlem, New York, took the most expensive and conservative designs of coveted labels and added an extra twist of 'street flavor.'"[54] The following year, British underground magazine *The Face* covered Dapper Dan's work.[55] The article featured a photo of him inside his Mercedes with the customized Gucci interior. They were one of the few press outlets to recognize his creativity and contribution to the design world during his career in the 1980s and 1990s. Dapper Dan garnered little press prior to 2017. Sharon Edelson of *New York Magazine* covered Day's work in a 1989 article titled, "Uptown Couture,"[56] and though *Yo! MTV Raps* provided a national platform for rappers to debut Dapper Dan ensembles on television, Day's clientele of gangsters, hustlers, and rappers did not align with the respectability politics of magazines such as *Jet* and *Ebony*. He notes, "the funny thing is I had to win over the Europeans to win over the white people, to win over the middle class black people."[57] Other designers had similar experiences, Patrick Kelly, for example, was more accepted and successful in Paris then in the United States.

MTV served as an outlet showcasing the visual culture of New York hip hop to people around the world and its influence spread. In 1987 Run DMC performed in Paris during their *Together Forever* tour.[58] Karl Lagerfeld—hired as creative director of Chanel in 1983—picked up on the sartorial language of hip hop and incorporated it into his fall 1991 runway show, a postmodern mash-up of Chanel signatures—costume jewelry, pearls, gold chains—with exaggerated wide-brimmed baseball caps, layers of gold wrestling belts, nameplates, and chains resembling the dookie chains worn by hip hop artists. One look featured gold cuffs, linked together by thin chains, unmistakably associating it with the history of slave shackles. Placing this accessory on the runway trivialized the history and suffering of Black people, yet it was showcased at a time when cultural insensitivities went largely unrecognized by the public and the press and for decades this was overlooked in fashion history. The over-the-top accessories transformed the conservative tweed suits and added the "fly" factor that Day's clients created in Harlem.[59] Grace Coddington, the New York-based fashion editor of *Vogue*, contextualized Lagerfeld's collection within hip hop culture for the December 1991 issue. The Peter Pan-themed photoshoot featured Linda Evangelista as Peter wearing layers of chains, including a Chanel nameplate. The copy reads, "Rap chains can't keep this fly-boy down. Here Peter promises to take Wendy and her brothers on a joyride if they quit their uptown digs for Never Never Land."[60] Another Chanel photograph shot by Karl Lagerfeld also featured Evangelista covered in layers of chains around her neck, arms, wrists, and waist, including a wrestling belt reminiscent of the belts worn by Day's customer, boxer Mike Tyson. The same year *Harper's Bazaar* featured an editorial entitled, "Street Smart," featuring layers of designer gold chains draped over black ensembles shot against backdrop of the city streets. The copy for the editorial reads, "Black leather and gold chains, short skirts and high boots. Hip hop meets top style in a witty take on street dressing."[61] Just as 1960s couturiers looked to youth culture and street styles for inspiration to stay relevant, mainstream fashion more readily referenced hip hop during the 1990s and also failed to credit the original designers or style-makers. After Gabrielle Chanel's death, Lagerfeld was tasked with reinventing and modernizing the brand to appeal to a younger demographic. Ironically, Day never used Chanel's logos in his designs. They existed outside of the realm of Harlem fashion as he explains, "I never wanna be in the traditional-runway zone, telling people how to feel. I want them to tell me how they feel, and then I want to extract those feelings and build fashion outta that."[62] Fashion certainly drew from Day and other hip hop styles. During this time Lil' Kim primarily wore Chanel and became friends with Karl Lagerfeld. She notes that he created a collection inspired by her.[63] Most recently, in a post postmodern rendition of the 1991 Chanel collection, Jeremy Scott designed a pre-fall 2020 collection for Moschino based on Lagerfeld's interpretation of hip hop fashion.[64] These designs come full circle when hip hop artists re-appropriate them—singer Rihanna recreated Evangelista's *Vogue* look for her 2013 *Pour It Up* music video and rapper Cardi B paid homage to the Chanel ensemble, substituting Versace jewelry for her 2018 performance on *The Tonight Show Starring Jimmy Fallon*.

In 1992 Day expanded his business by opening a studio in the basement of his brownstone and leased a 2,000 square-foot building on 120th Street between Second and Third Avenues. This space served as a small factory with eleven tailors and as a warehouse. At his peak, Day had thirty employees, spending $40,000 on payroll per month. During the holiday season he sold $32,000 of merchandise a day, which he never discounted.[65] Dapper Dan of Harlem was invisible to the fashion world until boxer Mitch Green, eager for a rematch of a 1986 fight, started an altercation with Mike Tyson outside the boutique in 1988.[66] News coverage of the fight led luxury brands to discover where the custom ensembles donning their logos originated. Gucci, Fendi, Louis Vuitton, and MCM initiated countless raids and lawsuits for years.[67] Self-taught as always, Day researched the legal issues and decided to represent himself in a lawsuit against Fendi who was represented by future Supreme Court Justice Sonia Sotomayor. The loss of this case and the exhaustion of constantly defending his designs led to the dissolution

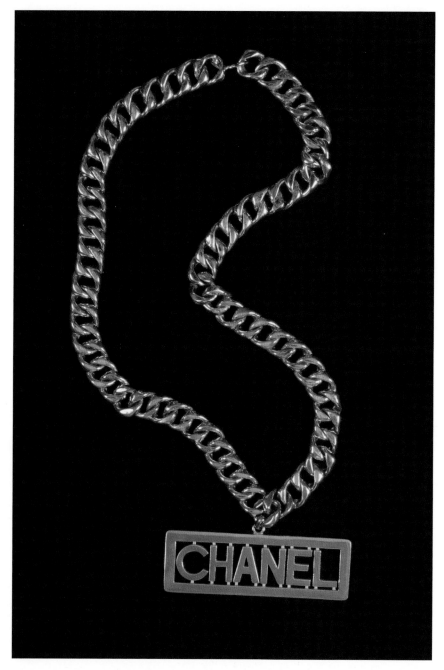

Figure 9.7 Karl Lagerfeld for Chanel, logo "dookie" chain necklace, fall 1991. Gift of Depuis 1924. © The Museum at FIT.

of his boutique in 1992. It is the legal duty of a brand to police its mark, otherwise it may face the loss of rights and use of the trademark. Luxury brands have always been aware of counterfeiting and are avid protectors of their logos. As Thomas notes, "the monogram pattern of interlocking LVs interspersed with Naïf-style diamonds, stars, and flowers, which Georges [Vuitton] designed in 1896 [was] also in response to counterfeiting and [he] registered it as a trademark in 1905."[68] Unfortunately, Day's innovative designs were not recognized as an opportunity for luxury brands to expand their market through collaboration. For the next twenty-five years, Day went underground, hidden from the fashion world at large and unrecognized for his influence on various luxury brands.

The third wave of logomania came to fashion at the end of the 1990s. David LaChapelle photographed Lil' Kim for a 1999 exhibition, titling the photograph, *Lil' Kim: Luxury Item.* Kim stood for hours as her entire body was painstakingly airbrushed with the Louis Vuitton monogram. LaChapelle says, "I was taking cues from Harlem designer Dapper Dan. Logos hadn't come back yet [into runway fashion]; that happened a season or two later."[69] The photograph caught the attention of *Interview* editor Ingrid Sischy, who decided to feature it on the November 1999 cover.

Another close friend of Kim's was John Galliano, who served as the creative director of Christian Dior and who introduced the monogrammed saddle bag in his spring 2000 collection. He later designed a fully monogrammed ensemble for Missy Elliot, complete with a flat cap, bustier, coat, and shoes. During the early twenty-first century, luxury brands tapped streetwear designers and artists for collaborations to infuse the "fly factor" into their brands. In 2000, for example, Louis Vuitton sent a cease and desist letter to the skate-brand Supreme for a skateboard deck they designed featuring the LV monogram. But seventeen years later, Louis Vuitton invited Supreme to collaborate on their fall 2017 collection. Over the years, Supreme had mastered the art of drop culture, creating hype around their limited-edition monogrammed items. Fashion brands began looking to streetwear brands and their marketing techniques as a guide on how to stay relevant. Supreme's business model and designs were based on Day's, but Louis Vuitton did not seek out the originator of monogrammed streetwear fashion or give credit.

Day's contributions to fashion were acknowledged in the 2005 book, *Gucci by Gucci,* in which he was credited as "the most famous converter of labels. Even though this trend was antithetical to trademark law … it was done in admiration. The benefit of Gucci's high unofficial approval rating among urban audiences came right back to Gucci ten or fifteen years later. When the hip hop outsiders

Figure 9.8 Rapper and producer Missy Elliott wearing John Galliano for Christian Dior monogrammed ensemble, 2004. Photo by Lawrence Lucier/FilmMagic.

became multi-millionaires, they put authentic Gucci at the top of their shopping list."[70] In this account, Gucci omitted the countless raids of Day's store and their lawsuit against him. The power dynamics of this situation are problematic; a powerful brand benefits from the sales of smaller-scale artists, while rejecting their interpretation of its brand. Yet the optics of such unbalanced dynamics have grown out of fashion. As an example, in fall 2016 Alessandro Michele, creative director of Gucci, struck a deal with the street-artist GucciGhost. Beginning in 2012, GucciGhost painted the brand's monogram on everything from boxing gloves to jackets and street signs. He posted the images on Instagram, stating, "I'm going to push this idea until Gucci either sues me or hires me."[71] Embracing the popularity of social media, the fall 2016 runway showcased the Double G logo painted onto leather bags, bomber jackets, and other garments. Unlike Day who developed a business, younger generations are now building hype around unoriginal ideas using social media platforms with no investment or risk.

Gucci's resort 2017 collection added further insult to Day's unrecognized legacy by including sweaters printed with a "counterfeit" Gucci logo. The following resort collection famously featured a jacket that was a carbon copy of Day's 1989 original designed for Diane Dixon. After seeing the runway show, Dixon criticized Michele on Instagram for copying Day's work. Twenty-five years later, Gucci finally gave Day the credit he deserved. He notes, "It is necessary for people to know where they are getting their inspiration from, especially for a Black person in America. When people don't, it hits home in a bad way. I want young people to know because that's aspiration for them. What makes America great is all the contributions. When you start denying who did what and who contributed, you separate us."[72]

Notes

1　Daniel Day received the name Dapper Dan from a former Harlem hustler named Dapper Dan. Impressed with Day's style and skills at dice, he transferred the title of Dapper Dan onto Day. Previous to receiving his new name, Day was referred to as Dancing Danny, alluding to his impressive dance moves. Daniel R. Day, *Dapper Dan: Made in Harlem: A Memoir* (New York: Random House, 2019), 57.

2　Daniel R. Day, Interview with author, September 4, 2019.

3　Day, *Dapper Dan: Made in Harlem*, 160.

4　Ibid, 164.

5　Day, Interview with author, 2019.

6　Ibid.

7   Ibid.

8   Day, *Dapper Dan: Made in Harlem*, 168.

9   Ibid., 172.

10 Ibid., 175.

11 Adam Bernstein, "Lois Alexander Lane; Founder of Harlem Institute of Fashion," *Washington Post*, October 27, 2007, accessed April 2, 2020, https://www.washingtonpost.com/wp-dyn/content/article/2007/10/26/AR2007102602221.html.

12 Day, Interview with author, 2019.

13 Day, *Dapper Dan: Made in Harlem*, 126.

14 Ibid., 106.

15 Ibid, 126.

16 Ibid.

17 Ibid., 174.

18 Day, Interview with author, 2019.

19 Shantrelle P. Lewis, *Dandy Lion: The Black Dancy and Street Style* (New York: Aperture, 2017), 9.

20 Day, Interview with author, 2019.

21 Day, *Dapper Dan: Made in Harlem*, 176.

22 Ibid., 178.

23 Ibid., 179.

24 Ibid., 182.

25 Ibid.

26 Sharon Edelson, "Uptown Haute Couture," *New York Magazine*, June 5, 1989, accessed April 2, 2020, https://blog.dapperdanofharlem.com/post/34723121490/new-york-magazine; Day, *Dapper Dan: Made in Harlem*, 184.

27 Day, *Dapper Dan: Made in Harlem*, 202.

28 This machine was seized in a raid before it was used on any garments for the boutique. Ibid., 230.

29 Colleen Hill, "Miss Dior," The Museum at FIT, April 6, 2017, accessed April 2, 2020, https://exhibitions.fitnyc.edu/paris-refashioned/.

30 Frida Giannini, ed., *Gucci: The Making of* (New York: Rizzoli, 2011), 56.

31 Sarah Mower, *Gucci by Gucci* (New York: Vendome Press, 2006), 26.

32 Dana Thomas, *How Luxury Lost Its Luster* (London: Random House, 2007), 9.

33 Day, *Dapper Dan: Made in Harlem*, 277.

34 Kim Hastreiter, *20 Years of Style: The World According to Paper* (New York: Harper Design, 2004), 34.

35 Day, Interview with author, 2019.

36 Giannini, *Gucci: The Making of*, 297.

37 "The dookie chain is a thick necklace that looks like a braided rope … For rap artists, it was a sign of success, and it was meant to disprove the racist stereotype

that all Black people in the US were poor." "Dookie Chains," *80s Fashion*, April 16, 2014, accessed April 2, 2020, http://www.80sfashion.org/dookie-chains/

38 Day, *Dapper Dan: Made in Harlem*, 189.

39 Ibid., 215.

40 Approximately $5,900 in 2020 values.

41 "Fendi Fall 1993," video file, 3:41, YouTube, posted by 90s Fashion, February 14, 2015, https://www.youtube.com/watch?v=E1yD48bvpSk; Meagan Fredette, "That Fendi Monogram Print is Taking Over 2018," *Paper*, April 11, 2018, accessed April 2, 2020, https://www.papermag.com/fendi-monogram-print-2018-2558871463.html.

42 Sarah Mower, "Fall 2018 Ready-to-Wear Fendi," *Vogue Runway,* February 22, 2018, https://www.vogue.com/fashion-shows/fall-2018-ready-to-wear/fendi/slideshow/collection#28; Lauren Alexis Fisher, "Kylie Jenner, Totally Average Mom, Matches Her Fendi Logo Stroller," *Harper's Bazaar,* April 13, 2018, https://www.harpersbazaar.com/fashion/designers/a19781355/kylie-jenner-fendi-stroller/.

43 Day, Interview with author, 2019.

44 Thomas, *How Luxury Lost Its Luster*, 45; *Dapper Dan: Made in Harlem: A Memoir*, 18.

45 Aria Huges, "The Naked Truth: How Lil' Kim Changed Hip-Hop Fashion," *ComplexCon(versations)*, December 10, 2019, accessed April 2, 2020, https://www.complex.com/pop-culture/2019/12/the-naked-truth-how-lil-kim-changed-hip-hop-fashion-complexconversations

46 "MCM Advertisement," *Vogue*, May 1, 1987, 261.

47 Day, Interview with author, 2019.

48 Huges, "The Naked Truth: How Lil' Kim Changed Hip-Hop Fashion," access online at https://www.complex.com/pop-culture/2019/12/the-naked-truth-how-lil-kim-changed-hip-hop-fashion-complexconversations.

49 Day, *Dapper Dan: Made in Harlem*, 193. Jeep featured a model in a 1990s look book with upholstered MCM seats and sun visors. Gary Warnett, "Luxury Vehicles," *Gwar Izm*, November 6, 2011, accessed April 2, 2020, https://garywarnett.wordpress.com/tag/ramen/

50 Approximately $118,627 in 2020 values.

51 Giannini, *Gucci: The Making of*, 319.

52 Day, *Dapper Dan: Made in Harlem,* 267.

53 Georgina Howell, "Gucci Again," *Vogue,* December 1, 1990, 322–7.

54 "Tracksuit," Victoria & Albert museum online collections, https://collections.vam.ac.uk/item/O138286/tracksuit/.

55 Paula Nessick and Butthy Matthias, "Harlem Reborn," *The Face* 2 no. 10 (1989): 50.

56 Edelson, "Uptown Haute Couture."

57 Day, Interview with author, 2019.

58 Robin Mellery-Pratt, "Run-D.M.C.'s 'My Adidas' and the Birth of Hip Hop Sneaker Culture," *The Business of Fashion*, July 18, 2014, accessed April 2, 2020, https://www.

businessoffashion.com/articles/video/run-d-m-c-s-adidas-birth-hip-hop-sneaker-culture.

59   Day defines fly as, "something intangible. It was about style, how you carried yourself in the street. It was about your shoes, the way you wore your hat. It was about the car you drove and how fly your girl dressed." Day, *Dapper Dan*, 31.

60   Grace Coddington, "Fashion: Peter Pan," *Vogue*, December 1, 1991, 224–9.

61   "Street Smart," *Harper's Bazaar*, September 1, 1991, 214–19.

62   Day, *Dapper Dan: Made in Harlem,* 271.

63   Huges, "The Naked Truth: How Lil' Kim Changed Hip-Hop Fashion," access online, https://www. complex.com/pop-culture/2019/12/the-naked-truth-how-lil-kim-changed-hip- hop-fashion-complexconversations.

64   Nicole Phelps, "Pre-Fall 2020 Ready-To-Wear Moschino," *Vogue*, December 9, 2019, accessed April 2, 2020, https://www.vogue.com/fashion-shows/pre-fall-2020/moschino.

65   Day, *Dapper Dan: Made in Harlem*, 217.

66   Mike Tyson was visiting the boutique to check the progress on a custom jacket at around 4:30 in the morning. Kelefa Sanneh, "Harlem Chic," *The New Yorker*, March 18, 2013, accessed April 2, 2020, https://www.newyorker.com/magazine/2013/03/25/harlem-chic.

67   The details of the raids are recalled in *Dapper Dan: Made in Harlem*, 226–32 and Sanneh, "Harlem Chic."

68   Thomas, *How Luxury Lost Its Luster*, 25.

69   Louis Vuitton sent a cease and desist letter after the photograph was made public. Nadja Sayej, "The Story Behind Lil' Kim's Iconic Louis Vuitton Logo-Print Portrait," *Garage*, November 18, 2018, accessed April 2, 2020, https://garage.vice.com/en_us/article/qvqde3/lil-kim-louis-vuitton-david-lachapelle/.

70   Mower, *Gucci by Gucci*, 30.

71   Ann Binlot, "The Man and Spirit Behind GucciGhost, Gucci's Renegade Line," *The New York Times*, September 2, 2016, accessed April 2, 2020, https://www.nytimes.com/2016/09/04/fashion/trevor-andrew-guccighost-brooklyn-fashion.html.

72   Day, Interview with author, 2019.

Bibliography

Bernstein, Adam. "Lois Alexander Lane; Founder of Harlem Institute of Fashion." *Washington Post*, October 27, 2007, accessed April 2, 2020. https://www. washingtonpost.com/wp-dyn/content/article/2007/10/26/AR2007102602221.html.

Binlot, Ann. "The Man and Spirit Behind GucciGhost, Gucci's Renegade Line." *The New York Times*, September 2, 2016, accessed April 2, 2020. https://www.nytimes. com/2016/09/04/fashion/trevor-andrew-guccighost-brooklyn-fashion.html.

Coddington, Grace. "Fashion: Peter Pan." *Vogue* (December 1, 1991): 224–9.

Day, Daniel R. *Dapper Dan: Made in Harlem: A Memoir.* New York: Random House, 2019.

Day, Daniel R. Interview with author, September 4, 2019.

"Dookie Chains," *80s Fashion*, April 16, 2014, http://www.80sfashion.org/dookie-chains/.

Edelson, Sharon "Uptown Haute Couture." *New York Magazine*, June 5, 1989, accessed April 2, 2020. https://blog.dapperdanofharlem.com/post/34723121490/new-york-magazine.

"Fendi Fall 1993." Video file, 3:41, YouTube. Posted by 90s Fashion, February 14, 2015, accessed April 2, 2020. https://www.youtube.com/watch?v=E1yD48bvpSk.

Fisher, Lauren Alexis. "Kylie Jenner, Totally Average Mom, Matches Her Fendi Logo Stroller." *Harper's Bazaar*, April 13, 2018, accessed April 2, 2020. https://www.harpersbazaar.com/fashion/designers/a19781355/kylie-jenner-fendi-stroller/.

Fredette, Meagan. "That Fendi Monogram Print is Taking Over 2018." *Paper*, April 11, 2018, accessed April 2, 2020. https://www.papermag.com/fendi-monogram-print-2018-2558871463.html.

Giannini, Frida. *Gucci: The Making of.* New York: Rizzoli, 2011.

Hastreiter, Kim. *20 Years of Style: The World According to Paper.* New York: Harper Design, 2004.

Hill, Colleen. "Miss Dior," The Museum at FIT, April 6, 2017, accessed April 2, 2020. https://exhibitions.fitnyc.edu/paris-refashioned.

Howell, Georgina. "Gucci Again." *Vogue*, December 1, 1990, 322–7.

Huges, Aria. "The Naked Truth: How Lil' Kim Changed Hip-Hop Fashion," *ComplexCon(versations)*, December 10, 2019, accessed April 2, 2020. https://www.complex.com/pop-culture/2019/12/the-naked-truth-how-lil-kim-changed-hip-hop-fashion-complexconversations./.

Lewis, Shantrelle P. *Dandy Lion: The Black Dancy and Street Style.* New York: Aperture, 2017.

"MCM Advertisement." *Vogue*, May 1, 1987, 261.

Mellery-Pratt, Robin. "Run-D.M.C.'s 'My Adidas' and the Birth of Hip Hop Sneaker Culture." *The Business of Fashion*, July 18, 2014, accessed April 2, 2020. https://www.businessoffashion.com/articles/video/run-d-m-c-s-adidas-birth-hip-hop-sneaker-culture.

Mower, Sarah. "Fall 2018 Ready-to-Wear Fendi." *Vogue Runway*, February 22, 2018, accessed April 2, 2020. https://www.vogue.com/fashion-shows/fall-2018-ready-to-wear/fendi/slideshow/collection#28.

Mower, Sarah. *Gucci by Gucci.* New York: Vendome Press, 2006.

Nessick, Paula and Butthy Matthias. "Harlem Reborn." *The Face* 2, no. 10 (1989): 50–3.

Phelps, Nicole. "Pre-Fall 2020 Ready-To-Wear Moschino." *Vogue*, December 9, 2019, accessed April 2, 2020. https://www.vogue.com/fashion-shows/pre-fall-2020/moschino.

Sanneh, Kelefa. "Harlem Chic." *The New Yorker*, March 18, 2013, accessed April 2, 2020. https://www.newyorker.com/magazine/2013/03/25/harlem-chic.

Sayej, Nadja. "The Story Behind Lil' Kim's Iconic Louis Vuitton Logo-Print Portrait," *Garage*, November 18, 2018, accessed April 2, 2020. https://garage.vice.com/en_us/article/qvqde3/lil-kim-louis-vuitton-david-lachapelle.

"Street Smart." *Harper's Bazaar* (September 1, 1991): 214–19.

Thomas, Dana. *How Luxury Lost Its Luster*. London: Random House, 2007.

"Tracksuit." Victoria & Albert Museum online collections. https://collections.vam.ac.uk/item/O138286/tracksuit/.

Warnett, Gary. "Luxury Vehicles," *Gwar Izm*, November 6, 2011, accessed April 2, 2020. https://garywarnett.wordpress.com/tag/ramen/.

Section 4

The Star Designer: National and International Impact

10

Color Story: Stephen Burrows's Impact on the World of Fashion

Tanya Danielle Wilson Myers

In the chronicles of fashion, Stephen Burrows will be recognized as a creator. His clothes crossed color lines, appreciated by a wide, international audience, regardless of ethnicity. More than any other designer during the 1970s, Burrows captured the vivacious energy of the New York disco scene. His practices and innovations transformed fashion culture. In an endless range of shapes and combinations, Burrows placed bright contrasting colors of chiffon or knit jersey fabric in a single ensemble. Instead of hiding the stitching, he celebrated and exaggerated it by using contrasting thread colors and by employing a narrow zigzag stitch to create his trademark "lettuce hem." The aesthetic of the visible seam is a recurring staple in Black visual and cultural practices dating back centuries and also speaks directly to the development of hip hop fashion a generation after Burrows. His fluid sexy separates are iconic of the individualist, confident woman of the 1970s. He showcased the "Black is Beautiful" philosophy through his use of African American models and his success as an African American fashion designer. This chapter explores Burrows's lasting impact on the fashion industry and his innovative design aesthetic that arose during the late 1960s and 1970s. Although his career continued into the twenty-first century, this text focuses on his early career and establishes Burrows as a significant and influential American fashion designer.

Early Life and Career

Stephen Gerald Burrows was born on September 15, 1943, in Newark, New Jersey, to Gerald Burrows and Octavia Pennington and was raised by both his mother and grandmother. His family had roots in the New York City garment district, the fashion capital of the United States by the mid-twentieth century. Burrows was taught to sew at the age of eight by his maternal grandmother Beatrice, a nurse who had also worked as a sample hand for the upscale New York designer and retailer Hattie Carnegie.[1] His grandmother remarked, "He used to watch me sew. He made his first dress for the girl upstairs when he was nine years old!"[2] It was at this early age, using his grandmother's machine, that the designer became fascinated with the merrow finish—a dense zigzag stitch used to finish hems and the technique that later became his signature. Burrows studied at Newark's Arts High School, the first public high school in the United States specializing in the visual and performing arts. Nurtured by a mother who liked to color in bold combinations as a hobby and a father who made nightclub caricatures, he developed an early interest in art.[3] In the hopes of becoming an art teacher, Burrows went on to study at the Philadelphia Museum College of Art from 1961 to 1963.[4]

During the 1960s, Burrows and his friends frequented the Palladium, a Latin club in New York located on 52nd Street and Broadway. "We went there every Sunday. We loved to Mambo," Burrows told *The Fader* magazine.[5] Burrows sketched dresses for his Mambo partners, practicing his fashion illustration skills in colored pencil, ink, marker, and crayon before rendering his glamorized sketches into fabric.[6] During his second year at the College of Art, he decided to change his major because he no longer liked the idea of sketching someone else's designs. Burrows opted to take a year-long sabbatical and worked in the display department of Bamberger's department store. He earned enough money to attend the Fashion Institute of Technology in New York City, where he studied fashion design from 1964 to 1966.[7] Burrows's senior year internship with the blouse company, Weber Originals, turned into a permanent position, earning him a salary of $125 a week, which Burrows claimed, "was a fortune back then."[8]

The 1960s was a decade dominated by youth, as seventy million children from the post-war "baby boom" became young adults. Within this generation, social attitudes moved away from the conservative ethos of the 1950s, eventually resulting in revolutionary ways of thinking and real change in the cultural fabric of American life. These momentous shifts were especially prevalent within Manhattan's youth culture, which was very much a part of Burrows's life and his early work. He experimented with a multitude of textiles, techniques, and finishes, disregarding the established conventions accepted by the previous

Figure 10.1 A group of Stephen Burrows's friends wearing Pepperland clothes from the Burrows collection for Bendel's Studio. Charles Tracy/Condé Nast via Getty Images.

generation of fashion designers. In finding his own expression, his youthful fascination with sewing machine techniques again took hold. Burrows recalled that he hated to put folded and stitched hems on jersey dresses as a fashion design student because they weighed down the garments. Consequentially, he used zigzag stitching at the ends to keep the fabric from unraveling.[9] During this developmental period, Burrows designed garments for his close college friends: models, artists, and fellow designers. This small inner circle was nicknamed "The Commune." His private garment sales to his Commune friends were such a success, Burrows was able to quit his job at Weber Originals. In 1967 he began selling linen dresses to Outrageous and feather vests to Allen & Cole, immersing himself in the New York boutique scene as a freelance designer. Burrows's first *Vogue* credit appeared in the October 1968 issue, which displayed his sexy, body-revealing, fringed leathers crafted for Allen & Cole and modeled by Naomi Sims.[10]

Burrows's first retail venture "O Boutique" opened in 1968 at 36 Park Avenue South. O Boutique, named for the Chinese symbol for eternity, was a small downtown New York boutique that housed both artwork and fashion. Supported by fifty communal workers, a group of creative types—actors, artists, and other designers—all sold their designs at the avant-garde store. It was unusual at the time for designers to have their own shops where they could exclusively market their designs. The boutique attracted artists and celebrities who frequented Max's Kansas City, a nightclub and restaurant across the street. From that moment, Burrows's traffic-stopping, stylish window displays, prominently placed in the heart of the city's hotspots, attracted an influx of customers. The "O look" represented a contemporary way of dressing that incorporated ethnic details, suede patchwork in rainbow hues, leather fringe to the floor, and metal studs. O Boutique extended its scope in 1969 by opening a sub-boutique in the "S'fari Room" at Bonwit Teller department store in New York City. The success of O Boutique led to a continuation of increased exposure and an expanding clientele. Stephen Burrows World opened in 1968 at the exclusive Upper Eastside retailer Henri Bendel. The in-store boutique intertwined artistic design, ready-to-wear manufacture, professional fashion promotion, and profit. The chic shop was decorated with black walls, nailhead studs, and full-length mirrors to provide a backdrop to the introductory collection. This was an elevated extension of Burrows's unisex Commune looks, including Cabretta leather pieces, jersey jigsaw-puzzle dresses, and trousers and tunics in heavy jersey, patched cardigans, and suede. The clothes fit like a second skin, and they were flexible enough that conventional sizing could be ignored. Many of the items sold for around $100, equivalent to approximately $724 in 2020.

The Battle of Versailles

Burrows's career was forever immortalized in fashion history by an invitation to present his collection at one of the most significant runway shows that had occurred to date, *Grand Divertissement à Versailles*, held on November 28, 1973. Gerald Van der Kemp, then curator of the Château de Versailles, and American fashion industry matriarch Eleanor Lambert, founder of both the Coty American Fashion Critics' Awards and the Council of Fashion Designers of America, together created and organized what began as a charity event to restore the seventeenth-century Palace of Versailles outside of Paris. Public relations pioneer and the force behind the International Best-Dressed List, Lambert had put American fashion design on the international map at a time when Paris was considered the only relevant fashion city. She coordinated the bi-annual New York fashion week shows that continue to this day.[11] Lambert recruited her client Burrows, along with other American designers Bill Blass, Oscar de la Renta, Halston, and Anne Klein, to show their designs alongside the French couturiers Marc Bohan for Christian Dior, Pierre Cardin, Hubert de Givenchy, Yves Saint Laurent, and Emanuel Ungaro.[12]

Burrows's presentation followed Anne Klein's, and his designs, which included his now-famous lettuce hem finish, bright knit jerseys, Pop Art bodices, and long skirts with sweeping trains, brought down the house. "My whole theme was about a train. Each dress, the train got longer and longer and longer," said Burrows.[13] American models, including eleven Black models, swung across the stage to contemporary music, against a single backdrop, a black velvet curtain on which an abstract pattern by artist Joe Eula was displayed. It was one of the first events in which an African American designer and African American models took to the high fashion stage collectively.[14] The French design community had never seen anything like it. The presence of African American models animated the stage. The diversity of the American models represented a major reversal of fashion industry attitudes on Black women and the concept of Black beauty. The models, adorned in Burrows's flowing frocks and coiffed with "feather bones"—long, thin feather hair ornaments—moved with a dance-like quality that electrified the audience. The Versailles fundraiser became a platform to recognize and celebrate American ready-to-wear fashion.[15]

Continuing Success

Energized by his success both before and after what became known as "The Battle of Versailles," Burrows expanded his business, branching out to design a multitude of fashion products that placed equal emphasis on simplicity and sexiness. Stevies, a line of loungewear, featured a collection of nightgowns, robes, and pajamas, and was sold around the country at Henri Bendel, Lord & Taylor, Bonwit Teller, Bloomingdale's, Marshall Field, Sakowitz, and I. Magnin, among other retailers. Furrier Michael Forrest partnered with Burrows on a 1974 fur collection, resulting in amusing concepts such as an enormous, brightly colored poplin poncho, hooded and lined in fur; a fox evening coat, fringed with tails; and a 1920s style coat of raccoon, edged with fox fur dyed purple. Burrows added another facet to his formidable list of accomplishments that year by designing for the home sewer. McCall's pattern company introduced four exciting "Carefree Patterns," that reflected the designer's fashion outlook: that clothes should have a line of humor, lots of color, and move easily. Designed for lightweight, knit jersey fabrics that clung to the body, these patterns epitomized easy living and easy sewing. Two famous Burrows fashion signatures were incorporated into the McCall's patterns: bright red stitching with options for both zigzag and straight stitches and the curling lettuce hems, also stitched in red, capturing the essence of his fluid designs. Priced at $1.25 each, the patterns were available in Misses sizes 6 to 16, depending on the style.[16] With the 1975 launch of Stephen B. fragrance for Max Factor, Burrows became the first Black designer with an eponymous perfume. The text, "Here comes Stephen B. Alive. Laughing. Dancing. Fresh. And Sexy," appeared diagonally across a photograph of the designer with smiling women on either arm in a November 1975 *Ebony* advertisement. Max Factor's list of ingredients included jasmine, hyacinth, rose, citrus, spice, musk, and amber. The fragrance retailed at $40 for an ounce of the perfume and $4.75 for a one-ounce bottle of the intensified cologne spray.[17]

By 1973 Burrows was at the top of his field with a showroom located at 550 Seventh Avenue.[18] His talent and ingenuity were recognized by the American fashion industry, and he won many awards for his distinctive artistry and achievements as a fashion designer. Stephen Burrows, at the age of twenty-nine, was announced the winner of the 1973 Coty American Fashion Critics' Award. The star of the 31st Annual Coty Awards ceremony, Burrows was the first African American to be so honored by the industry.[19] Fluid and exotic matte jersey, clinging like a second skin, and bias-cut, lettuce-edged gowns, were displayed at the awards show on "the Burrows girls," as the designer's friends and models were often called. Fashion photographer and journalist Bill Cunningham equated the color impact with that of a Leon Bakst-designed ballet.[20] Burrows would go on to receive a special Coty Award for lingerie in 1974. The next year, he won both the Council of American Fashion Critics Award and the coveted Crystal Ball Award from the Knitted Textile Association (now known as the National Textile Association). He won the original Coty Award, called the "Winnie," for the second time in 1977 for his significant contributions in the women's wear category.

The Stephen Burrows Design Aesthetic

Stephen Burrows's designs betray his deep belief in the dressmaking art, while he simultaneously rejects both the high luxury tradition and the accepted techniques of mass production. Therefore, no two custom Stephen Burrows dresses are exactly alike. Burrows selected seven colors each season and used them in select combinations or all at once, creating a complete look, which included handmade accessories. Burrows's accessories, such as his popular over-the-shoulder bag, often became symbols of fashion-insider status all on their own. While most designers work to master a single trait, the signatures in Burrows's designs are multiple, drawn from his surrounding environment, and continually evolving the craft of fashion design. This chapter explores four design characteristics in which Burrows created innovative and influential signatures: silhouette, texture, color, and hem finishing. These characteristics connect Stephen Burrows's garments with his design process and a larger vocabulary of global design aesthetics, providing evidence that the "Burrows look" cannot only be clearly defined, but also continues to be duplicated by designers around the world.

Silhouette and Movement

It was during his time at the Fashion Institute of Technology that Burrows recognized his preference for designing and producing garments by draping fabric directly onto a dress form, finding it very relaxing.[21] His approach to the cut of clothing and modern silhouettes put him at the forefront of fashion and style during the late 1960s and 1970s. His clothing skimmed the body, enhancing the curves and flow of the bodyline with rhythmic movement. This emphasis on the body through silhouette, enhanced by seam work, reflected freer social attitudes around both male and female bodies and the increasingly important idea of the freedom of youth. Movement and simplicity were of primary concern throughout his design process. "I like sweater clothes that pull on, move easy and have nothing but useful fastenings like industrial zippers and raincoat snaps, no buttons or little zippers," Burrows explained.[22] The

Figure 10.2 Stephen Burrows, yellow, blue, pink, lavender, and off-white rayon evening dress, circa 1973. Gift of Mary W. Delany. © The Museum at FIT.

clothes needed to look good in motion and facilitate the movement of the body beneath the garment. Early in his career, Burrows designed with his Mambo dance partners and Studio 54 club-goers in mind. Gradually, his designs began to cater to a new archetype, the independent woman on the go, accommodating her active daily lifestyle.

With the use of finely knitted stretch fabrics such as rayon jersey, Burrows crafted a close fit and slim silhouette, often described as slithery and slinky. He stated, "A woman should appreciate her femininity and use it to constantly experiment with herself."[23] With this design philosophy, Burrows chose to create styles sized only for slim figures, in line with the attitudes of many high fashion designers of the period, "I don't believe in designing above a size 12," he stated, and his size 12 did not usually fit anyone above a size 10.[24] Burrows's exciting designs, however, were much coveted because they stood out, "I consider what I do the new haute couture," he said, "No one wants standardized clothes, but clothes with strong simple lines and humor. The most important thing is to have fun with your clothes, be calm in your cut, and exaggerate in details here and there."[25] Aligned with articulated movement, Burrows always had an appreciation for and nuanced understanding of fabric and texture, both major influences on his silhouettes.

Fabric and Texture

Fabric selections for each design season consisted of a vast variety of combinations inspired by the contrasting grit of New York City streets and the glitz of the city's nightlife. Mixed media conjured the mood of the moment; this evocation was carried throughout Burrows's brand image. The "Vogue's Own Boutique" column featured an article entitled, "A Head of Hair" in February 1969 that solidified Burrows as "one of the first to design any-sex, completely modern, clothes."[26] Featuring his eclectic mix of looks available at O Boutique, the same column in the April 15, 1969 issue depicted both men and women in multiple Burrows looks including herringbone tweeds, a cobra-hooded wool jersey tunic with strips of snakeskin, and a suede weskit with bands of cobra.[27] The emerging counterculture of the late 1960s broke all of high fashion's previously established rules, embracing a more folk- and internationally inspired iteration of handcrafting, hand-dyeing, and surface embellishment. This energy carried over to the designs for the Henri Bendel boutique, Stephen Burrows World, firmly placing the new aesthetic within the high fashion realm.

The January 1, 1970 "Vogue's Own Boutique" column described Burrows as "one of the most interesting leather designers anywhere," and his featured skirt consisted of fringes, patches of animal patterned leather, and multicolored suede.[28] For his spring 1971 collection, the spotlight was on his deft cutting skills, exemplified by a new version of the shawl comprised of white leather with cut-outs to resemble a giant spider's web.[29] He also created a technique of cutting bias suede strips and stitching them together for an effect that resembled the inside of a fur coat. This technique was also used for T-shirts worn with the designer's wide-leg trousers, which he designed two years before the rest of the fashion world caught onto the trend. Elements— such as the use of leather and suede in combination with heavily textured fabric such as tweed—put together with seemingly simple construction methods, created a classic rather than trendy quality in his garments. His debut collection at Stephen Burrows World featured vivid matte jersey color blocking and tightly fitted studded leather, directly reflecting his East Village boutique sensibility. Working with matte jersey—a fabric that had been previously used almost exclusively for lingerie—distinguished him as a hands-on designer, as slinky jersey fabric is notoriously difficult to work with. Unfortunately, his obsession with jersey also worked to his detriment. "Stephen knew that his dresses, like sweaters, had to be folded. But in department stores they had to be hung," said former model and creative director Bethann Hardison, "but matte jersey doesn't live well hanging on a hanger. It starts to shrink in and grow long. So if it arrived as a 4, 6, or 8, after a while it wouldn't fit. All you have to have is a store telling you your clothes don't fit. Forget it. Stephen knew that would happen, but he couldn't convince the department stores."[30]

Burrows's atelier looks evolved over time into flowing sensual garments. He simplified his approach and featured linear, monochromatic designs, more explicitly sensual womenswear, and lighter fabrics, notably chiffon. "His chiffons are still the most innovative around," said Robert Sakowitz, then president of the Texas specialty chain Sakowitz's, who praised the clothes for being more wearable than previous styles, yet highly innovative.[31] Fearless, Burrows explored silk crêpe separates, velvet eveningwear, and nylon and Lycra fabrics, seen in his second-skin swimsuit designs. Burrows also experimented with fun, bright, multicolored prints on dresses, as well as separates and accessories. The high-spirited, sweetly campy motifs were often hand-painted by Peter Fasano, who was adept at interpreting the effervescent fervor of the Burrows brand.[32]

Figure 10.3 Stephen Burrows, multicolor leather and knit jacket, fall 1970. Gift of Stephen Burrows. © The Museum at FIT.

Figure 10.4 Stephen Burrows, color-blocked, two-piece polyester chiffon evening dress, 1973–1974. Gift of Mrs. Savanna Clark. © The Museum at FIT.

Color Blocking and Color Combinations

Stimulated by Pop Art's graphic boldness, Burrows had an absolute disregard for the established laws of color. His designs were a combination of purposeful plays on color combinations, and the cut and piecing together of patterns was more artfully abstract than practical. *Vogue* captured the designer at his Stephen Burrows World boutique where he was photographed helping the singer Cher into his rainbow-colored jersey jumpsuit of green, yellow, and black, as well as a zip-front coat of yellow, green, red, and orange against black.[33] "The girl he designs for is young, daring, eager to experiment, and individual,"[34] noted fashion critic, Anne-Marie Schiro. Bernadine Morris concurred on Burrows's exuberant and playful colors, "Does a dress have a red top? He'll make the sleeves lime, the middle peach—and he'll add orange stockings for good measure. The strangest thing is, it works."[35] Every garment was truly artistic, lively, and unique.

"Stephen Burrows is in Pepperland: He must be—look at the way he understands colour—the way he puts together all the happy palette of the rainbow—hue-ing it and shaping it into totally contemporary clothes … what a wonderful designer Stephen Burrows is."[36] This *Vogue* column headline painted the mood of the time and captured the amusement that Burrows's garments evoked. When asked about the inspiration for his collections, Burrows said,

> I concentrate on things that are part of the body. The colors of course were bright and highly saturated strong colors. I had a tendency to gravitate toward bright, strong colors. I didn't care if they went together or not, but I would put them together. It didn't matter to me; I just wanted this color with this color and people found it exciting. I just did what I wanted to do.[37]

The use of intense colors in unexpected combinations suggests the surreal, and the vivid qualities of Burrows's designs make them a continuing presence in contemporary fashion. Sociologically, Burrows captured a moment. His colors were bright to the point of assault. He heightened and popularized a fashion trend that still resonates, brilliantly colored, close-fitting dresses and pants put together like mosaics from patches of fabric or leather. Golden yellow, mossy green, tangerine orange, hot pink, deep purple, and metallic colors were combined with leather, suede, and knit fabrics. To these, he added his own invention: body-hugging jersey dresses with rippling hems of uneven length.[38]

Figure 10.5 *Glamour* 1970: Model wearing black midi dress with sleeves of different colors and a band of color at the hem under a vest, both by Stephen Burrows. Photo by J. P. Zachariasen/Condé Nast via Getty Images.

Hemlines and Stitching

Burrows's hemlines were ingenious and playful; quite unique. His clothes caught the chaos of the disco years; his lines were never quite clean or orderly. Referred to as "Inside out chicness" by *New York Magazine*, his looks, dresses, and skirts in particular, varied in length and were comprised of uneven hemlines.[39] Even the necklines on his sequin halters billowed and sloped.[40] Burrows created a unique lettuce hem, a finishing method in which a zigzag stitch is sewn over a stretch fabric that is pulled taut, resulting in the fabric curling. The effect is a garment with a flirtatiously undulating hemline. Although Burrows acknowledged that the hem style was his single greatest achievement, he remarked that, "Lettucing was a mistake … but I liked the way it looked."[41] Diana Vreeland, then editor-in-chief of *Vogue*, reportedly asked for one of Burrows's garments in "lettuce green." He pulled the green-colored fabric as he sewed creating a rippled lettuce leaf effect that turned into one of the designer's greatest mistakes.[42] "The material he selected is something you have to be engaged by. You have to handle the material. A lettuce hem, if you just sent it through the machine, it wouldn't do that," said Harold Koda, chief curator of the Costume Institute at the Metropolitan Museum of Art. "It requires the intervention of a person."[43]

A confident customer was essential to Burrows, who stated in 1977, "My customer has to know who she is. Or else she's going to put my things on and say, 'I can't wear this! Everything's showing!' My customer wants to show it."[44] Everything about his design is daring and bold, even the threading of his garments is vibrant. He used red thread to stitch along the hemline regardless of the garment's hue. "Red is like the blood vessels," explained Burrows, "It shows you're a hard and fit worker."[45] Burrows's influence is felt in many examples of late twentieth and early twenty-first-century fashion design, both high and low, in which visible, contrasting thread is shown and enhanced by a fancy stitch such as a zigzag. The way Burrows turned the details of his design—the silhouette, fabric, color, and stitching—into signatures helped distinguish his work, kept it recognizable, and visually portrayed his philosophy, which contributed to his brand image. These four characteristics illustrate not only Burrows's design sense but also portray how his strong and consistent viewpoint bolstered his brand. Burrows worked within, and developed, a framework that was based on his own beliefs about the purpose of clothing. Throughout his career, he expressed strong ideas about the practicality of clothing. Burrows emerged onto the New York fashion scene during the late 1960s as an original; his cut was clean, strong, and masterly. His use of color was bold, daring, and skillful. His eye for detail was impeccable. The results were clothes that became contemporary classics, reflecting the changes of each season and year, but always with a clear Stephen Burrows identity.[46] Yet these characteristics were not formed in a vacuum. Burrows's aesthetics draw from a long lineage.

A Black Thread

From the seventeenth century, Africans were transported to the United States with generations of knowledge regarding the cultivation of textile and dye materials and textile production. For many years, researchers have documented the links between African American cultural aesthetics and those of West African peoples. Africa's multiregional, multiethnic traditions of adornment generally encompass ideas about self and community expression and spirituality. Textiles were and continue to be integral parts of various African cultures.[47] The use of large shapes and strong contrasting colors are related to the communicative function of African fabrics. Historians Jacqueline Tobin and Raymond Dobard note, for example, that historically in West Africa it was important for tribes to recognize patterns from a distance.[48] Stephen Burrows's patterns, which were similarly used in his fabrications, communicated the aesthetics of a new American generation. He drew inspiration, not just from the "ethnic" or the "exotic" influences that were popularly mined by Western fashion designers during the 1960s and 1970s, but also from simple forms enriched with color and texture. The innate boldness and contrasts in his designs connect him to the larger African Diaspora, as well as African American communities during the late 1960s and 1970s.

While the Civil Rights Movement had a political and social foundation, it also prompted a change in the social behavior and bodily appearance of African Americans. New attitudes that embraced the beauty of Black people and culture were embodied in attention-grabbing clothes that pushed for and celebrated Black visibility in American society. Additionally, some African American designers such as Burrows were able to benefit from the political and social ground gained by activists of the 1950s that resulted in increasing acceptance of Black professionals in many fields, including fashion. Taking this opportunity, Burrows helped to illustrate the need to rethink what had been previously defined by mainstream fashion, showing how clothing reflected a culture, as well as its power to connect multiple social worlds. Burrows's work often challenged the dichotomies of conventional fashion. His work flirted with boundaries between elegant and rugged, raw and sophisticated. There was a kind of oppositional aesthetic operating within his designs that may or may not be related to his diasporic heritage.

While Burrows's unisex designs and work in leather and metal embellishment anticipated two dominant fashion trends of the seventies, androgyny, and punk,[49] his use of the visible seam spoke directly to the development of hip hop fashion a generation later. The visible seam is a recurring "stitch" in Black visual and cultural practices with roots in West Africa. For example, the rich history of African American quilting, a practice that regularly incorporates the exposed seam, relies on West and Central African design aesthetics that were often read as mistakes to the untrained eye. These colorful and bold design irregularities came from purposeful and long-rooted cultural aesthetics in West African music, art, and dance, and were used in antebellum America as secret communicative tools between enslaved people.[50]

The use of strips of fabric, a common construction technique in Burrows's work, as well as in nineteenth- and twentieth-century African American quilts, is also a significant and symbolic construction technique and design element in West African textiles. Throughout West Africa, the narrow strip design is an identifier of one's prestige and social status as the narrower the strip, the greater the skill, the higher the price, and, therefore, the more esteem to the man or woman wearing it.[51] Yoruba *aso oke*, or high status cloths, made up of more than one strip pattern were once quite common, and this type of African textile can be directly traced to African American strip quilts.[52] The first element of West African textile artistry is breaking up an otherwise plain surface, highlighting ornamentation, and also the contrast between plain and multicolored backgrounds. The second element of this aesthetic involves the manipulation of the cloth texture to enhance movement, and the third is revealed in reworking traditional forms. Cloth serves its social purposes, not just in ceremonial and ritual occasions but also as an expression of one's ideas.[53] All of these elements can be traced to African American textile traditions and are especially present in Stephen Burrows's design practice.

Burrows carried these aesthetics and practices into twentieth-century fashion through several elements, especially the visible seam, a technique and a look that resurfaced in hip hop clothing during the 1990s in the designs of Cross Colours, Karl Kani, and FUBU (For Us By Us). These apparel lines were also known for asymmetrical contours and patterns. Much of their clothing incorporated bold or contrasting stitch work on pants pockets, sweaters, shirts, and jackets.[54] As music served as a dominant influence on the development of fashion trends, it was only a matter of time before the fashion industry recognized and co-opted the style of hip hop culture. FUBU was a brand that consciously attempted to raise awareness and support of Black-owned businesses. Designer Karl Kani (born Carl Williams) found inspiration in his urban, youth culture roots much like Burrows did during the 1960s.

Conclusion

As a master cutter of fabric, Stephen Burrows was at his best creating his designs on a limited scale. He expanded into a larger manufacturing business, but after three short years, the Seventh Avenue venture ended in 1976. "I thought I wanted to dress everyone," Burrows reflected, "It took a while to realize that that wasn't for me."[55] "Seventh Avenue was a disaster," he continued, "No one knew how to make knit clothes. They considered it lingerie. Seventh Avenue considered it cheap."[56] After running his own company from 1970 to 1982, Burrows left the fashion business, though he continually resurfaced and relaunched collections into the twenty-first century. In 2002, Burrows was inducted into the Fashion

Figure 10.6 Nine models all wearing Stephen Burrows clothes and holding umbrellas, lifting the designer over their heads. Photo by Oliviero Toscani/Condé Nast via Getty Images.

Walk of Fame. With his own plaque embedded into the very groundwork of New York's historic fashion district, he brought his family's garment district heritage full circle. In 2006, at the same time that he celebrated forty years as a designer, Burrows received The Board of Directors Special Tribute from the Council of Fashion Designers of America. Burrows's legacy, however, is impactful beyond awards. His fashions were praised as expressing the Black experience: an innate gaiety, exuberance, and joy in dressing up. Yet his clothes also crossed color lines and were appreciated by a mainstream fashion audience. Burrows was one of the first Black designers to reach the level of visibility and success that he achieved in the mainstream fashion industry, and he undoubtedly helped pave the way for other Black people in the fashion field. Not only hip hop designers such as Karl Kani, but also later designers such as Patrick Kelly, Tracy Reese, and Patrick Robinson, walk in his footprints. Burrows was also important in creating the American sportswear tradition that defined contemporary fashion during the 1970s and does so into the present. As for how he sees his role in the fashion world, he said, "The essence of Stephen Burrows: be happy when you're in the clothes and have fun with what you're wearing."[57] Enormously successful during the 1970s, Burrows has come and gone and come again, but his design sensibility has been consistent. He stretches a rainbow over the body. His rainbow is extraordinary and unexpected, juxtaposing the deepest hues.

Notes

1   "Fashion Designer Stephen Burrows (interview by *Star-Ledger*)," video file, 1:18, YouTube, posted by *NJ.com*, February 5, 2007, http://www.youtube.com/watch?v=uys2IrQEZbI.

2   Marian Christy, "Burrows Makes a Splash," *Boston Globe*, November 16, 1971, 23.

3   Joan Cook, "When the Dress is the Label," *The New York Times*, October 7, 1973, 118.

4   "Fashion Designer Stephen Burrows (interview by *Star-Ledger*)."

5   Alex Frank, "Stephen Burrows: The Dancing Designer," *The Fader*, April 25, 2013, accessed February 18, 2020. https://www.thefader.com/2013/04/25/stephen-burrows-the-dancing-designer.

6   "Vogue's Own Boutique of Suggestions, Finds, and Observations: Mambo," *Vogue*, May 1, 1971,191.

7   Cook, "When the Dress is the Label," 118.

8   Rosemary Feitelberg, "Stephen Burrows Reminisces in Rhythm," *Women's Wear Daily*, March 20, 2013, 12.

9   Bernadine Morris and Barbara Walz, *The Fashion Makers* (New York: Random House, 1978), 52–3.

10 "Vogue's Own Boutique of Suggestions, Finds, and Observations: Indian Summer," *Vogue*, October 1, 1968, 248.

11 Enid Nemy, "Eleanor Lambert, Empress of Fashion, Dies at 100," *The New York Times*, October 8, 2003, accessed February 18, 2020. https://www.nytimes.com/2003/10/08/nyregion/eleanor-lambert-empress-of-fashion-dies-at-100.html.

12 *Versailles '73: American Runway Revolution*, directed by Deborah Riley Draper (Versailles '73: American Runway Revolution Films, 2012), DVD.

13 Ibid.

14 Eugenia Sheppard, "Yanks Pull Off Fashion Heist in Paris," *Los Angeles Times*, December 2, 1973, D1.

15 *Versailles '73: American Runway Revolution*.

16 "Award Winner Burrows Designs for Homesewer," *Atlanta Daily World*, April 9, 1974, 3.

17 Walter Jackson, "New Fragrances—Five to Know About Now," *Harper's Bazaar*, October 1975, 42

18 Cook, "When the Dress is the Label," 118.

19 Nina S. Hyde, "'Winnies': Plaudits for the Designers," *The Washington Post*, October 18, 1973, B3.

20 Bill Cunningham, "Seventh Ave. Swells Attend Coty Fashion Critics' Awards," *Los Angeles Times*, October 29, 1973, C6.

21 Todd Plummer, "Stephen Burrows Reflects on the Past and Present," *Style* (blog), May 19, 2014, accessed April 15, 2015. http://www.style.com/trends/industry/2014/stephen-burrows-reflects-past-present.

22 Plummer, "Stephen Burrows Reflects on the Past and Present," access online at http://www.style.com/trends/industry/2014/stephen-burrows-reflects-past-present.

23 Betty Ommerman, "Putting Bits and Pieces Together," *Newsday*, August 28, 1972, 12A.

24 "Capturing the Coty," *Newsday*, June 28, 1973, 1A.

25 "Young Designer Puts Zest into His New Designs," *Chicago Daily Defender*, December 1, 1971, 19.

26 "Vogue's Own Boutique of Suggestions, Finds, and Observations: A Head of Hair," *Vogue*, February 15, 1969, 144.

27 "Vogue's Own Boutique of Suggestions, Finds, and Observations: We Love This Park," *Vogue*, April 15, 1969, 126–7.

28 "Vogue's Own Boutique of Suggestions, Finds, and Observations: Rome/New York/London," *Vogue*, January 1, 1970, 173.

29 Bill Cunningham, [no title], *Chicago Tribune*, December 27, 1971, B2.

30 Robin Givhan, "Déjà vu: Stephen Burrows Woos Seventh Avenue–Again," *The Washington Post*, August 1, 2005, C01.

31 Nina S. Hyde, "Back to Basic Burrows," *The Washington Post*, May 2, 1977, B3.

32 "Table Wear," *New York Magazine*, January 10, 1977, 66.

33 "Vogue's Own Boutique of Suggestions, Finds, and Observations: The Blue-jean Look," *Vogue*, October 1, 1970, 203.

34 Anne-Marie Schiro, "For the Young and the Daring," *The New York Times*, September 20, 1970, 268.

35 Bernadine Morris, "The Look of Fashions for the Seventies in Colors That Dazzle," *The New York Times*, August 12, 1970, 44.

36 "Vogue's Own Boutique of Suggestions, Finds, and Observations: Stephen Burrows is in Pepperland," *Vogue*, August 1, 1970, 138–9.

37 "Interview with Stephen Burrows," *SJ Chronicle* (blog), June 28, 2013, http://sjchronicle.com/2013/06/28/interview-with-stephen-burrows/.

38 Chelsea Zalopany, "André Leon Talley Honors Stephen Burrows at SCAD," *Vogue*, May 19, 2014, accessed February 18, 2020. https://www.vogue.com/article/andre-leon-talle-stephen-burrows-exhibition-scad.

39 "The Bendel," *New York Magazine*, March 5, 1973, 58.

40 Nicole R. Fleetwood, *Troubling Vision: Performance, Visuality, and Blackness* (Chicago: University of Chicago Press, 2011), 157–8.

41 Plummer, "Stephen Burrows Reflects on the Past and Present," access online at http://www.style.com/trends/industry/2014/stephen-burrows-reflects-past-present.

42 Ibid.

43 *Versailles '73: American Runway Revolution*.

44 Jean Butler, "Fashion," *The New York Times Magazine*, June 5, 1977, 89.

45 Ommerman, "Putting Bits and Pieces Together," 12A

46 "Fashionscope '77," *Afro-American*, October 22, 1977 A1.

47 Philip M. Peek and Kwesi Yankah, *African Folklore* (New York: Routledge, 2004), 27.

48 Jacqueline Tobin and Raymond G. Dobard, *Hidden in Plain View: The Secret Story of Quilts and the Underground Railroad* (New York: Doubleday, 1999), 42.

49 Valerie Steele, *Fifty Years of Fashion: New Look to Now* (New Haven: Yale University Press, 2000), 91.

50 Eli Leon, *Accidentally on Purpose: The Aesthetic Management of Irregularities in African Textiles and African-American Quilts* (Davenport, Iowa: Figge Art Museum, 2006), 45.

51 Bernhard Gardi, Kerstin Bauer, and Rogier Michiel Alphons Bedaux, *Woven Beauty: The Art of West African Textiles* (Basel: Museum der Kulturen, 2009), 56.

52 John Picton, *The Art of African Textiles: Technology, Tradition, and Lurex* (London: Barbican Art Gallery, Lund Humphries Publishers, 1995), 14; Gardi, Bauer, and Bedaux, *Woven Beauty*, 122.

53 Gardi, Bauer, and Bedaux, *Woven Beauty*, 17–18.

54 Fleetwood, *Troubling* Vision, 157–8.

55 Morris and Walz, *The Fashion Makers*, 52–3

56 Ibid..

57 Rosemary Feitelberg, "Stephen Burrows Reminisces in Rhythm," *Women's Wear Daily*, March 20, 2013, 12.

Bibliography

"Award Winner Burrows Designs for Homesewer." *Atlanta Daily World*, April 9, 1974, 3.

"The Bendel." *New York Magazine*, March 5, 1973, 58.

Butler, Jean "Fashion." *The New York Times Magazine*, June 5, 1977, 72–3, 86–9.

"Capturing the Coty." *Newsday*, June 28, 1973, 1A.

Christy, Marian. "Burrows Makes a Splash." *Boston Globe*, November 16, 1971, 23.

Cook, Joan. "When the Dress is the Label." *The New York Times*, October 7, 1973, 118.

Cunningham, Bill. No title. *Chicago Tribune*, December 27, 1971, B1–2.

Cunningham, Bill. "Seventh Ave. Swells Attend Coty Fashion Critics' Awards."
    Los Angeles Times, October 29, 1973, C6.

"Fashion Designer Stephen Burrows (interview by *Star-Ledger*)." Video file, 01:18,
    YouTube. Posted by *NJ.com*, February 5, 2007. http://www.youtube.com/
    watch?v=uys2IrQEZbI.

"Fashionscope '77." *Afro-American*, October 22, 1977, A1.

Feitelberg, Rosemary. "Stephen Burrows Reminisces in Rhythm." *Women's Wear Daily*,
    March 20, 2013, 12.

Fleetwood, Nicole R. *Troubling Vision: Performance, Visuality, and Blackness*. Chicago:
    University of Chicago Press, 2011.

Frank, Alex. "Stephen Burrows: The Dancing Designer." *The Fader*, April 25, 2013,
    accessed February 18, 2020. https://www.thefader.com/2013/04/25/stephen-
    burrows-the-dancing-designer.

Gardi, Bernhard Kerstin Bauer, and Rogier Michiel Alphons Bedaux, *Woven Beauty:
    The Art of West African Textiles*. Basel: Museum der Kulturen, 2009.

Givhan, Robin. "Déjà vu: Stephen Burrows Woos Seventh Avenue–Again." *The
    Washington Post*, August 1, 2005, accessed November 27, 2020. https://www.
    washingtonpost.com/archive/lifestyle/2005/08/01/deja-vu/11437396-026d-497f-
    a589-a64a64a00673/.

Hyde, Nina S. "Back to Basic Burrows." *The Washington Post*, May 2, 1977, B3.

Hyde, Nina S. "'Winnies': Plaudits for the Designers." *The Washington Post*, October 18,
    1973, B3.

"Interview with Stephen Burrows." *SJ Chronicle* (blog), June 28, 2013, accessed February
    18, 2020. http://sjchronicle.com/2013/06/28/interview-with-stephen-burrows/.

Jackson, Walter. "New Fragrances—Five to Know About Now." *Harper's Bazaar*,
    October 1975.

Leon, Eli. *Accidentally on Purpose: The Aesthetic Management of Irregularities in African
    Textiles and African-American Quilts*. Davenport, Iowa: Figge Art Museum, 2006.

Morris, Bernadine. "The Look of Fashions for the Seventies in Colors That Dazzle." *The
    New York Times*, August 12, 1970, 44.

Morris, Bernadine and Barbara Walz. *The Fashion Makers*. New York: Random House,
    1978.

Nemy, Enid. "Eleanor Lambert, Empress of Fashion, Dies at 100." *The New York Times*, October 8, 2003, accessed February 18, 2020. https://www.nytimes.com/2003/10/08/nyregion/eleanor-lambert-empress-of-fashion-dies-at-100.html.

Ommerman, Betty. "Putting Bits and Pieces Together." *Newsday*, August 28, 1972, 12A.

Peek, Philip M. and Kwesi Yankah, *African Folklore*. New York: Routledge, 2004.

Picton, John. *The Art of African Textiles: Technology, Tradition, and Lurex*. London: Barbican Art Gallery, Lund Humphries Publishers, 1995.

Plummer, Todd. "Stephen Burrows Reflects on the Past and Present." *Style* (blog), May 19, 2014, accessed April 15, 2015. http://www.style.com/trends/industry/2014/stephen-burrows-reflects-past-present.

Schiro, Anne-Marie. "For the Young and the Daring." *The New York Times*, September 20, 1970, 268.

Sheppard, Eugenia. "Yanks Pull Off Fashion Heist in Paris." *Los Angeles Times*, December 2, 1973, D1.

Steele, Valerie. *Fifty Years of Fashion: New Look to Now*. New Haven: Yale University Press, 2000.

"Table Wear." *New York Magazine*, January 10, 1977, 66.

Tobin, Jacqueline and Raymond G. Dobard. *Hidden in Plain View: The Secret Story of Quilts and the Underground Railroad*, New York: Doubleday, 1999.

Versailles '73: American Runway Revolution. Directed by Deborah Riley Draper. Versailles '73: American Runway Revolution Films, 2012. DVD.

"Vogue's Own Boutique of Suggestions, Finds, and Observations: A Head of Hair." *Vogue*, February 15, 1969, 142–6.

"Vogue's Own Boutique of Suggestions, Finds, and Observations: The Blue-jean Look." Vogue, October 1, 1970, 200–4.

"Vogue's Own Boutique of Suggestions, Finds, and Observations: Indian Summer." *Vogue*, October 1, 1968, 248–50.

"Vogue's Own Boutique of Suggestions Finds and Observations: Mambo." *Vogue*, May 1, 1971, 190–2.

"Vogue's Own Boutique of Suggestions, Finds, and Observations: Rome/New York/London." *Vogue*, January 1, 1970, 172–6.

"Vogue's Own Boutique of Suggestions, Finds, and Observations: Stephen Burrows is in Pepperland." *Vogue*, August 1, 1970, 138–42.

"Vogue's Own Boutique of Suggestions, Finds, and Observations: We Love This Park." *Vogue*, April 15, 1969, 126–30.

"Young Designer Puts Zest into His New Designs." *Chicago Daily Defender*, December 1, 1971.

Zalopany, Chelsea. "André Leon Talley Honors Stephen Burrows at SCAD." *Vogue*, May 19, 2014, 19, accessed February 18, 2020. https://www.vogue.com/article/andre-leon-talle-stephen-burrows-exhibition-scad.

11

Scott Barrie: Designing 1970s New York

Elizabeth Way

"We're 'in' now and the only thing to do is stay there."[1] When Scott Barrie was interviewed in 1973 by *Women's Wear Daily* (*WWD*), the American fashion industry's most widely read trade paper, he observed, "The gap between black and white designers is beginning to close."[2] Barrie and other Black fashion insiders would often express such positive outlooks for the future of African American designers in the New York fashion industry during the 1970s, and judging by Barrie's position—the co-owner and head designer of his own label— he had reason to be optimistic. The 1970s was a groundbreaking decade for Black American fashion. Barrie was among a group of designers, including Stephen Burrows and Willi Smith, who had been able to build on the overwhelmingly anonymous work of Black fashion makers of previous decades to become known names on Seventh Avenue.

Barrie was crucial in creating the new American look of the 1970s. If American fashion was characterized as practical and sporty during the 1940s and 1950s, it had taken a decidedly sexy and glamorous turn by the late 1960s. Barrie's sophisticated aesthetic evolved over the decade, but he was most known for soft, unstructured, draped silhouettes, executed with precise technical skill in difficult fabrics such as silk jersey and chiffon. This style helped define the look of American fashion at this time, differentiating it from the established authority of Parisian haute couture. From the late 1960s through the 1970s, Barrie's designs regularly appeared in *WWD*, *Vogue*, and *The New York Times* in editorials, reviews, and department store advertisements. His clothes also lent a contemporary fashionability to advertisements for products such as Revlon makeup and Virginia Slims cigarettes. He dressed celebrities and costumed actors and musicians, and was a minor celebrity in his own right, well established in the New York nightlife scene and appearing in televised interviews. Scott Barrie became a respected representative of the fashion industry, lending his opinions to reporters seeking knowledge on upcoming fads or business trends.

Figure 11.1 Scott Barrie, 1973. *Denver Post*. Denver Post via Getty Images.

Yet by the turn of the twenty-first century, Barrie was largely forgotten as a significant and influential fashion designer of the 1970s.

Early Career

Few details of Barrie's early life were published during his lifetime, and those that did appear reinforced a persona that Barrie seemed to carefully and self-consciously construct. He was candidly aware of the image of the creative and artistic fashion designer that lived in the popular imagination. As one of the few prominent Black designers, he had no intention of disappointing expectations. Yet his showmanship, evident in his carefully composed portraits and his oft-referenced Art Deco style townhouse, contended with his experiences as a hard-working designer in a mercurial industry. In June 1974 Barrie was more than a decade into his professional career. His success was confirmed by his recently purchased Manhattan home, his nomination for a Coty Award (Seventh Avenue's highest honor), and a dedicated feature by reporter Ki Hackney for *WWD*. Barrie begins the interview by disappearing into his bathroom to "finish his 'morning face,'" and tells Hackney that his planned ensemble was waylaid at the dry cleaner,

> I pictured myself lounging in white and beige for these photographs ... I wanted
> to try to live up to some kind of image people have of a designer living the life
> of glamor. People really think that's all we do ... They don't know about working
> 'till 3 in the morning and putting collections together over and over again.[3]

In this scene, choreographed for Hackney, Barrie's white jacket—his own prototype for a future men's line—is finally delivered and he "assumes his glamour image."[4] During this interview Barrie winks at the audience—mostly other New York industry professionals—and Hackney happily plays along, writing, "Glamor has been a part of Barrie's life since childhood in Philadelphia,"[5] where his grandmother and godmother worked as dressmakers to Black celebrities such as Della Reese, Sarah Vaughn, and Dinah Washington. Yet any reader familiar with working in the New York fashion industry, or even vaguely cognizant of American racial politics, was certainly aware that the life of an entrepreneurial designer and a Black man in mid-century America would be more complex.

Scott Barrie was born Nelson Clyde Barr in Apalachicola, Florida, in 1946. He grew up in Philadelphia where his family "indoctrinated [him] into the business of clothes."[6] He recalled he "practically grew up" under his grandmother's sewing machine, and "Naturally, by instinct you pick up the basics very early on."[7] His sister Christine Walker later remembered his early interest and talent in design, sketching "very futuristic drawings" from six years old and beginning to sew at age ten.[8] Barrie supplemented these basics with a more formal design education at the Philadelphia Museum College of Art—he later attributed his understanding of the body to his study of art and life drawing classes.[9] In 1962 he moved to New York where he attended the Mayer School of Fashion. Barrie noted that he apprenticed with Arthur McGee, but he soon struck out on his own. He ran his first business out of his apartment, cutting and sewing jersey dresses, while supporting himself with various fashion jobs.

From the beginning of his career, Barrie was aware of the designer image he wanted to project and the power of marketing himself. His first job as a designer was at the Allen & Cole boutique, and it coincided with one of his earliest appearances in the fashion press. He made a cameo in an August 1965 cover story in *WWD* about a young socialite shopper at Allen & Cole, which was described as, "an off-the-beaten-track boutique Marisa Berenson has told her about."[10] Barrie, the designer of the socialite's custom, bell-bottom and over-blouse ensemble, was late for a fitting and delivered the wrong top. However, the design proved a hit, and Barrie, only about twenty years old, was already positioning himself as a designer of young, sexy clothes. The socialite commented, "I love the color and the way the pants sit on the hip," adding that she wore them "wherever I can get away with them for dinner."[11] At a transitional period in fashion when trousers on women in public was far from the norm, Barrie was designing cutting-edge clothes for young, stylish women seeking modernity and ease and selling to ultra-fashionable, upscale retailers. Barrie designed a similar silhouette in the form of a white, cotton lace jumpsuit pictured in *Vogue* two months earlier. He was credited as the designer of the made-to-order ensemble, available at the Nancy Reals Boutique located at 110 East Fifty-fifth Street.[12]

Barrie's work in the mid-sixties was youth-oriented, fresh, and in line with the most creative fashion being presented in New York and Paris. Haute couturier André Courrèges, for example, had shown lace evening trousers for spring 1964. However, when Barrie began to sell under his own label, he experimented with new fabrics and the slinkier, body-conscious styles for which he, and the decade of the 1970s, would later be known. A July 1966 *WWD* article reported that Barrie "and his partner are in the process of designing, making, and selling their first collection" under the name Windham Couture, run out of Barrie's "airy second floor apartment with a workroom in back."[13] The article stated that this was Barrie's first time working with his soon-to-be signature fabric, matte jersey, and cited the renowned couturier Madame Grès as his inspiration. One of the illustrated designs featured in the article was a draped, bifurcated "harem dress," inspired by a traditional ensemble he had seen on the Indonesian delegate to the United Nations. Barrie commented, "Why not? … I am going to do things which you haven't seen before."[14]

Both this and the August 1965 *WWD* article created a romantic picture of a youthful and eager designer, one who was resourceful, talented, and undeniably on the pulse of fashion's next phase. Also notable was that neither article mentioned that Barrie was Black. By the mid-1970s the concurrent success of a group of Black designers would create a "trend" on which the fashion and mainstream press would frequently remark. The 1970s was a tumultuous and contradictory period. After the height of the Civil Rights Movement, Black Americans were still largely segregated in practice. African Americans were routinely denied housing, educational, and economic opportunities, a situation exacerbated by the economic recession. Yet Black people, actors, singers, sports stars, and politicians, were more visible than ever in American society. This visibility was crucial in normalizing the presence of Black professionals in every industry. Barrie's celebrated label, sold all over the country, and his precisely crafted press coverage helped make Black designers more accepted in the fashion industry and Blackness in general more acceptable in mainstream society. However, Barrie was conscious of the prejudice within his profession, and his initial optimistic tone, captured by *WWD* in 1973, would shift as his career progressed beyond this period of popularity for Black designers.

Starting the Business

Despite Barrie's early press and successful made-to-order designs, he told Hackney "'I couldn't get a job on SA [Seventh Avenue],' ... adding, 'maybe I was a little too far out.'"[15] Barrie was unwilling to design under someone else's vision. He wanted independence and creative control. However like many designers, he was not able to maintain the business side of his operation alone. In 1976 reporter Sandy Parker wrote an article for *WWD* titled, "Black firms on SA: Financing is Key," which explored the future of Black-owned fashion companies given the recent success of several Black designers. The article revealed contemporary attitudes that mainstream society generally accepted about African Americans, as well as the almost painful optimism of some Black designers that racism was no longer prevalent. Parker quoted Percy Sutton, described as "a black who is borough president of Manhattan," who offered the grossly oversimplified statement that, "blacks 'have not had a history of being in business or an understanding of business'" as a reason that few Black designers owned their operations. James Daugherty, a Black designer who attracted an investor to his company after years of success working for a manufacturer, offered a contradictory, though no less overgeneralized view, stating, "Years ago, I might have had difficulty getting even a designer's job. But times are different and people are more open—to any color."[16]

Although Black designers in the New York industry were more visible than ever before, creating a profitable business was still a difficult undertaking, one that Parker attributed to the lack of access to capital. Discrimination from banks and other investors, as well as a general distrust within the Black community to invest in an unsteady business such as fashion, made it difficult for Black designers to access the money they needed to buy supplies and manufacture their designs. Since the 1940s New York designers typically showed seasonal collections approximately six months ahead of the retail season. Buyers for department stores and boutiques from all over the country attended the New York fashion shows or met with designers to view the collections and place orders. With these orders in hand, a designer who did not already possess the necessary capital to produce could approach a bank for a loan to buy materials, hire cutters and sewers, and pay for shipping to the stores. The designer would be paid by the store after delivery. However, banks were hesitant to loan money to fashion designers because any glitch in the production process would likely result in delays, canceled orders, and a default on the loan. Private investors were also wary of putting money into ventures that relied on young or inexperienced designers. Stores, fearful of delayed or non-existent deliveries might not place orders at a new designer's fashion show or might even cancel orders during the production period. The inflation and economic stagnation of the 1970s compounded the uncertainty of the system, and an added layer of racial discrimination made it extremely difficult for Black designers to maintain their own businesses.

Scott Barrie's company Barrie Sport Ltd. set an encouraging example, not only to Black designers, but also anyone looking to create a successful fashion business in New York. By 1976 the company was doing approximately three million dollars' worth of business a year. Barrie praised his business partners, telling Parker that seven years previously, when he failed to secure a Small Business Administration loan, "I was lucky to find Robbie Marks, who really cared. I had a small business going, but I had a finance problem to the point where I was delivering dresses and waiting for the check. Those were tough times."[17] Marks was a recent graduate of the Fashion Institute of Technology, majoring in merchandising and buying, and she managed the Allen & Cole boutique while pursuing a career in modeling and acting. Marks recalled meeting Barrie,

> Scott would come every once in a while to design something, to try to sell his clothing, and I just loved what he did. And so we became friends. And then he'd tell me his story, that he went through a couple of partners and just couldn't make it with them in business … he said, "I can't get my things into the bigger stores."[18]

Marks offered to accompany Barrie to meetings with buyers in exchange for clothing loans to wear for her portfolio photographs,

> I figured, let me help, and I just had a feeling that he wasn't getting through any doors. And he wasn't … so I would go with him and it was a kind of validation because [the store buyers] were afraid that they'd give him an order, they'd be spending their open-to-buy money, and they weren't going to get the clothes. [They] liked his stuff, but … [reliability] was very important for the buyers at that time.[19]

The combination of Scott's design talent and Marks's educational experience and determination helped the duo overcome the discrimination they faced as a Black man and young, white woman starting out in the fashion business. Ironically, men dominated the womenswear industry at this time, and sexism was a part of the business. At a meeting with a fabric supplier, for example, Marks recalled that the group sat in silence waiting for the meeting to begin until finally one of the older male reps asked her when her father would arrive.

The big break the partners needed came from Elaine Monroe, the buyer for the "Place Elegance" department of Bloomingdale's. Marks noted, "She was a major help to get us going and believed in us."[20] After about a year, Marks's husband Stephen Marks also joined the business, and the three partners began an era of exciting expansion for Barrie Sport Ltd. Robbie and Stephen Marks ran all aspects of the business, while Barrie designed several collections, both in-house and for manufacturing licenses. The label's offerings expanded from the main Scott Barrie line to include Barrie Sport; Scottie; a silk separates line; swimwear introduced in 1975; furs introduced in 1976; a blouse line; lingerie; accessories; and patterns for Vogue Patterns. Robbie Marks remembered the first office, "we had set up in a small place over a Blimpie's [sandwich shop] … we had a little office showroom in the front, then we had a couple of the cutting tables."[21] They employed a cutter named Bennie Squires and two seamstresses, "that was how we started … Scott would draw it … and Bennie would cut. That's how little it was and it always smelled from Blimpie's sandwiches. To get buyers to come up there was interesting. It wasn't on Seventh Avenue, it was nearby, but not on Seventh."[22] Stephen and Robbie Marks noted that the business expanded quickly. Barrie's collections were featured in the fashion press, garnering favorable reviews, and stores all over the country placed orders. After two years they moved into a premium location at 530 Seventh Avenue—Robbie Marks commented, "we became a big boy."[23] In this space they employed a design room manager named Young-Joo Kwon, who translated Barrie's sketches into patterns, and at least a dozen seamstresses, in addition to two showroom managers and Barrie's assistant. As well as selling to major stores, such as Henri Bendels, Lord & Taylor, Bergdorf Goodman, Barneys New York, Joseph Magnin, Bonwit Teller, and Saks Fifth Avenue, Barrie also sold to smaller boutiques around the country and in the United Kingdom.

The success of the company made Scott Barrie and the Markses well-established personalities in the thriving New York social scene, and also fostered relationships with prominent celebrities. Barrie dressed musicians such as Liza Minelli, the Pointer Sisters, Ashford and Simpson, Roberta Flack, Chita Rivera, Nina Simone, and Dionne Warwick, as well as actresses such as Cicely Tyson and Faye Dunaway. Barrie's pieces were also featured in films, including *The Way We Were* (1974), and he designed over a hundred costumes for *The Whiz* (1978). The showroom frequently hosted stylists, such as Patricia Field, and editors, including Eunice Johnson and Audrey Smaltz of *Ebony*, who featured the styles in the magazine and in the annual Fashion Fair. Jacqueline Onassis admired Barrie's clothes at Bloomingdale's and had their sales staff arrange a showroom visit, prompting the Secret Service to close the office to any other clients.

Barrie's showroom functioned as a salesroom, a venue to host important clients, and a rarified community space where the most prominent Black models of the era worked and socialized. Robbie Marks commented on the showroom's casual atmosphere, energized by the two Marks children, their dogs, and frequent visits by models such as Pat Cleveland. Black models were the first and most visible trailblazers into the New York fashion industry. A few faces made an impact during the 1960s, but the 1970s saw the success of a group of Black models that mirrored and overtook the popularity of Black designers. Scott Barrie worked with established stars, such as Naomi Sims, as well as models on the rise. The company was not only early in hiring Black models to walk runway shows, it specifically sought them out. Robbie Marks, herself contracted with Ford Models, spoke with the agency's founder Eileen Ford about hiring Black models for Scott Barrie shows. She remembered working with models such as Alva Chinn, Bethann Hardison, Iman, and Grace Jones, stating, "it was a wonderful time, we had such fun. The girls were great, and we were so happy that it got them going. Very few houses used [them], and at least half or more of our models were Black girls."[24]

Supporting a Black community within the fashion industry was important because, although Black designers and models were working and being recognized more than ever before, issues of racial discrimination were also significant elements of their experiences. Even Barrie's family doubted that the industry would allow him to succeed. Barrie recalled their sentiments,

Figure 11.2 Audrey Smaltz wearing a black Scott Barrie gown at the 1971 Ebony Fashion Fair. Photographer unknown. Image courtesy of Audrey Smaltz.

"Oh, you want to be a designer? … That's a white boy's game, you're not going to get anywhere being a designer."[25] In a 1975 televised interview produced by Anton Perich, Barrie told interviewer R. Couri Hay that he mostly ignored discriminatory actions and focused on his work, "People would give you reasons why things were not done, but you could never really pinpoint and say that that was the reason why, and I never took the time to give it that much of

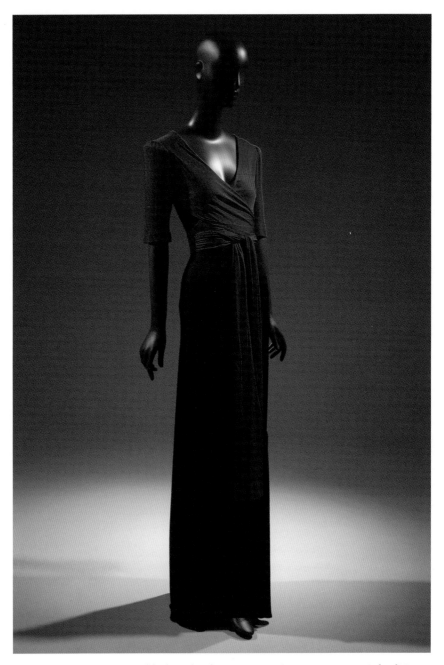

Figure 11.3 Scott Barrie, black and red rayon jersey dress, circa 1973. Gift of Naomi Sims. © The Museum at FIT.

a thought … [though] there were occasions that it was made pretty obvious."[26] Robbie Marks commented, "[during] the seventies, there was still a lot of racial tension going on. We had letters and phone calls, threats at times because we were a Black and white company."[27] One specific outburst of racism occurred when Barrie appeared in a nationally circulated print advertisement for the label's line of denim jeans. In the ad Barrie was posed as the designer at work, fitting a white model. Stephen and Robbie Marks recalled that the company received hate mail from around the country in response to the ad. Stephen Marks commented, "The country was so different then. Us getting hate mail because he's in a picture with a white woman … New York wasn't that way, but a lot of the country was in the 1970s."[28]

Despite direct and indirect incidents, Barrie stated, "a few of us stuck it out, and I think now the market has opened up and … there are several black designers on Seventh Avenue … I think there are a few of us that are responsible for this."[29] By recognizing his achievement as a successful Black designer, Scott referred to the spoken and unspoken hardships he endured. He told Ki Hackney in 1974,

> Now, because I am black and made it, it's a lot easier for other black designers to not be fearful of going into design or any other career. Black designers in schools don't have to worry now. Success depends on how good they are. At some point, being black actually helped. People like Bill Smith, Willi Smith, Jon Haggins, Stephen Burrows and myself are the path-blazers. That's too few, but there will be more. They won't be considered just black designers anymore as we were. And thank God that's over.[30]

The optimistic tone of both Barrie's statements and Marks's reference to New York as a safe haven from racism speak to the excitement over Black designers in the fashion industry during the 1970s. However, this would not last. In 1989, when there were fewer Black designers working in the New York industry compared to the previous decade, Barrie told reporter Constance White, "I find that kind of sad … I never thought only of my Blackness as a designer but we get less help than some of the other boys who are less talented."[31]

The Designs

The success of Barrie's collections ultimately rested on his designs. His clothing spoke to the fashion-forward woman of 1970s New York and, to a certain extent, the rest of the country. He noted that by 1975, his brand was also selling in

Europe and Japan.[32] Although most known for his matte jersey dresses, Barrie worked a range of fabrics into his signature, unstructured silhouette. He stated, "I believe in clothes, even if they aren't made in jersey fabrics … [that] have a certain softness to them. Even if it's a wool flannel … or gabardine, it can be worked into something that's quite soft."[33] Barrie paid close attention to the materials he used, buying European textiles, but also supporting American fabric producers. He might even design his own motifs to achieve his desired look, "I get involved with absolutely everything, not just the making of the garment, but also designing the fabrics and making sure that the colors are right."[34] These soft fabrics tended to be delicate and difficult. He explained to R. Couri Hay, "I really have a load of nerve to choose such fabrics [as crèpe de chines, matte jerseys, and chiffons] to work with, but I've been doing this for a long time now, and my factory understands how the fabrics work."[35]

His adeptness and frequent use of these materials pointed to his technical skill as a designer—Bernadine Morris, fashion critic for *The New York Times*, called him "a master at draping mat jersey and chiffon."[36] Despite the laborious process of draping these fabrics, Barrie's clothing was very much a part of the Seventh Avenue fashion industry, based solidly on ready-to-wear manufacturing, much of which he produced in-house. Barrie's company was a staple on Seventh Avenue and represented the best of what could be designed and made in New York. The Markses compared Barrie's clothes to one of the most famous New York designers of the period, stating "He was a little more in the caliber of Halston, but we weren't priced as high as Halston."[37] Barrie wanted to create clothes that were "timeless, something that [the customer would] love and want to keep, not to toss out at the end of each season. I don't believe in disposable dresses."[38] Examining a few of Barrie's extant garments, held in the collection of The Museum at the Fashion Institute of Technology (MFIT), reveals the details of his designs that ranged from minimalist, to soft and layered, to experimental. Barrie utilized a number of stitching and finishing techniques to complement his fabrics, but overall kept his construction as simple as possible. His clothing bears the marks of off-the-rack manufacture in keeping with modern American dressing. He asserted that, "hand-made garments are for another period, another era,"[39] and his designer label, "Scott Barrie New York," showed that Barrie Sport Ltd. was fully integrated into the ready-to-wear industry that the city made world famous.

A circa 1974 navy, rayon jersey evening dress is one of the most minimal Barrie designs in MFIT's collection, yet it illustrates Barrie's control over fabric and manufacturing quality. It is a sleeveless tank-style dress with a deep scoop neckline in front and back, and its floor-length skirt flares to fullness at the hem. The heavy knit fabric creates a body-conscious fit at the bodice and the skirt's fullness provides dynamic movement for the wearer. The dress was constructed in four pieces with seams at the sides, the center front, and center back and with a center back zipper. This dress was made with as light of a touch as possible to honor the minimalist style and to accentuate the body of the wearer. The long vertical seam allowances were left raw, for example, as the jersey would not unravel and a ridge from a heavy seam finish would be visible from the outside of the dress. However, the neckline and armhole edges were serged, turned, and stitched to make them inelastic and strong. This, as well as the vertical seams, is extremely important in supporting the heavy weight of the dress, maintaining a snug fit, and preventing unsightly stretching at the neckline and armholes. Here Barrie demonstrated his mastery over jersey—this design exploits the fabric's stretch and clinging qualities, but the construction controls the unwieldy weight and prevents overstretching, hence the use of a zipper in a knit garment.

A 1971 black halter-neck evening gown fabricated in light synthetic jersey exemplifies another minimalist Barrie design. Audrey Smaltz wore this dress when she served as the commentator for the 1971 Ebony Fashion Fair (*see* figure 11.2), and later donated it to MFIT. This dress features a prominent waistband with two separate bodice panels forming a deep plunging neckline. The bodice pieces were shirred for shaping and fit and angled and pleated to lie flat against the body when criss-crossed and tied at the back neck. A full-length skirt was also gathered into the waistband. As the anchor of the dress, the waistband was reinforced with interfacing and was fully faced, with serged finishing at the seam allowances. The bodice panels were fully lined and the skirt's vertical seams left raw. The skirt hem was serged, turned, and stitched, and there are hand-finishing stitches around the zipper at the center back waistband. Here, Barrie used variety of construction techniques to take advantage of the jersey's sensuous, clinging qualities, while again controlling the stretch of the fabric.

Barrie's other work incorporated shirring, layering, and draping of geometric elements. A black jersey, short evening dress, circa 1974, features a spaghetti strap bodice with a seam at the natural waist and a semicircular skirt. The dress consists of a double layer of two different weights of jersey in the body and an additional rectangular, sheer jersey layer over the bodice, which was sewn into the neckline. The effect, when hanging on the body, was a voluminous dress of deep folds, which was enhanced by the uneven skirt hem. This design privileges the movement of the fabric around a body in motion.

Figure 11.4 Scott Barrie, black rayon jersey dress, circa 1974. Gift of Naomi Sims. © The Museum at FIT.

Two of Barrie's most spectacular ensembles in the MFIT collection are a red and black rayon jersey gown with a layered wrap bodice, circa 1973 (*see* Figure 11.3) and a circa 1974 silk faille dress with a halter-neck bodice and pannier-silhouette skirt (*see* Figure 11.5). These works show the full range of Barrie's talent, as well as the competence and nimbleness of his manufacturing team, from pattern makers to sewers. Barbara Streisand wore a version of the two-tone jersey dress (Figure 11.3) in *The Way We Were*, and Robbie Marks noted that it was one of their most popular styles. The base of the dress is made up of a sleeveless black V-neck body with a slightly nipped waist. The elbow-length sleeves are made of red jersey and a wrap front was sewn into the front armhole and shoulder line seams. These layered bodice pieces include long ties that angle down from the shoulder to follow the V-neckline and wrap around the waist. The finishing was again minimal; however, the sleeves were supported at the shoulder with padded sleeve heads to create volume and a stronger shoulder line. This subtle detail points to Barrie's fastidiousness for the perfect silhouette, which he incorporated into an unrestrictive garment that was adjustable to the wearer. It was this type of clothing—pared-down, easy, sexy, and chic—that represented the best of New York design.

The red faille dress is more unusual in Barrie's oeuvre. It has a distinctive skirt that extends into sharp points at the hips and narrows down to a pegged hem, yet it still maintains softness in the cowl neckline and draped wrap of the skirt. Barrie chose the perfect fabric for this design—the faille is stiff enough to maintain the shape but is surprisingly soft for its weave. This design also incorporated the layering and geometric pattern pieces seen in his other work. The bodice was made from an inverted triangular pattern piece, mounted onto a simple underdress with a straight, horizontal neckline that collapses into the cowl when worn. The bodice's upper points were pleated into the halter straps that tie around the neck. The bodice was sewn into a pointed waistline, inset into the wrap skirt, which was created from pattern pieces that extend up to sharp points. These points are inverted down into themselves to create the pannier-like silhouette at the hips. Although this dress is complex, the pattern making simplified the construction as much as possible, adhering to the design and construction principles observed in Barrie's other work. This piece was more experimental and showed Barrie's comfort in creating structured and avant-garde designs. As early as 1966, Barrie noted his admiration for the great couturier Madam Grès, revealing his knowledge of fashion history. His work can be seen as an updated, "Americanized" version of the intricate draped jersey gowns she created during the 1930s and her more experimental and geometric work of the 1960s and 1970s.[40]

Figure 11.5 Scott Barrie, red silk faille dress, circa 1974. Gift of Bill Cunningham. © The Museum at FIT.

Conclusion

Barrie, like so many Black dressmakers and designers before him, drew on the knowledge and skills amassed by his family and passed down generation to generation. His remarkable achievement was that he transformed that knowledge—previously practiced anonymously—into mainstream success. His work, which came to define the look of New York at a critical time in its ascendency as a fashion capital, was admired and sought after. He joined the ranks of mainstream Seventh Avenue designers as a New York celebrity, interviewed by the press and depicted as living a life of glamor. He was also well respected as a fashion insider. When the poor economy was projected to depress fashion sales in 1975, *Women's Wear Daily* sought out sixteen New York designers, including Barrie, to gather information on how to weather the slow season. Barrie's inclusion exemplified his company's established and respected standing in the industry. Although the mix of designers who were interviewed, including five women and two other designers of color, showed the growing diversity on Seventh Avenue, Barrie was the only Black designer represented.[41] Sadly, he was not able to define his impact in more concrete terms. His *WWD* interview in 1974 on the eve of the Coty Awards marked a high point in his career, yet he lost that award to Ralph Lauren.[42] His work remained strongly acclaimed through the end of the decade, but he split with the Markses as early as the end of 1979, and he liquidated Barrie Sport Ltd. in 1982.[43] Barrie moved to Milan, where he continued to design, working for the Italian fashion firm Krizia from 1986 to 1988, and later for Kinshido, a Japanese manufacturer. He relaunched eponymous lines in 1983, 1984, and again in 1989, this time with Kinshido's backing.[44] His career came to an abrupt end upon Barrie's untimely death in 1993.[45] The 1970s represented an unfortunately short-lived period of excitement for and acceptance of Black designers, a momentum that was not carried into the next decades. However, Barrie's influence on fashion cannot be restricted to ten years. His popular designs helped create the look of 1970s New York, making his legacy undoubtable and reverberating.

Notes

1   Ki Hackney and Keitha Mclean, "The American Spirit of '73," *Women's Wear Daily*, June 21, 1973, 4.

2   Ibid.

3   Hackney, "Great Scott," *Women's Wear Daily*, June 25, 1974, 4.

4   Ibid.

5   Ibid.

6   Ibid.

7   André Leon Talley, "Black Designers Surviving in Style," *Ebony*, November 1980, 171.

8   Constance C. R. White, "Scott Barrie Dies at 52; Made Mark on SA in 70s," *Women's Wear Daily*, June 10, 1993, 14.

9   "B. Altman & Co. advertisement for Scott Barrie swimwear," *The New York Times*, June 22, 1975, 7.

10   "Brownstone Boutique," *Women's Wear Daily*, August 19, 1965, 1.

11   Ibid.

12   "Vogue's Shop Hound," *Vogue*, June 1, 1965, 162.

13   "Fashion RTW: We Want Individuality," *Women's Wear Daily*, July 26, 1966, 23.

14   Ibid.

15   Hackney, "Great Scott," 4.

16   Sandy Parker, "Black Firms on SA: Financing is Key," *Women's Wear Daily*, September 1, 1976, 10.

17   Ibid, 45.

18   Robbie Marks and Stephen Marks, interview by author, Denver, August 3, 2018.

19   Ibid.

20   Ibid.

21   Ibid.

22   Ibid.

23   Ibid.

24   Ibid.

25   Anton Perich, *The Anton Perich Show Presents Scott Barrie with R. Couri Hay* (1975, New York), video file, 50:07, YouTube, posted by Anton Perich, February 15, 2008, accessed November 2, 2019, https://www.youtube.com/watch?v=O2zGcYFEZZg.

26   Ibid.

27   Robbie Marks and Stephen Marks, interview by author.

28   Ibid.

29   Perich, *The Anton Perich Show Presents Scott Barrie with R. Couri Hay*.

30   Hackney, "Great Scott," 4.

31   Constance White, "Scott Barrie Back and Renewed," *Women's Wear Daily*, November 20, 1989, 11.

32   Perich, *The Anton Perich Show Presents Scott Barrie with R. Couri Hay*.

33   Ibid.

34   Ibid.

35   Ibid.

36 Bernadine Morris, "A Master of the Draped Dress Won't Rest on His Laurels," *The New York Times*, June 21, 1975, 53.

37 Robbie Marks and Stephen Marks, interview by author.

38 Perich, *The Anton Perich Show Presents Scott Barrie with R. Couri Hay*.

39 Ibid.

40 "Fashion RTW: We Want Individuality," 23.

41 Catherine Bigwood, Ki Hackney, Keitha McLean, and Bobbie Queen, "1975—A Challenge for SA's Designers," *Women's Wear Daily*, December 30, 1974, 4.

42 "Eye," *Women's Wear Daily*, June 27, 1974, 10.

43 "Marks Leaves Scott Barrie," *Women's Wear Daily*, December 20, 1979, 15; White, "Scott Barrie Back and Renewed," 11.

44 "Scott Barrie Contemporary Advertisement," *Women's Wear Daily*, February 28, 1983, 70; "Scott Barrie Now," *Women's Wear Daily*, February 3, 1984, 15.

45 White, "Scott Barrie Dies at 52; Made Mark on SA in 70s," 14.

Bibliography

"B. Altman & Co. advertisement for Scott Barrie swimwear." *The New York Times*, June 22, 1975, 7.

Bigwood, Catherine, Ki Hackney, Keitha McLean, and Bobbie Queen. "1975—A Challenge for SA's Designers." *Women's Wear Daily*, December 30, 1974, 1, 4–5.

"Brownstone Boutique." *Women's Wear Daily*, August 19, 1965, 1.

"Eye." *Women's Wear Daily*, June 27, 1974, 10.

"Fashion RTW: We Want Individuality." *Women's Wear Daily*, July 26, 1966, 22–3.

Hackney, Ki. "Great Scott." *Women's Wear Daily*, June 25, 1974, 4–5.

Hackney, Ki and Keitha Mclean. "The American Spirit of '73." *Women's Wear Daily*, June 21, 1973, 4–5.

"Marks Leaves Scott Barrie." *Women's Wear Daily*, December 20, 1979, 15.

Marks, Robbie and Stephen Marks. Interview by author. Denver. August 3, 2018.

Morris, Bernadine. "A Master of the Draped Dress Won't Rest on His Laurels." *The New York Times*, June 21, 1975, 53.

Parker, Sandy. "Black Firms on SA: Financing is Key." *Women's Wear Daily*, September 1, 1976, 45

Perich, Anton. *The Anton Perich Show Presents Scott Barrie with R. Couri Hay*. 1975. New York. Video file, 50: 07.YouTube. Posted by Anton Perich, February 15, 2008, accessed November 2, 2019. https://www.youtube.com/watch?v=O2zGcYFEZZg.

"Scott Barrie Contemporary Advertisement," *Women's Wear Daily*, February 28, 1983, 70.

"Scott Barrie Now." *Women's Wear Daily*, February 3, 1984, 15.

Talley, André Leon. "Black Designers Surviving In Style." *Ebony*, November 1980, 170–4.

"Vogue's Shop Hound." *Vogue*, June 1, 1965, 162–3.

White, Constance. "Scott Barrie Back and Renewed." *Women's Wear Daily*, November 20, 1989, 11.

White, Constance C. R. "Scott Barrie Dies at 52; Made Mark on SA in 70s." *Women's Wear Daily*, June 10, 1993, 14.

12

Race WERK: WilliWear and Patrick Kelly Paris

Eric Darnell Pritchard

Critical explorations of the challenges facing Black creatives navigating the minefield of American race, racism, and racial identity—its histories, ideologies, and discourses—have existed for decades, and yet very few of these works, save for those within fashion studies, have been attentive to how the unique experiences of Black fashion designers might inform such considerations. Perhaps one of the most well-known treatises on the state of the Black creative was written by world-renowned poet, Langston Hughes. In 1926 Hughes wrote a now oft-cited essay in which he posited the ways that race, racism, and racial identity—as an experience and discursive formation—contributed to unique pressures bearing down upon the work of Black creatives across a wide range of artistic forms. Originally published in *The Nation*, Hughes's essay, "The Negro Artist and the Racial Mountain," intended to function as a work, "in defense of the freedom of the black writer."[1] Perhaps the most provocative of Hughes's theses, the essay considers the work of Black creatives who chose to make "racial art," art that included, illuminated, or emerged from parts of Black life which might be considered disreputable. Hughes describes such subjects as,

> the low-down folks, the so-called common element, and they are the majority—may the Lord be praised! The people who have their hip of gin on Saturday nights and are not too important to themselves or the community, or too well fed, or too learned to watch the lazy world go round. … [T]hey do not particularly care if they are like white folks or anybody else. … They furnish a wealth of colorful, distinctive material for any artist because they still hold their individuality in the face of American standardizations. And perhaps these common people will give to the world its truly great Negro artist, the one who is not afraid to be himself … and they accept what beauty is their own without question.[2]

What Hughes posits as the conditions under which Black artists work is illuminating as an illustration of a set of circumstances that cross a wide range of Black creative fields.

This chapter will extrapolate the specific resonance and persistence of the racial mountain, of which Hughes speaks, and which many Black fashion designers have confronted in order to make their work. It does this by centering fashion design and style as its focal object. Press and scholarship noting the long existing ways that fashion has not addressed historic and ongoing matters of racism and exclusion are legion, and represent an umbrella under which a long list of absences, erasures, and offenses might be included.[3] And yet, despite the industry's perpetual failure to address matters of racial justice and institutional racism, Black creatives in fashion have navigated these matters in creating, nurturing, sustaining, and disseminating a vibrant Black fashion history, culture, and aesthetic within and without the fashion system, as documented by numerous scholars in the interdisciplinary field of Black fashion studies.[4]

Among the many effects of these circumstances, and how they have been addressed by Black creatives, are the specific challenges they present to Black fashion designers. Fashion historian Rikki Byrd writes that,

> [i]n an industry that doesn't like to talk about race (let alone blackness), it's rare for designers, who identify as black, to readily insert identity politics into their brands. The fear, perhaps, emerges from the fact that doing so could pigeonhole them into a singular narrative of blackness—one that could result in them being unattractive to customers, investors, and the media.[5]

Despite this, both historically and contemporarily, many Black fashion designers overtly or implicitly reference race, racism, and Black cultural traditions in their designs and advertising campaigns; some even as they express ambivalence about "Black" being attached to their occupation or the essentialism of such a phrase, noting astutely that one never sees designers who are not people of color identified as "white fashion designers."

For instance, in an interview with Byrd, fashion designer Kerby Jean-Raymond, designer of the award-winning fashion label Pyer Moss, expressed his desire to not be labeled a "Black designer." The work of Jean-Raymond, a Haitian American, is, however, unapologetically Black and proud, as well as overt in its commentary on race and social justice. His spring 2016 collection, for example, used fashion design as a way of raising consciousness and protesting against police brutality, and subsequent collections have been celebrations of Black diasporic cultural productions and traditions. This illustrates Jean-Raymond's recognition that Blackness is central to who he is *and* to his work, and shows his emphasis on Blackness on his own terms, as demonstrated when he says to Byrd, "If I'm going to be the Black designer, I'm going to tell it my way."[6]

Therefore, this chapter pursues the following questions: How are Black fashion designers' race- and class-consciousness being produced in and through their work, presence, and knowledge? What can be learned about designers' relationships to race in fashion design when their focus is on interests that include, but do not amplify, the themes of visibility or respectability that have directed many examinations of Black American cultural production for more than a century? This chapter argues that in these moments, Blackness is not preoccupied with whiteness, white supremacy, and class elitism. Rather, Blackness is free to be what it is, when it is, which is a self-reflexive conversation between the creative and a designer's deep considerations of Blackness and the discourses of race relevant to their artistic expression. Such engagement with the discourses around race and class politics are thus honest, bubbling over with critical, creative, social, political, cultural, and yes, economic possibility.

To explore these questions, this chapter rewinds to the 1970s and 1980s, and specifically to the work of fashion designers Willi Smith and Patrick Kelly and their eponymous labels WilliWear and Patrick Kelly Paris. Smith, born and raised in Philadelphia, was the youngest person ever nominated for the Coty Award (the precursor to the Council of Fashion Designers of America's Award for Womenswear Designer of the Year). He went on to win that award in 1983 for WilliWear. Kelly, born and raised in Vicksburg, Mississippi, became in 1988 the first American admitted into the prestigious *Chambre syndicale du prêt-à-porter des couturiers et des créateurs de mode*, the Paris-based organizing body of French ready-to-wear designers.

Smith and Kelly, sadly, both passed away at the height of their success from illnesses due to AIDS-related complications, in 1987 and 1990 respectively. But, during their too-brief careers, Smith and Kelly became, unarguably, two of the most successful and famous Black fashion designers in history. As such, Smith and Kelly are fruitful examples for the exploration of how race- and class-consciousness are reflected in design in a myriad of ways. For instance, in their work and work environments, Patrick Kelly and Willi Smith each approach race and class as the inverse of one another. Kelly had a very outwardly camp and affirmative take on Blackness in his fashion designs, and Smith was equally overt in his display of his sensibilities of race and class. However, for Smith, his expression embraced and was interpreted through the vessel of American sportswear and, thus, was much subtler. On the other hand, while Smith's showroom was designed to effect an urban streetscape, including a sidewalk, a street, a fire hydrant, fences, and brick walls, all of which he used to display clothes, Kelly's showroom centered a variety of objects of Black memorabilia—Black dolls, wood sculptures from Nigeria and South Africa, throws created in kente and ankara fabrics, and lithographs of Black performers—alongside ornate objects aestheticized as European and bourgeois, including gold gilded frames and Chiavari chairs. Both Smith and Kelly are each conversing on race and class identity, but in very different ways, as demonstrated in their clothing and showrooms as objects of analysis.

Examining the work of Smith and Kelly also provides an opportunity to examine how Black fashion designers navigated the politics of race in fashion during the late twentieth-century post-Civil Rights era. This leaves significant historic and critical distance to posit the implications of their contributions to fashion design and the role of race, racial identity, and racism as they exist in the early twenty-first century. To aid this analysis, the "race werk" concept is used as a theoretical shorthand by which the intersections of the biographical, philosophical, political, and aesthetic can be explored. These concentric circles chronicle the ways in which fashion designers make work and make history in the face of the harsh and complex "racial realities" in which they live, to quote critical race theorist and legal scholar, Derrick Bell.[7]

Race Werk

The term "race werk" refers to a constellation of practices through which Black creatives in the fashion and style industries harness the tools, vocabularies, and grammars of the sartorial and ornamental that are pivotal to fashion and use them to make work through which they become successful within the American and international fashion system. They achieve this while simultaneously providing the literal and figurative material through which the consumers, critics, and spectators can historicize, critique, disrupt, and reinvent systems and discourses of race and racism. "Werk" rather than "work" is used because it is a term that originates in Black queer language and vernacular practices and is used by many to denote their recognition of, and that they take pleasure in, a social presence or act. UrbanDictionary.com, for example, defines "werk" as "a congratulatory exclamation of approval" or "a congratulatory declaration of support, praise or approval, for an outstanding achievement in any area of life. Probably for original, sensational or courageous accomplishments in the fields of art, fashion, music, sport and friendship."[8] Indeed, there has been some version of werk in Black queer language and vernacular practices for some time. During the 1980s, for example, some Black gay men would say that something was "ovah," carrying with it the same effect as werk, as it communicated the element of congratulations, exclamation, recognition, and encouragement to keep carrying on being sensational and fierce.

Both Willi Smith and Patrick Kelly, as Black gay men, and especially as Black gay men who frequented the artistic circles and nightlife of New York City during the 1970s and 1980s, belong to this language and vernacular tradition—both its cultural roots and contemporary expressions. Thus, the spelling "werk" rather than "work" is especially used to characterize this aspect of their contributions as Black fashion designers. Werk is also used as a way to highlight the various kinds of labor that Smith, Kelly, and other race-conscious fashion designers perform; that is, they not only perform the work of the fashion designer but also, in calling it race werk, provide through their designs a serviceability to explorations of race, racism, and racial identity within and without the fashion system. For these designers and other creatives who engage in this, race werk is how they do critical race commentary, but make it fashion.

In order to characterize the myriad and complex types of race werk that might be performed, three especially frequent examples that have emerged in fashion historically and contemporarily will be codified. First, in some instances, race werk might be positioned from the inside out—meaning it can develop from an agentive positionality that locates itself as within the fashion system and thus contributing to its betterment or rehabilitation. A second example includes those performances of race werk that develop from an agentive positionality that locates itself outside the fashion system and, thus, is less interested in rehabilitating or bettering that system. Instead, it simply makes work that contributes to a vocabulary, theorization, commentary, and action with regards to race and racism, leaving the matter of implications on the industry to those who identify with it. A third example of race werk is a direct reflection of what the performance studies scholar José Esteban Muñoz, theorizing the subversive performances of queer of color creatives, called "disidentification." He describes this as a "mode of dealing with dominant ideology, one that neither opts to assimilate within such a structure nor strictly opposes it; rather, disidentification is a strategy that works on and against dominant ideology."[9]

Attention to disidentification as an ingredient in or codification of some instances of race werk also creates space to recognize the complex personal politics of the fashion designers and other creatives whose work might be located under the umbrella of race werk. Disidentification leaves room for us to illuminate and grapple with the messiness of such performances, their meanings and implications. This is especially imperative when, again, the race werk being explored intersects the biographical, political, philosophical, and aesthetic. As such, it may be more epistemologically honest and conceptually effective to mete out and understand the various dimensions of race werk relationally to each of those intersections than to invest in the concept to achieve a neatness that flattens out the contributions of race werk and its agents.

Thoroughly Modern Willi: Race Werk in WilliWear

In 1976 Willi Smith, with his friend Laurie Mallet, founded the fashion label, WilliWear. Primarily a womenswear designer, Smith built his first collections for WilliWear around thirteen silhouettes that "captured the spirit of pragmatic leisurewear."[10] Smith's design methodology was one in which he would draw ideas from being on the streets of New York, especially Harlem and the Lower East Side, as well as his hometown of Philadelphia. As his design house grew, he would take to the streets, and if he saw clients wearing his clothing he would stop and ask for feedback on his work or use ideas of how they would take his garments into their personal style as a way of informing his future designs. In this way, Smith's design process was one of a call and response between himself and the streets. Smith called the unique style that emerged from this methodology "street couture." In addition to womenswear, Smith's label offered a wide range of other products, including menswear, a line for boys and girls, and accessories. At the height of its success, WilliWear had gross sales in excess of $25 million.

One place in which to begin identifying and examining Smith's race werk is in his own commentary on the phrase "Black fashion designer." Smith too was reluctant to adopt the term, noting, as does Kerby Jean-Raymond, that he did not like being called a Black fashion designer when white designers were not identified as "White fashion designers." However, Smith did note that being Black was a critical ingredient to his work, as he stated in the *New York Daily News*: "Being Black has a lot to do with my being a good designer. My eye will go quicker to what a pimp is wearing than someone in a gray suit and tie. Most of these designers who have to run to Paris for color and fabric combinations should go to church on Sunday in Harlem. It's all right there."[11] In this statement, Smith illustrates an affirmative stance toward Blackness while simultaneously refusing essentialism. Such commentary invites an observer or reader to self-reflexivity about universalizing the occupation of "designer" as white, but Smith's commentary also provides a positive valuation of Blackness in respect to the work of design. Relatedly, Smith's comments illustrate how, for him, the abundance of Black life, culture, and history functions as mission-critical not only as inspiration but also in terms of the specific skills he applies to design. But what are those skills? One consideration is that, as fashion and style are reliant on vision and visuality, Smith is highlighting a kind of critical *seeing* that has nuance in terms of how the eye is drawn to resonances and performances of Black style. However, he does so in a way that is at risk—but stops short—of essentializing Black people and Black life as a whole. This is evident in the above quote in which Smith traverses Black life from the secular to the sacred—the pimp to the Black church—as equally significant sites of Black style. Such an informed, nuanced, and thus complex view escapes turning to Blackness as a literal uptake or inspiration, which, one might argue, is surface level at best in its impact upon color, cut, fit, and style.

Smith's race werk is also evident in his approach to whiteness and class politics in his design work. His fall 1986 collection most evidences this. *Women's Wear Daily* (*WWD*) called it "a good WilliWear collection reflecting a more serious Smith."[12] The collection included thick knit pullover sweaters, jumpers, overalls, and jersey coats in fabrics of "wool flannel, jersey, gabardine and bulk knits for day; rayon taffeta, polyester organza and cotton velvet for night."[13] The collection also marked a departure from the usual cottons from India and Hong Kong that Smith was known for using. *The New York Times* fashion critic Bernadine Morris noted that Smith "added European fabrics to his repertory as his clothes look more grown-up."[14] The clothing presented an array of colors marking, "a newly sophisticated palette of navy, gray, wine and black plus royal and kelly."[15] Bonwit Teller, a highly sought-after retailer at the time, noted that their buyers enjoyed the collection and the "grown-up Willi," while Bloomingdale's buyers said they liked "the new so-called sophistication."[16] This WilliWear collection was featured multiple times in *WWD*'s fall 1986 collection previews, summaries, and editorials.[17]

The constant repetition of the description of Smith's fall 1986 presentation and collection as "grown-up" echoes some of the language included in the invitation and other promotional materials released during the run-up to the show. For instance, for the fall 1986 collection, WilliWear distributed a pamphlet called *The WilliWear News*, made to look like a newspaper with mock news reports about the collection and its influences. The headline for this edition of *The WilliWear News* was "Totally Serious," a phrase that was repeated throughout the pamphlet and also referenced in reviews of the WilliWear presentation and collection. As fashion critics, retailers, and other industry professionals ran with Smith's all-grown-up collection, the tongue-in-cheek way in which being "Totally Serious"

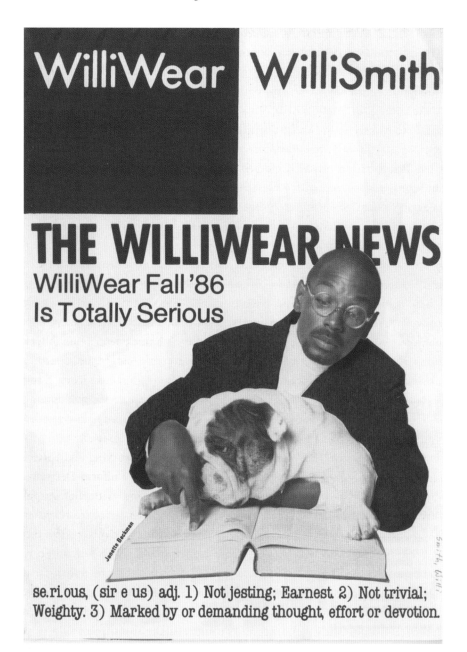

Figure 12.1 Designer Willi Smith on the cover of *The WilliWear News*. Photo by © Janette Beckman, with permission of Janette Beckman. Courtesy of The New School Archives and Special Collection, The New School, New York, NY.

was "proclaimed with irony"[18] seemed to have flown over many people's heads. The collection was celebrated as a more sophisticated Smith. Implicit in Smith's irony, however, was his race werk in the "Totally Serious" collection and its promotional material.

According to *The WilliWear News*, the collection was to be understood as split into two sections: "Varsity," which was "inspired by Willi's college days … represents WilliWear's version of current and post-college dressing," and "Nanny/ Chauffeur," which consisted of clothes "inspired by English nanny and chauffeur uniforms. Serious suits with a twist. Anyone wearing these clothes will only be taken TOTALLY SERIOUSLY."[19] One of the instances of race werk in "Totally Serious" is the association of the fall 1986 collection with racialized and classed social identities and practices that are highlighted in the news articles. One piece is titled "To a Tea," with the standfirst, "Be civilized and wear WilliWear to a tea."[20] Beside the story is an image of a woman wearing WilliWear while holding a humongous tea cup and saucer, which is captioned, "Rachael is serving a big cup of tea but her mind is on her proper classic poodle suit which should always be worn with a white silk turtleneck."[21] The story is a thick description of how to brew and enjoy tea in a way that is authentically cultured, including advice like "[d]rinking tea with your pinky straight up in the air is both incorrect and silly" and "Serious Tea. At four o'clock in the afternoon, every day, this is an activity which you must do yourself. Nanny cannot help you here," along with a reminder that preparing tea "is an exercise in civilization and poise."[22]

Other sections of *The WilliWear News* parodied the working and service classes in relationship to dress. A brief article titled, "A Uniform Decision," focused on "Willi's inspiration for a uniform way of dressing," with photographs of workers, including a police officer and a hotel worker, whose uniforms it describes as comprising, "a distinctive outfit. It consists of clothing intended to identify those who wear it as members of a specific group. Any uniform can be considered a 'classic' and can be worn day after day."[23] The Nannies and Chauffeurs section of the fall 1986 collection is "an example of such 'classics.' It has revived yesterday's uniforms into becoming part of today's hottest fashions."[24] There are also images of two models, one woman and one man, playing the role of Nannie and Chauffeur, wearing WilliWear gabardine suits staged as their uniforms in burgundy and navy, respectively. These images are alongside other images of the same models in a daydream sequence focused on eveningwear, with the woman wearing a little black dress and the man wearing a tuxedo, noting that "you don't really have to be rich" to afford it, and that both look "seriously happy."[25]

A Uniform Decision

Here's Willi's inspiration for a uniform way of dressing.

The uniform is a distinctive outfit. It consists of clothing intended to identify those who wear it as members of a specific group. Any uniform can be considered a "classic" and can be worn day after day. WilliWear sees the Nannies and Chauffeurs group of the Fall Collection as a perfect example of such "classics." It has revived yesterday's uniforms into becoming part of today's hottest fashions.

Here are some hardworking New Yorkers whose classic looks have inspired Willi this season.

To A Tea

Be civilized and wear WilliWear to a tea.

SERIOUS TEA

At four o'clock in the afternoon, every day, this is an activity which you must do for yourself. Nanny cannot help you here. Even the preparation of the tea is something you must oversee because you want everything to be just so. Although this is an exercise in civilization and poise, always remember that if you do fumble a bit, the best medicine is a simple polite peel of laughter and everyone will overlook what minor catastrophe that may have arisen.

YOUR TEA TRAY

Should have on it: lemon slices, milk, sugar lumps, extra hot water, and cakes and/or tea sandwiches. (Cookies are too casual as a rule, however, if someone has dropped-by unexpectedly they are adequate).

WHAT SORT OF TEA?

Willi's favorite team for a cool September afternoon is Hu Kwa. Although this delicious woody-flavoured Chinese tea can prove difficult for you to find, it is well worth the search. If you can't find it, the next best thing is Lapsang Soochong which is even heartier in flavor. Earl Grey, a popular favorite, is an aromatic Indian tea which is grand enough and light enough to be served all year long.

BREWING

Catch your water just before it comes to a boil. Pour just a touch of water into your tea pot and swirl it around so that the pot becomes warm to the touch (this is known as scalding the pot). Toss that water out. Now, scoop in one heaping teaspoon into the pot per guest. Then you add one scoop extra "for the pot." Allow the tea to steep (stand) for five minutes before serving.

PINKIES UP!

Drinking tea with your pinkie straight up in the air is both incorrect and silly. A crooked pinkie is correct and turns your hand into a lovely crab shape. While pouring the tea, use a strainer so your guests don't get any tea leaves in their cups! (Unless you plan to do a reading). Ask your guests what they wish to have in their tea and YOU put it in for them even on refills. You may use a footman to deliver the cups to your guests as the only servant on hand in the proceedings, but this can make matters more clumsy than they need be and the idea is to make your guests feel special by your serving them personally.

"One lump or two? Do you take milk? May I offer you a lemon? You take nothing at all? How abstemious of you!"

Betsey Phelan

For more loose leaves open the WilliWear News and see our Varsity inside.

Rachael is serving a big cup of tea but her mind is on her proper classic poodle suit which should always be worn with a white silk turtleneck.

Willi loves dogs so much he chose special dalmatian scarves to accessoriz his poodle coats.

WILLI'S JEWEL-TONE FASHIONS FOR FALL DON'T COST A FORTUNE.

Figure 12.2 (This page, and opposite) Two sections of WilliWear fall 1986 collection as presented in *The WilliWear News*: Varsity, as discussed in "A Uniform Decision," "To A Tea," and "Nannies and Chauffeurs." Photo by © Janette Beckman, with permission of Janette Beckman. Courtesy of The New School Archives and Special Collection, The New School, New York, NY.

NANNIES & CHAUFFEURS

A Formal Daydream

Willi's nannies and chauffeurs won't feel like working when they're wearing Willi's proper uniform-like garbardine suits.

Here Gail and Walter are on their dream date and both look seriously happy in Willi's latest addition to his collection . . . eveningwear. You don't really have to be rich to afford Gail's sexy little black dress or Walter's WilliWear tuxedo.

Although Nanny Gail's mind certainly isn't on the dusting, she still looks like she means business in her basic burgundy gabardine suit with its long straight skirt.

Waiter, the chauffeur looks dreamy in his uniform-like perfect WilliWear navy gabardine fall suit.

A Good Vision

Singers Ashford and Simpson love Willi's good taste and vision in uniforms.

Several months ago, Nick Ashford and Valerie Simpson approached Willi about clothing the waiters, waitresses and bartenders at their new restaurant, Twenty, Twenty, located appropriately at 20 West 20th Street in Manhattan. Willi chose the black and white group of his summer '86 collection, that was featured in the last edition of the WILLI-WEAR NEWS. So, if you're in town, drop in and enjoy some great American Regional cooking and be served by some of the best dressed waiters in town.

Janette Beckman

These details and excerpts from WilliWear's fall 1986 collection and *The WilliWear News* are highlighted because they provide a great surface upon which to explore Smith's race werk. First, the discussions of tea drinking and collegiate culture are racialized and classed in a way that functions as a commentary on whiteness and elitism via a parody of wealth and privilege. This is evident of the juxtaposition between the more urban—nonwhite and working-class—aesthetic with which WilliWear is most associated. Smith was aware of and embraced this understanding of his aesthetic enterprise, as evidenced in his own commentary on his work. Recall his note about the influence of Harlem on his design, but also, in one often-quoted statement by Smith, in which he says, "I don't design clothes for the Queen, but for the people who wave at her as she goes by."[26] As such, Smith designed the "Varsity" look which is frequently referred to as "classic" with the signature elements of the WilliWear "street couture" look, including oversized jackets, loose-fitting shirts and trousers, and baggy pants. This application of his own design aesthetic on "classic" serves to illuminate the erroneousness of these raced and classed categories of dressing. Similarly, through the nannies, chauffeurs, and other uniform apparel mirroring the working classes depicted as fashionable apparel, Smith is saying that fashion and stylishness is not defined by or is the exclusive provenance of the wealthy—again racialized in the "Totally Serious" parody as white. All in all, WilliWear evidences the ways in which an American sportswear brand during the late twentieth century developed an approach to design that enabled Smith to work on the cutting edge of the fashion industry while navigating the complex histories, ideologies, and discourses of race and racism as important material in the making of his designs.

Black and Proud: Race Werk in Patrick Kelly Paris

The race werk in WilliWear's street couture was informed by the northern, urban metropolis in which Smith was born and raised. However, Patrick Kelly's race werk embodies a distinctly Black, Southern, poor and working class, and rural milieu. Born and raised in Vicksburg, Mississippi, Kelly came to love fashion at the age of five through the help of his maternal grandmother, Ethel Rainey. Rainey, a domestic worker who cleaned the homes of wealthy white families in and around Vicksburg, encouraged Kelly's love of fashion by giving him fashion magazines such as *Vogue* and *Harper's Bazaar* that she would get from the homes where she worked. From that early age, Kelly sought to pursue

Figure 12.3 In Paris, fashion designer Patrick Kelly, alongside models, is exuberant in showing fun, youthful clothes and accessories from his womenswear collection. The looks include a few adorned with his signature multicolored buttons and bows. Photo by julio donoso/Sygma via Getty Images.

a career in fashion, making it part of his scholarly pursuits as well. He enrolled at Jackson State University, a historically Black college and university in Jackson, Mississippi, where he took a keen interest in African American art history. The melding of these two scholarly fields—Black studies and art history—form the basis of the substance of Kelly's race werk in design later in his career. Kelly did not complete his studies and relocated from Jackson to Atlanta, finally settling in New York City where he enrolled in fashion school for a brief time in pursuit of his goals. While he attempted to get work in the design studios of New York, he ultimately found America to be an almost impossible place in which to establish himself in the fashion industry. At the encouragement of supermodel Pat Cleveland, who gave Kelly a plane ticket to Paris and advice that France might be more open to his work, Kelly left the United States in 1979. After working for five years in numerous jobs within the industry, he made a star appearance in French *Elle*, where he and his signature tubular jersey dresses, adorned with buttons and bows, were photographed by Oliviero Toscani for a fashion editorial by Nicole Crassat. In 1985, Kelly with the support of his business and romantic partner Bjorn Amelan, formed the fashion label, *Patrick Kelly Paris.*

Although it took going to Europe to finally achieve all he desired in fashion, Kelly saw Black cultural, social, and religious spaces as the height of style and fashion. One of Kelly's oft-quoted statements, which was both shocking and beloved by fashion insiders, was when he said that one could learn more about fashion in any Black church in the American South on a Sunday morning than could ever be learned from a runway in Paris.[27] It is worth noting how Kelly's sentiment here echoes that of Willi Smith's comment quoted earlier. Part of what made Kelly's work so noteworthy and memorable was that

> Kelly's original and controversial visual vocabulary blended the real, painful, and also traumatic histories of race in America, including racial terror and racist iconography—watermelon hats and bandanas like those featured in representations of Mammy's and Aunt Jemima pancake ads, maid uniforms stylized as those worn by Black domestic workers on clothing racks, and perhaps most controversially, the logo of Kelly's company—a golliwog, a character in British children's literature reviled for the racism in the depiction of its features, with the company name Patrick Kelly Paris written around it—and the aesthetics of the South's Black poor and working classes with the joy and fantasy of nightlife, the value of noted works of visual art, and the glamour of celebrity and superstardom of Black pop icons.[28]

Given the ways in which Kelly so regularly and overtly engaged discourses and images related to race and racism in his work, he presents an especially unique challenge to tease out the dimensions to his design and craft as race werk. In pursuit of this challenge, however, the examples that resonate most with Kelly's race werk are not those that are most associated with his visual vocabulary—the golliwog, buttons, bows, or even how Kelly dressed himself regularly in denim overalls, clothing that has been historically associated with sharecroppers and agricultural workers.[29] Instead, interest is focused on garments that show Kelly operating at the intersection of race, class, and labor, which was central to his family's history and the history of Black Americans in Vicksburg and beyond. One such garment is the Kelly "Nail Ensemble." First shown in the presentation for Kelly's fall/winter 1988 collection, the ensemble consists of a jacket made of black cotton velveteen with silver metallic machine embroidery and a skirt also in black cotton velveteen. The embroidery upon the fabric depicts nails and has an almost three-dimensional quality so that they look like real metal nails fastened to the garment. The jacket and skirt were paired with black gloves made of a black wool and spandex knit and embellished with actual metal nails. Kelly

Figure 12.4 "Nail" ensemble from Patrick Kelly Paris fall/winter 1988 collection as photographed for the 2014 exhibition, *Patrick Kelly: Runway of Love*. Courtesy of Philadelphia Museum of Art: Gift of Bjorn Guil Amelan and Bill T. Jones in honor of Monica Brown, 2014, 2014–207-12a-e.

Figure 12.5 Bandana skirt from the Patrick Kelly Paris spring/summer 1988 collection as photographed for the 2014 exhibition, *Patrick Kelly: Runway of Love*. Philadelphia Museum of Art: Gift of Bjorn Guil Amelan and Bill T. Jones in honor of Monica Brown, 2014, 2014–207-1a-e.

takes a nail—a tool of manual labor, building, and repair work that exists so far away from the luxury fashion world—and reappropriates it for a high fashion look. Should the metal nails alone not evidence the reference point Kelly sought, the accessories for this garment might. Among them are a necklace with a nail charm and a pair of earrings and matching bracelet depicting miniature tools, including a hammer and a wrench.

Other garments that illustrate Kelly's race werk are his various dresses that reference the mammy, a raced, gendered, and sexualized stereotype or "controlling image," to quote Black feminist sociologist Patricia Hill Collins.[30] A controlling image "applied to U.S. Black women ... the mammy—the faithful, obedient, domestic servant"—was "created to justify the economic exploitation of house slaves and sustained to explain Black women's long-standing restriction to domestic service, the mammy image represents the normative yardstick used to evaluate all Black women's behavior."[31] Depictions of mammies in popular culture include Aunt Jemima, a fictional spokesperson for pancake mix, depicted as a smiling Black woman, and the character of the enslaved Black woman named Mammy played by actress Hattie McDaniel in the 1939 film adaptation of Margaret Mitchell's 1936 novel, *Gone with the Wind*.

Kelly, having grown up in America, would have been aware of these depictions and others. More importantly, he was also the grandchild of a domestic worker, and Kelly's personal collection of Black memorabilia contained dozens of Aunt Jemima dolls, advertisements, and other materials. In a reported incident, a woman told Kelly that she did not like the Aunt Jemimas he had displayed, to which Kelly told her, "My grandmother was a maid, honey. My memorabilia means a lot to me."[32] For Kelly, the Aunt Jemima depiction did not signify the shame intended by the stereotype, but a revised meaning upon which he associated love for his grandmother and other Black domestic workers.

It is unsurprising then that Kelly would reference the mammy and Aunt Jemima characters in his designs for multiple collections. For spring/summer 1988, Kelly created a dramatic skirt made of the red bandana fabric often worn by mammies and Aunt Jemima. The skirt was a red printed cotton plain weave, which he paired with shoes by legendary accessories designer, Maud Frizon (Maud Frizon DeMarco). The shoes were red leather with a bow made out of the red bandana fabric. Kelly's spring/summer 1987 collection also featured an off-white cotton ribbed knit dress, with red bandana handkerchiefs with rhinestone buttons hanging from the hem. Kelly also referenced mammy and Aunt Jemima in other dresses, hats, shoes, and even a screen-printed T-shirt called the "Mississippi Lisa," one of several T-shirts in which Kelly remixed Leonardo da

Vinci's iconic portrait, *The Mona Lisa* (*La Giodonda*), into different reference points connected to his aesthetic enterprise. For example, the "Mississippi Lisa" T-shirt depicts a Black woman with large gold hoop earrings wearing a red bandana scarf tied around her head and a top also made of bandana fabric. She is smiling widely while stirring something in a mixing bowl, a nod to the Aunt Jemima pancake ads and to Black women domestic workers and cooks. Such garments and images are only a small example of the many ways in which Kelly's race werk sought to create counternarratives that enabled him to be resilient, inspired, and ultimately an inspiration to others, rather than crushed by the dominant stories that were painful and marginalizing to him.

As illustrated through the work of fashion designers Willi Smith and Patrick Kelly, race werk illuminates how the intersections of the biographical, philosophical, political, and aesthetic dimensions of a creative's life illuminates the critical race labor of culture workers in fashion. Per the examples of the fashion designers presented in this chapter, the tools and implications of race werk are not exclusively the needle and thread, but the kinds of race, class, and other forms of identity-based consciousness that the designer brings to their work. In this case, race werk provides the conceptual framework by which fashion designers and other creatives within and without the fashion system can be seen to reclaim the subtleties of race and cultural production.[33] This intervention is imperative for the necessary current and continued discussions on the legacies of Black fashion designers and the pervasive racism and resistance to equity, justice, and difference that have outlived generations of artists who have used fashion, style, and beauty culture as a mode of redress and race werk.

Notes

1   "Langston Hughes," in Henry Louis Gates and Nellie Y. McKay, eds., *The Norton Anthology of African American Literature*, 2nd ed. (New York: W. W. Norton & Company, 2004), 1290.

2   Ibid., 1312

3   See Robin Givhan, "Why Fashion Keeps Tripping Over Race," *New York Magazine*, February 10, 2011, accessed November 27, 2020. https://nymag.com/fashion/11/spring/71654/; Vanessa Friedman, "Fashion's Racial Divide," *The New York Times*, February 11, 2015, E1, E8–9; Jeremy Lewis, "Accounting for Race in Fashion, pt. 1" *DIS Magazine*, 2015, accessed November 27, 2020. http://dismagazine.com/discussion/59332/accounting-for-race- in-fashion-pt-1/.

4   Barbara Summers, *Black and Beautiful: How Women of Color Changed the Fashion Industry* (New York: Amistad Press, 2001); Noliwe Rooks, ed.,"Black Fashion: Art. Pleasure. Politics." *Nka: Journal of Contemporary African Art*, no. 37 (November 2015): 4–5; Carol Tulloch, *The Birth of Cool: Style Narratives of the African Diaspora* (London/New York: Bloomsbury Academic, 2016); Rikki Byrd, ed., "Open Space: Black Fashion Studies," *International Journal of Fashion Studies* 4, no. 1 (April 2017), accessed November 27, 2020, http://libproxy.fitsuny.edu:3207/10.1386/ infs.4.1.103_7; Constance C. R. White, *How to Slay: Inspiration from the Kings and Queens of Black Style* (New York: Rizzoli, 2018).

5   Rikki Byrd, "On the 'Black Designers,'" *Fashion Studies Journal*, no. 1, 2016, accessed January 7, 2020, http://www.fashionstudiesjournal.org/essays/2016/9/11/ on-the-black-designer.

6   Ibid.

7   Derrick Bell, *Faces at the Bottom of the Well: The Permanence of Racism* (New York: Basic Books, 1992); Derrick Bell, "Who's Afraid of Critical Race Theory?" *University of Illinois Law Review* (1995): 893–910.

8   "Werk," UrbanDictionary.com, accessed January 22, 2020, https://www. urbandictionary.com/define.php?term=Werk.

9   José Esteban Muñoz, *Disidentifications: Queer of Color and the Performance of Politics* (Minneapolis: University of Minnesota Press, 1999), 11–12.

10   Marnie Fogg, "Willi Smith," lovetoknow.com, accessed January 23, 2020, https:// fashion-history.lovetoknow.com/fashion-clothing-industry/fashion-designers/willi-smith.

11   Richard Martin, ed., "Willi Smith," in *Contemporary Fashion* (New York: St. James Press, 1995), 482.

12   "N.Y. NOW: Willi Smith," *Women's Wear Daily*, April 29, 1986, 15.

13   Ibid.

14   Bernadine Morris, "Willi Smith Gets Fall Off to a Good Start," *The New York Times*, April 29, 1986, B6.

15   Ibid.

16   Ibid.

17   "So Suitable," *Women's Wear Daily*, April 9, 1986, 24.

18   Martin, *Contemporary Fashion*, 482.

19   *The WilliWear News*, WilliWear Limited, Willi Smith Papers, The New School Archives and Special Collections, New York. Original emphasis.

20   Ibid.

21   Ibid.

22   Ibid.

23   Ibid.

24   Ibid.

25   Ibid.

26   Martin, "Willi Smith," 482.

27   Robin Givhan, "Patrick Kelly's Black Radical Cheek," *The Washington Post*, May 31, 2004, C01, accessed January 24, 2020, https://www.washingtonpost.com/wp-dyn/articles/A3561-2004May30_2.html.

28   Eric Darnell Pritchard, "Overalls: On Identity and Aspiration from Patrick Kelly's Fashion to Hip Hop," *Funambulist* 15 (2018): 32.

29   Ibid.

30   Patricia Hill Collins, *Black Feminist Thought* (New York: Routledge, 1990), 80.

31   Ibid.

32   Givhan, "Patrick Kelly's Black Radical Cheek."

33   My thanks to Professor Tiffany Patterson, a scholar of African American history at Vanderbilt University, for her feedback on this specific claim of mine at a critical time in my research and writing this chapter. My deep gratitude also goes to Tracy Sharpley-Whiting, Director of the Callie House Center for the Study of Global Black Cultures and Politics at Vanderbilt University, and the other attendees of the Callie House Work-in-Progress Seminar in July 2019 for their helpful questions, comments, and feedback on this project.

Bibliography

Bell, Derrick. *Faces at the Bottom of the Well: The Permanence of Racism*. New York: Basic Books, 1992.

Bell, Derrick. "Who's Afraid of Critical Race Theory?" *University of Illinois Law Review* (1995): 893–910.

Byrd, Rikki. "On the 'Black Designers.'" *Fashion Studies Journal* (2016), accessed January 7, 2020. http://www.fashionstudiesjournal.org/essays/2016/9/11/on-the-black-designer.

Byrd, Rikki. ed., "Open Space: Black Fashion Studies," International Journal of Fashion Studies 4 no. 1 (April 2017), accessed November 27, 2020. http://libproxy.fitsuny.edu:3207/10.1386/infs.4.1.103_7.

Collins, Patricia Hill. *Black Feminist Thought*. New York: Routledge, 1990.

Fogg, Marnie. "Willi Smith." lovetoknow.com, accessed January 23, 2020. https://fashion-history.lovetoknow.com/fashion-clothing-industry/fashion-designers/willi-smith.

Friedman, Vanessa. "Fashion's Racial Divide," *The New York Times*, February 11, 2015, E1, E8–9.

Givhan, Robin. "Patrick Kelly's Black Radical Cheek." *The Washington Post*, May 31, 2004, accessed January 24, 2020. https://www.washingtonpost.com/wp-dyn/articles/A3561-2004May30_2.html.

Givhan, Robin. "Why Fashion Keeps Tripping Over Race," New York Magazine, February 10, 2011, accessed November 27, 2020. https://nymag.com/fashion/11/spring/71654/.

Hughes, Langston. "The Negro Artist and the Racial Mountain," (1926) in *The Norton Anthology of African American Literature*, 2nd ed., ed. Henry Louis Gates and Nellie Y. McKay, 1311–14. New York: W. W. Norton & Company, 2004.

"Langston Hughes," in *The Norton Anthology of African American Literature*, ed. Henry Louis Gates and Nellie Y. McKay, 2nd ed. New York: W. W. Norton & Company, 2004.

Lewis, Jeremy. "Accounting for Race in Fashion, pt. 1." *DIS Magazine*, 2015, accessed November 27, 2020. http://dismagazine.com/discussion/59332/accounting-for-race-in-fashion-pt-1/.

Martin, Richard. Ed., "Willi Smith," in *Contemporary Fashion*. New York: St. James Press, 1995.

Morris, Bernadine. "Willi Smith Gets Fall Off to a Good Start." *The New York Times*, April 29, 1986, B6.

Muñoz, José Esteban. *Disidentifications: Queer of Color and the Performance of Politics*. Minneapolis: University of Minnesota Press, 1999.

"N.Y. NOW: Willi Smith." *Women's Wear Daily*, April 29, 1986, 15.

Pritchard, Eric Darnell. "Overalls: On Identity and Aspiration from Patrick Kelly's Fashion to Hip Hop." *Funambulist* 15 (2018): 32.

Rooks, Noliwe. ed.,"Black Fashion: Art. Pleasure. Politics." *Nka: Journal of Contemporary African Art*, no. 37 (November 2015): 4–5.

"So Suitable." *Women's Wear Daily*, April 9, 1986.

Summers, Barbara. *Black and Beautiful: How Women of Color Changed the Fashion Industry*. New York: Amistad Press, 2001.

Tulloch, Carol. *The Birth of Cool: Style Narratives of the African Diaspora*. London/New York: Bloomsbury Academic, 2016.

White, Constance C. R. *How to Slay: Inspiration from the Kings and Queens of Black Style*. New York: Rizzoli, 2018.

The WilliWear News. WilliWear Limited, Willi Smith Papers, The New School Archives and Special Collections, New York, accession number: PC.08.04.01.

Postscript

Elizabeth Way

Any fashion scholar knows to be wary of "firsts." It is rare to find definitive documentation of the very first designer to create a specific style or achieve a certain milestone, though this does not stop mainstream culture from embracing this narrative. In that vein, this volume offers a long list of "firsts," designers who should be readily incorporated into fashion culture and curriculums—not because the initiating achievement has always been unequivocally proven, but because the title indicates the radical and groundbreaking nature of the accomplishment. Wesley Tann was "among the first Blacks to have a successful and visible clothing business in the country's fashion center on Seventh Avenue in New York."[1] Jay Jaxon was the first Black American to head a Parisian couture house. Patrick Kelly was the first American to be admitted into the *Chambre syndicale du prêt-à-porter des couturiers et des créateurs de mode* in Paris. Scott Barrie and Stephen Burrows were the first nationally recognized Black fashion designers. These statements are the tip of a fashion history iceberg that offers fresh perspectives and a more complete understanding of the American fashion industry. The chapters on Wesley Tann, Jay Jaxon, Scott Barrie, Stephen Burrows, and Willi Smith illuminate New York's fashion culture during the early 1960s and into the 1980s—a period that shaped American fashion into an internationally respected creative industry. Black designers were there, building New York into a fashion capital, and even taking their talents to Paris.

These studies also document the diverse career trajectories of designers both on and off Seventh Avenue—narratives vital to understanding how New York fashion functioned in the past and how it has changed in the twenty-first century. Yet, Deihl's chapter on Tann also exemplifies the way in which Black professionals created their own networks and opportunities. Tann organized fashion shows for fellow designers outside of the official New York fashion week, and mentored students of color at the High School for Fashion Industries and the Harlem Institute of Fashion. He, along with Ruby Bailey before him, were active members of the National Association of Fashion and Accessories Designers. They, like Black professionals around the country, were creating inroads to mainstream industries and pathways for their own success. Tann may not have been as well-known as Scott Barrie, but Barrie credits Tann's mentorship, emphasizing the generational connections between Black designers as critical.

Lisby's chapter similarly reveals the intricacies of a changing Parisian fashion system during the late 1960s and early 1970s through Jay Jaxon's career, but his chapter also underscores the boldness of the decision to even pursue fashion design for a Black man—a career that Scott Barrie's family told him was "a white boy's game."[2] Like Burrows who initially trained to be a teacher, or Art Smith who was encouraged to pursue architecture, Jaxon initially followed a more traditional professional career path into law school and worked in a bank before and while he worked in fashion. He, like Patrick Kelly, also took a calculated risk in recognizing the limitations of the New York industry and moving to Paris. Against the background of the Civil Rights era, these designers' decisions to invest in their own creativity and abilities were acts of resistance and empowerment.

The designers of the late twentieth century were pivotal in making Black designers visible. They drew from the past and influenced the future. Wilson Myers draws on the visual culture of centuries of Black makers, tracing Stephen Burrows's design and color signatures back to West African aesthetic roots, through antebellum quilters, and up to his grandmother, a veteran of the New York industry. His designs electrified 1970s fashion, embodying youth, freedom, and experimentation, and have set tropes that have inspired hip hop designers and mainstream fashion into the twenty-first century.

Beyond writing Black designers back into fashion history, the authors throughout this volume have demonstrated how the history and visual and material culture of Black fashion makers are vital resources in illuminating, not just the American fashion industry and fashion culture, but the experiences of Black Americans and the history of the United States. These authors have applied their insightful scholarly analysis to deepen the understanding of the work of these Black makers, and their chapters have expanded accepted perceptions. Knowles, for example, redefines the fast fashion concept, bringing its origins back into the nineteenth century and tying a fashion issue that is urgent to the twenty-first century into a wider conversation about Black people's relationship to capitalist systems. Her research is important to contemporary discussions of how the fashion industry treats people of color, not only in the United States, but globally. Knowles also argues that "the people who develop products used to make apparel, and who use textiles and clothing to stylize existing apparel in inventive ways, should also be considered as designers." This idea jumps from her analysis of nineteenth-century Southern enslaved makers to late twentieth-century Harlem. Elia's study of Dapper Dan, which she defines as a case study that "focuses on an alternative point of view on the history of fashion, broadening the idea of who creates fashion, what fashion can be, and when and where this occurs," fills an obvious gap in the history of international style. Streetwear and logomania, ideas that Dapper Dan redefined and exponentially expanded, are two defining characteristics of late twentieth-century global fashion that frequently reassert themselves on mainstream designers' runways and on the streets of fashion centers.

Davis and Owens also enlarge the definition of designer. Ruby Bailey's work predates trends in twenty-first-century contemporary art that use fashion and textiles as vehicles to express cultural identity, while also reflecting folk art practices. Her work deserves a place in art historical scholarship, as well as in fashion studies, and creates opportunities to further connect these fields from new angles. Jewelry designers, especially those outside the realm of high-end luxury, are not often considered among fashion designers, yet Art Smith's focus on the body represented a significant shift that anticipated the clothing styles of the rest of the twentieth century. This focus on the unrestricted body guided the designs of both Scott Barrie and Stephen Burrows. Owens's reevaluation of Smith's experiences and work through the lens of Afrofuturism beautifully exemplifies the ways in which fashion studies is truly an interdisciplinary pursuit. Pritchard also shows the wide range of perspectives available to the fashion scholar by utilizing a "race werk" framework to analyze Willi Smith's and Patrick Kelly's designs as disruptive to racist structures. Pritchard weaves their work into broader discussions within queer theory—an intersectional methodology with enormous potential for future fashion studies scholars.

Square's chapter on dressmakers as activists highlights the importance of dressmaking and fashion production as a source of empowerment and income. As a valued skill during enslavement and one of the few professions available to Black women after emancipation—as outlined in Chapter 3—dressmaking supported abolitionism, often invisibly. While Harriet Jacobs and Rosa Parks are rightfully honored as leaders in the ongoing fight against anti-Black racism, their occupations form an important part of their histories. Visibility also cannot be undervalued as a form of resistance to discrimination. Fannie Criss's skills and talents as a designer made her visible to both white and Black society in Richmond and New York. She leveraged them to become a property owner and employer. Stewart ties Criss's intricate and beautiful material culture into a social and political history that places Criss's success—comparable to a Black female bank president—in confrontation with the rise of the Lost Cause rewriting of Southern American history and the discriminatory laws of the Jim Crow era, including the 1904 segregation of Richmond's street cars, specifically enacted to target Black businesses.

Many of the designers examined in this volume and many more Black designers throughout the twentieth and twenty-first century have expressed discomfort or dissatisfaction in being labeled a Black designer. One of many examples is Pulitzer Prize-winning journalist Robin Givhan's description of Kerby Jean-Raymond's "fatigue over being described as a 'black' designer. Not because he isn't proud of his heritage and not because he doesn't bring his full self to his work, but because the nomenclature is limiting. It puts him in a category and suggests that he isn't trying to reach the widest audience and that his clothes somehow are not universal."[3] As Square and Pritchard explain, Jean-Raymond is the talented and provocative designer of Pyer Moss, a fashion brand that unabashedly carries on the activism of earlier fashion makers. Fashion has always served as an outlet for complex personal identities, and Black Americans have always participated, both as wearers and makers. As more and more diverse designers become visible in fashion industries, and as more scholars restore and add their narratives to fashion history, perhaps the designation of ethnic background—accentuated in this volume as a corrective to invisible histories—will no longer be needed. Lois Alexander's sentiment, quoted in the introduction, that Black fashion history tends to begin with the current generation of designers, is thankfully changing. This collection of scholarship can serve as a resource to students, scholars, designers, and lovers of fashion culture that documents the rich and detailed history of Black American fashion makers. More importantly, it stands as a challenge to extend and deepen scholarship that normalizes diverse and wholistic histories.

Notes

1   Michael Henry Adams, "How Black Style Became Beautiful," *Ebony*, September 1, 2007, 75.

2   Anton Perich, *The Anton Perich Show Presents Scott Barrie with R. Couri Hay* (1975, New York), video file, 50:07, YouTube, posted by Anton Perich, February 15, 2008, https://www.youtube.com/watch?v=O2zGcYFEZZg.

3   Robin Givhan, "Pyer Moss Designer Steps Outside Fashion and Into the Conversation about Race," *The Washington Post*, August 21, 2015, accessed July 10, 2020, https://www.washingtonpost.com/news/arts-and-entertainment/wp/2015/08/21/pyer-moss-designer-steps-outside-fashion-and-into-the-conversation-about-race/.

Bibliography

Adams, Michael Henry. "How Black Style Became Beautiful." *Ebony*, September 1, 2007, 74–5.

Givhan, Robin. "Pyer Moss Designer Steps Outside Fashion and Into the Conversation about Race." *The Washington Post*, August 21, 2015, accessed July 10, 2020. https://www.washingtonpost.com/news/arts-and-entertainment/wp/2015/08/21/pyer-moss-designer-steps-outside-fashion-and-into-the-conversation-about-race/.

Perich, Anton. *The Anton Perich Show Presents Scott Barrie with R. Couri Hay.* 1975. New York. Video file. 50: 07. YouTube. Posted by Anton Perich, February 15, 2008. https://www.youtube.com/watch?v=O2zGcYFEZZg.

Index